The World Book Student Handbook
Student Guide

The World Book
Student Handbook

Student Guide

Published by

World Book Encyclopedia, Inc.

a Scott Fetzer company

Chicago

The World Book Student Handbook
Copyright © 1981, 1978 by
World Book-Childcraft International, Inc.
Merchandise Mart Plaza, Chicago, Illinois 60654
All rights reserved. This volume may not be reproduced in
whole or in part in any form without written permission
from the publishers.
Printed in the United States of America
ISBN 0-7166-3121-0 (Volume 1)
ISBN 0-7166-3120-2 (2-volume set)
Library of Congress Catalog Card No. 81-51365
e/hc

Using the Student Guide

The years you spend in school are probably your most important years. During this time, you will develop many of the skills you will need throughout the rest of your life. Your school years are the key years of your development and growth.

Most schools and teachers do a very good job of presenting the information and skills you need to learn. They present you with material in mathematics, science, social science, language arts, and many other subject areas. But no matter how well your teachers teach, you have to do your part. You have to study and practice the information and skills presented in school. And often you have to learn how to do this on your own, because teachers may not have the time to help you learn how to learn.

How to study; how to learn; how to make the most of your school years; these are what *The World Book Student Handbook: Student Guide* has been designed to help you to do. *The World Book Student Handbook: Student Guide* has been carefully planned and executed to meet the need for practical advice that would enable both junior high and senior high students to make the most effective use of their school experience. It can also give parents a tool to use in helping their children improve in school.

Each unit of *The World Book Student Handbook: Student Guide* is a self-contained whole. Each unit concentrates on a particular area that has been identified as a problem area by students themselves. And each unit has been written by experts in the unit's area of concern.

The self-contained approach means you will not find it necessary to read this book from cover to cover. Instead, you may choose those areas in which you feel you need help or wish to improve the level of your performance.

Unit 1 introduces you to many of the problems that will be discussed in depth throughout the remainder of the book. The importance of careful planning of your educational career is described. And tips are given as to who can help you develop and then carry out both your short-range and your long-range educational plans.

Different kinds of classroom situations require students to behave and respond differently. Often, a student does poorly simply because he or she does not know what a teacher expects. Unit 2 discusses the skills you need to function successfully in different kinds of classroom situations.

If asked what is the most serious and widespread learning

problem among students today, most educators would answer "reading." Unit 3 concentrates on various aspects of the reading problem. Both comprehension and reading speed are considered.

Throughout your school years and the rest of your life, you will be required to put your thoughts and feelings or present information in writing. Your future success or failure can depend on your ability to express yourself in writing. Unit 4 concentrates upon writing skills.

Unit 5 considers another communication skill, speaking. The impression you make on others, either positive or negative, is vitally important. Often, this impression can be affected by the way you are able to handle yourself in both formal speaking and conversational situations. Unit 5 presents you with a variety of techniques and strategies that can help you to become a more effective speaker.

However, it is difficult to improve communication skills if you do not have a good vocabulary. You can neither express yourself nor understand the ideas and feelings of others if you do not know the meaning of the words being used. Unit 6 can help you to develop a more precise vocabulary.

Your library is one of the best study tools you have. And yet many students are unaware of how to best use this tool. Unit 7 tells you what the library is all about, how it is organized, what it contains, and how you can use it efficiently.

Many pupils look upon study as a "hit or miss" proposition. They waste a great deal of time with unnecessary tasks and end up doing poor quality or average work even though they seem to spend a great deal of time studying. Planned and organized study will help you to use your study time efficiently and effectively. And Unit 8 will help you to plan and organize your available study time.

School is not all class time and study time. Extra-curricular activities are an important part of every well-rounded education. Unit 9 discusses extracurricular activities and gives you many tips on how you may use such activities to increase the value of your educational experience.

The years you spend in school are not an end in themselves. These years are preparation for the rest of your life. Unit 10 describes the kind of career planning you should be doing *now* to increase your chances of success in the future.

Taken together, the 10 units of *The World Book Student Handbook: Student Guide* will help you to improve virtually all phases of your school career. And they will also help you to lay the basic foundation upon which you can build a happy and successful life in the future.

Contributors

Jerry J. Anderson, Ph. D.
Instructor and Student Council Advisor,
Oak Park and River Forest High School,
Oak Park, Illinois

Margaret Jane Bicek, M. A.
Secondary Reading Specialist,
Forest Lake Area Schools,
Minneapolis, Minnesota

Edgar Dale, Ph. D.
Emeritus Professor of Education,
The Ohio State University,
Columbus, Ohio

Nicholas P. Georgiady, Ph. D.
Professor in the Department of Educational Leadership,
Miami University,
Oxford, Ohio

Richard J. Jensen, Ph. D.
Assistant Professor of Speech Education,
University of New Mexico,
Albuquerque, New Mexico

Jeanette E. Mitchell, M. S. L. S.
Instructor in Library Sciences,
University of Hawaii,
Honolulu, Hawaii

Joseph O'Rourke, Ph. D.
Research Associate in the College of Education,
The Ohio State University,
Columbus, Ohio

Dominic J. Piane, M. M. E.
Instructor,
University of Chicago Laboratory Schools,
Chicago, Illinois

Timothy G. Plax, Ph. D.
Associate Professor of Speech Communication,
University of New Mexico,
Albuquerque, New Mexico

Louis G. Romano, Ph. D.
Professor in the Department of Administration and
    Higher Education,
Michigan State University,
East Lansing, Michigan

Betty Jane Wagner, M. A.
Chairperson of the English-Philosophy Department,
National College of Education,
Evanston, Illinois

Staff

Editorial director
William H. Nault

Editorial

Executive editor
Robert O. Zeleny

Managing editor
Dominic J. Miccolis

Senior editor
Seva Johnson

Assistant editor
Gail Rosicky

Administrative assistant
Janet T. Peterson

Index editor
Theresa Kryst Fertig

Art

Executive art director
William Hammond

Art director
Joe Gound

Design director
Ronald A. Stachowiak

Senior designer
Bernard Arendt

Designer
Free Chin

Production artists
Hans W. Bobzien
Susan T. Wilson

Contributing artist
Robert Keys

Product production

Manufacturing
Joseph C. LaCount

Research and development
Henry Koval

Pre-press services
J. J. Stack

Product control
Carmen Adduci
Barbara Podczerwinski

Composition
John Babrick

Film separations
Alfred J. Mozdzen
Barbara J. McDonald

Editorial services

Director
Susan C. Kilburg

Editorial research
Mary Norton, Head
Frances L. Fu
Robert Hamm
Max R. Kinsey

Rights and permissions
Paul E. Rafferty

Contents

Getting the most out of school

Do you like school? Do you enjoy going to class? For many students the answer to these questions is "No!" And this means problems. Like it or not, the years you will spend in school are among the most important years of your life.

This unit explains to you why this is true. And it gives you some tips as to how you can make your years in school more satisfying and productive.

1

The contributor of this unit is Dr. Jerry J. Anderson, Instructor and Student Council Advisor, Oak Park and River Forest High School, Oak Park, Illinois.

1. How can you succeed in school?

Education is important

You live in a world that is getting more and more complex. Science and technology are advancing daily. Jobs are becoming more specialized and demand greater skills and training. Competition for advancement is becoming fierce.

It is an active, competitive, and exciting world. To succeed in this world, you must be well prepared and well trained.

Your training and preparation begins in school. Today, more than ever before, the amount of future satisfaction a person may expect will depend upon his or her educational training. Getting a good education has become the most important goal today's young person can achieve.

What an education means

There are few jobs today that do not require at least a high school diploma. So a high school education is an important and necessary part of anybody's education.

High school is a sort of testing ground. You are given a lot of freedom in what you will choose to study. High school programs give you the chance to find out what your interests and aptitudes are. High school is a place where you will prove yourself. So it follows that your high school record is going to depend partly on your abilities. But even more than this, what you will achieve in high school will tell others much about your attitudes and your determination.

Planning can help

A word of caution is necessary at this point. Since high school is a testing ground, some students are confused by the freedom of choice they have in course offerings. Other students are overwhelmed by the number of extracurricular activities, such as athletics and clubs, they may participate in. Students often wander into courses or activities for no other reason than a course title, club's name, or friend's recommendation.

No one would seriously recommend a rigid, straitjacket program of courses and activities for any beginning junior high or high school student. But it is important for you to recognize that some planning is needed if you are to get the most out of your school experience.

All too often, students do not begin serious planning of their academic program until the last year or two of high school. This is a great mistake. Planning should begin in junior high. And this planning should include not only course choices, but also extracurricular activities. Many successful careers have been the outgrowth of an extracurricular interest developed in a school-sponsored club or activity.

Success in school requires discipline and commitment. Students often feel that these are qualities that they will acquire and apply once they have a job. What is important for you to understand is that you already have a job—that of student. The work habits and attitudes toward responsibility that you developed in school will be the ones carried over to your first job.

School is your job

Employers usually look for young people who have skills that are useful to the business. But employers also emphasize a person's ability to take responsibility and to get along with others. Many of the problems which employees have on the job center around an inability to get along with fellow employees.

Your school is an excellent laboratory in human relations. You meet all kinds of students and teachers. Learning how to keep a good relationship with many different kinds of people is a very important part of your school experience. In fact, the social part of your job as a student is almost as important as the academic part.

Your job as a student includes many responsibilities. You must attend classes. This is important since many employers feel that school attendance records provide a clue to a prospective employee's absentee rate. You must prepare class assignments. This helps you to develop good work habits. Doing your assigned schoolwork as well as you can and on time is the best training you can get for future employment.

Another important responsibility of your job as a student is learning to do your assigned work as well as possible. This is especially true for work that you find uninteresting or for work you do not feel like doing. Even the most glamorous job has many boring, dull, and repetitive tasks that must be done. The habit of doing what you have to do, when you have to do it should be developed early.

Success at your school job is often a good predictor of success at other kinds of jobs. In fact, some employers will not even give employment interviews to individuals whose school record shows poor performance. These employers believe that if you have ability, but did not use it in school, you are probably not serious about your future.

Set some general goals

Lack of general goals is one reason why some students do poorly in school. You may be years away from a definite career choice. Even so, you should try to set as early as you can what general fields you feel you would like to work in. And you should try to find out what those fields have in the way of requirements for entry.

This leads to a difficult question. How can you plan when you are not sure of any particular career choice? There is no easy answer to this problem. But here are a few suggested guidelines.

Keep in mind that you should plan what is best for you. The tendency to cave in to pressure from friends is very strong in junior high and high school. Try to ignore the career plans that your friends are making.

Choose the career goal you feel will make you happy in the future. To do this, you must know yourself and what your interests are. There is no single list of questions that you can ask yourself. But here are a few items that many career counselors recommend that the student think about.

1. Who am I?
2. What would I like to be doing 15 or 20 years from now?
3. What are my abilities?
4. What attitudes do I have?
5. How can I get where I want to go?

The answers to these questions should give you an idea of who you are. And they should help you to discover what your interests are. Junior high school and high school is a time when you will have the opportunity to think about such questions and hopefully to settle them.

2. Who can help you?

Your career choice is probably the single most important decision you will ever make. To choose wisely, you must understand yourself. And you must have knowledge of the job opportunities that are available to you.

Understanding yourself helps you discover the vocations and careers for which you are best qualified. Only when you understand yourself will you see what your aptitudes and abilities are. A wise career choice means matching aptitudes and abilities to some occupation.

An understanding of job opportunities also requires self-awareness. To evaluate job opportunities you must know what various jobs will require of you. And you must be able to judge if you have the aptitudes and abilities needed to do these jobs.

Many studies have been done of people working at various jobs. These studies all show that many people are unhappy in their career. The same studies show that employers have great difficulty getting people who can fill responsible jobs.

There can be many different reasons for unhappiness in a job or for career failure. But most of these reasons come down to the same thing. The people who are having career problems are usually those who waited too long before making a career decision. They are the people who failed to begin career preparation while in school. They are the people who depended upon chance or luck to "get them through." Or they are the people who have been unwise and uncertain in their decisions while in school.

Planning will help you prepare for the kind of work for which you are best suited. And planning will help you identify the kind of work in which you are most likely to have the

Career choice and school

Help in planning

17

greatest opportunity for success and happiness.

The first, and most important, step in the planning process is the selection of an educational program designed to help you achieve both short-range and long-range educational goals. Many junior high and high school students feel that planning is not necessary unless they intend to go to college. Nothing could be further from the truth. Planning is just as necessary for the student enrolled in a vocational educational program as it is for the college-bound student. In fact, early planning is even more important for the vocational education student. High school may be the last formal education for this student. He or she must be prepared to get every bit of help and training high school has to offer.

Planning your educational program should include discussions with your parents or guardians. Older brothers and sisters can also be helpful.

You certainly will not want to overlook the counseling service offered by your junior high or high school. A trained counselor can point out many things about your educational and career plan that you did not think of or felt were unimportant.

There are people outside of your family and school who can help you plan for the future. Area colleges will have guidance counselors. Contact a college close to you and arrange to meet with a counselor. He or she will be happy to give you information about the kind of academic program you should be planning if you intend to go to college.

Most state governments include a department of employment services. This is a valuable planning resource that is ignored by many people. You should take advantage of the guidance services offered by this department.

State employment services usually do four basic things.

1. Distribution of job information.
2. Employment counseling.
3. Referral to job training programs.
4. Job placement.

Cooperative school programs provide employment-related services to graduating seniors, school dropouts, and potential dropouts who desire to enter the labor market. These programs provide employment counseling, job development, referral to job or job training, and follow-up services and testing.

3. Are you a good student?

Surveys of junior high school students usually show that many young people feel they have to do too much studying outside of school. Many students believe the kind of homework they are given is not interesting or challenging. Although they seem to find time for parties, dates, television, and sports, students never seem to have enough time for homework. They are usually behind with their notebooks, special reports, and daily lesson assignments.

You cannot avoid homework

However, some students, who have just as many outside interests and no greater mental ability are able to keep up with their assignments. The difference is usually a matter of the way these students feel about homework and the way they manage their time.

Most schools require students to do some homework. Take a reasonable view of homework. Think of it as necessary practice in the development of certain skills, and for mastering and recalling what you have learned in the classroom. Doing homework is good preparation for the future. It helps you to develop work habits that will be useful either in future academic training or "on the job."

Learning is a very individualized process. What may work to help one student learn may not help another. But many learning and study problems can be overcome through the application of certain techniques and disciplined work. While the information that follows will be covered in much more detail in the remainder of this book, here are a few tips that will help you to become a better student.

Tips for learning

1. Do not trust your memory to remember daily assignments. Record your assignments daily. You will save time and know exactly what is required if you have a

special place in your notebook for recording daily assignments. Make accurate notes about your daily assignments. Before leaving school, make sure that you have all books and materials that you will need for studying at home.

2. Make a time schedule for homework. Work out a daily schedule. Consider the amount of time you normally need to spend on each of your assignments. Your homework time schedule will vary depending upon the number of study periods you have at school, and the approximate length of time you have for study at home each day.

3. Have a definite place to work. If possible, a quiet, private spot, which is not too warm, and in which you can have a table or desk, a straight chair, and good lighting is the most desirable. Some students insist that they are not bothered by radio, television, or conversation when studying. But many studies have shown that it takes more energy and power of concentration to study with such distractions than it does to study in a quiet place.

4. Begin to study immediately. Do not wait for some sudden inspiration. Begin whether you are in the mood or not. Some students begin with their favorite subjects and spend most of their time on those subjects. They then neglect subjects that are hard or that they do not like. It is better to plan to work first on the lessons that you find the hardest. Do the more difficult work while your mind is fresh. Subjects that you like least often become interesting when you spend more time on them.

5. Make an effort to understand and remember what you have read. Review previous lessons as a background for your present assignment. Then scan the new lesson to get an idea of the entire assignment before studying it in detail. Read the material, one section at a time, and make an effort to keep important points in mind. Try to get the main idea of each paragraph and take notes as you read. Then review your notes and any parts of the assignment that you do not understand or remember.

6. Take notes. Form a habit of making neat, readable notes in class that can be reviewed easily and quickly. Do not scribble notes on odd pieces of paper. Keep notebooks or set-aside part of a general notebook for each subject. Make notes brief, using short sentences, phrases, and abbreviations. Do not try to copy too much from a book or take down every word a teacher says.

Activity

The unit-end activity has been designed to help you to practice and gain the ability to use the various classroom and study skills described in this unit. Please do not write in this book, but place your answers on a separate sheet of paper. Answers to the activity can be found on page 290 of the **Answer Key.**

Study habits checklist

Check your study habits by answering the following questions. An incorrect answer may indicate a study habit deficiency that should be corrected.

1. Do you have a definite place to study in your home?
2. Do you have a definite time set aside for study every day?
3. Do you study alone?
4. Do you have a dictionary in the room in which you study?
5. Do you have a TV, radio, record player, or tape player on when you are studying?
6. Do you study for more than one hour at a time?
7. Do you keep a notebook listing your daily assignments?
8. Do you take notes while you are studying?
9. Do you make a list of questions for the things you do not understand?
10. Do you study every night?
11. Do you have good lighting in the room in which you study?
12. Do you usually study the subject that you like best first?
13. Do you skim reading assignments before reading them thoroughly?
14. Do you review classwork on a regular basis?
15. Do you take notes during classtime?
16. Do you have a notebook that is carefully organized by subject matter?
17. Do you have a weekly schedule that organizes your time for study and other activities?

A guide to classroom skills

Most of your time in school is spent with a teacher in a classroom. But there are many different kinds of teachers. And there are many different kinds of classroom organizations. Do you have trouble getting along with some teachers? Can you adjust to differences in classroom organizations?

This unit describes the different kinds of classroom arrangements and some of the many different kinds of learning activities. And it discusses the student-teacher relationship and what you can do if you fall behind in classwork.

The contributors of this unit are Dr. Nicholas P. Georgiady, Professor in the Department of Educational Leadership, Miami University, Oxford, Ohio; and Dr. Louis G. Romano, Professor in the Department of Administration and Higher Education, Michigan State University, East Lansing, Michigan.

1. How are your classes organized?

- Are you worried about your work in school?
- Do you have trouble concentrating on your studies and your classwork?
- Do you have trouble remembering what you learned in class?
- Do you find yourself falling behind in your study assignments?
- Do you find yourself wasting time when you should be studying?

If the answer to one or more of these questions is "yes," then read this unit. It is definitely for you!

Actually, this unit is for everyone in school! Even though your school marks are pretty good, chances are you can do even better. If your marks are not so good, the information here will be even more important for you. Nearly everyone can do better by knowing how best to use the time he or she spends in the classroom.

Just think, most young people spend 10 or more years of their lives attending schools! That represents a lot of time. The education that you get during this time can be very important to your future. A good education can mean several important things to you. For one, it can mean a better job for you. Today's jobs call for more education than was needed years ago. Besides a better job, an education can make you a happier person. You will understand yourself, other people, and the world you live in much better.

Understanding how to make the best use of your class time can help you get more out of your education. How you plan your work in school is just as important as how much ability you have. On any football team, there are probably several players who can throw a football as far as the quarterback can. But can they throw it accurately, into the hands of a down-field receiver? The quarterback is playing his position because he trained for it. He *learned* to play the position! In the same way, you can learn to play your "position" in school better by knowing *how* to work better in class.

This unit is for students who are having trouble with class work and want to earn better grades and learn more. It is also for the good student and the average student who want to improve their work.

The next pages will give you a great deal of information that will help you as a student. Go over the ideas carefully. Think about them. Then try them out. The results will take time. But if you are willing to spend the time, the results will please you. Remember, work smarter, not just harder!

Few students understand what is expected of them in the classroom. This is because students are not aware of the reasons behind the organization of the class they may be in.

There are different kinds of classroom organizations. Each of these organizations has different purposes. Knowing why your class is arranged in the way it is will help you to work better in that class. What follows is a description of some typical classroom arrangements as they are used at different school levels.

Elementary school. Many elementary schools have what are called "self-contained classrooms." Here, your teacher works with a class of 25 to 35 students. Together, you all study a number of subjects such as reading, language arts, science, mathematics and social studies. You and your classmates may also study art, music, and physical education as well. In some elementary schools, there may be special teachers for these last three subjects. These are teachers who have been specially trained to teach art, music, or physical education.

In the elementary school, much of the school day is spent in one classroom with one teacher. Teacher and students get to know each other quite well during the year that they are together.

The teacher knows you are different from other students. Some students learn more slowly than other students. So the teacher works carefully with each one, helping each student to learn at his or her own pace. If you need special help with some part of a lesson, the teacher is there to help with the job of learning the lesson. When you have a ques-

Understanding your class

tion or a problem, you can turn easily to the teacher for help.

In the self-contained classroom, the teacher may teach some lessons to the whole class at the same time. Students and teacher talk about the topic they are studying. Each student has a chance to take part in the discussion. Sometimes, a few students may talk more than the others. Quiet or shy students may hesitate to take part in the discussions. A good teacher will know who the shy students are and will try to encourage them to take part in the class discussions. Listening is important in class discussions, too. Much can be learned by listening to what the teacher says and what the students say, too.

For other learning activities, the class may be divided into small groups. Four, six, or eight students may work on a project together. They plan their work and decide who will do each part. Then each student carries out his or her assignment. Students are encouraged to help each other when there are difficult tasks to be done.

Still other learning activities are individualized. You work alone on an assignment. The assignment is usually planned just for you. You work at your own rate. You may use books, magazines, filmstrips, and other sources that contain needed information. The teacher acts as a guide, providing help and direction whenever it is requested. Individualized activities permit you to use initiative and to show a sense of responsibility. Such activities also help to increase your sense of accomplishment.

Middle school or junior high school. After spending five or six years in the elementary school, you may move on to either a middle school or a junior high school. The middle school may include grades five through eight or grades six through eight. The junior high school may include grades seven and eight or grades seven, eight, and nine.

In the middle school or junior high school, classes are organized differently from classes in the elementary school. The middle school and junior high school help you make the change from elementary to high school.

Middle school or junior high students are supposed to be more mature than students in elementary school. Middle school or junior high students are supposed to be ready to make decisions or choices of the subjects they will study.

For example, you may be given the choice of either art or music to study. Some schools offer foreign language classes if you are interested. Or you may choose to study algebra if you are interested in mathematics.

In the middle school or junior high each teacher teaches the subject he or she knows best. As you move from one subject to another, you also meet different teachers.

In some schools, a class of students will stay in one room with the same teacher for two or more periods. They will study more than one subject together. It may be a combination of social studies and language arts or it may be science and mathematics. But even in this arrangement, you will meet with several different teachers during the day. This is different from elementary school where you worked with one teacher for most of the school day.

The middle school or junior high student learns to work in a schedule and assumes more responsibility for his or her school work. Special interests and abilities are used to guide students into programs most suitable for them.

Most middle schools and junior highs schedule an activity period at the end of the school day. During this period, you may meet in clubs to work with such things as photography, dramatics, the school newspaper, music, chess, checkers, and other kinds of activities.

There are also athletic teams of various kinds. These usually include basketball, baseball, football, swimming, track, and soccer for both boys and girls.

The team activities may be intramural, with a chance for every student to take part, or they may be interscholastic, with the best players on a team playing for their school against teams from other schools.

Middle school and junior high students are usually given much more homework than elementary school students are. You will have to take your books and paper home with you to work on assignments that are part of your class studies. Homework assignments help you learn more about the subjects you are studying.

Senior high school. When you go on to the senior high school, you will find yourself in a much larger school than the junior high or middle school you left. For many students, their formal education will end in the high school. High school for them should be a preparation to enter the job market. Many high schools offer vocational education for students who will soon be looking for jobs.

Other high school students will continue their education by going on to a college or university. These students will take courses to help them get ready for college. Depending on what your plans for the future are, you will take courses to help you prepare.

High school programs are departmentalized. This means that you must move from class to class to study different subjects. You meet with different teachers during the school day. Teachers are assigned to teach the subjects in which they have been trained.

Each state has a list of required courses that high school students must take. These required courses usually are two years of English, one or two years of social studies including U.S. history, one year of science, and one year of mathematics. Physical education may also be required for two or more years.

In addition to the required courses, high schools also offer many different elective courses. These are courses you may choose to take or not to take. The choice usually depends upon your interests or needs.

The school day is divided into periods. Periods may last from 45 to 60 minutes each. Two to five minutes are allowed for passing from classroom to classroom. A lunch period of about 30 minutes is included during the school day. Many high schools also have study periods when students are given time to work on homework or class assignments.

Some high schools have a special activities period one or more days each week. During this time, clubs of various kinds meet.

Activity periods may also be used for student council meetings. The student council gives students a chance to practice student government. It encourages students to participate in making their high school a better place for learning and living together.

Athletic events are an important part of the high school day. When an athletic event such as a pep rally is scheduled, some period may be dropped to let students attend the rally. Athletic teams in football, basketball, track, and baseball, as well as other sports, represent the high school in contests with other high school teams. Most high schools now have girls' teams as well as boys' teams. In addition to the interscholastic teams, intramural teams make it possible for many students to have the fun of competing against their friends.

Special assemblies are also part of the high school program. For these, the student body is gathered in a large assembly hall to hear a speaker, a program of music, or to see a play.

As you can see, high school can be a "special" experience. It offers many benefits if you are willing to take advantage of them.

Different kinds of classes. Several kinds of classroom organizations are used in the middle school, junior high, and high school. One kind is called a lecture class. Here, the teacher speaks to the students about a topic. The teacher explains the important ideas you must learn. Then he or she asks questions to make sure that you understand the topic. You will usually have a chance to ask questions and to explain your own ideas on the topic. The questions and answers help in the exchange of information between teacher and students.

Another kind of class is a seminar. Here, the teacher does not lecture. Instead, he or she acts as a discussion leader. Ideas are exchanged and discussed informally.

Instead of sitting in rows of seats, you and other students usually sit in a circle, often around a large table. The teacher does not stand in front of the class. He or she joins the seated group. This usually helps the students to feel more at ease.

Each person in a seminar has a chance to ask questions and to give his or her own ideas. Such open discussion between teacher and students usually leads to a better understanding of the topic.

Different kinds of study groups. There are several kinds of groups for study. Some groups are class-sized. Others may be made up of six to eight students. Sometimes, two or three students will work together as a team.

You may also study alone using a study carrel, a small enclosed place for individual study. In the carrel, you can view filmstrips or motion pictures on special projection equipment. You can also listen to tape and disk recordings that describe or explain the topics being studied.

Of course, much additional information comes from books and magazines found in a library or media center. Today's schools use a variety of media for study purposes. And they use many different kinds of classroom and study arrangements to help you succeed at the job of learning.

2. What to do in class?

Educators all around you

Education goes on in many places. In the home, your parents educated you when they helped you learn to walk, to talk, to get along with others, and to avoid hurting yourself.

In the neighborhood, young people get another kind of education. There, you learn about other families and other people. You learn about shopping and services you can use. You learn about games and recreation.

Churches educate, too. They help young people learn about religion and deciding right from wrong.

Much education takes place in schools. Reading, writing, and using numbers are important parts of this education. In school you gain knowledge, information, and skills that help you live successfully in society. The most important job a school has is to help each of its students become able to use his or her education in daily life. And your most important job as a student is to take advantage of the education offered by your school.

Making the most of your time in school

You will spend many years in school. How much you learn will be important in your later life as an adult. And how much you learn will depend on how well you use your time.

Knowing how to study can help to make the time you spend in school more valuable. Here are some ideas on how you can do better work in your classes.

Be there! First of all, to get the most out of an education, you must be there, in school, attending class, as much as possible. Some students feel that it is smart to "cut classes," to purposely miss classes. Such students are only cheating themselves. Except for illness or other real emergencies, you are better off in school than anywhere else.

Take care of yourself! When you are not feeling well, it is difficult to keep your mind on school work. The important thing is to take care of yourself until you feel better.

People think most clearly when they feel well. An auto engine runs smoothly when all the engine parts are in good order and working together as they are supposed to. Spark plugs are clean and adjusted correctly. The carburetor is clean and working smoothly. So is the fuel pump. When one of these parts breaks down, the engine shows it by running raggedly.

Just like an engine, your body needs certain care to function well. Good food, taken regularly, is the fuel the human engine runs on. You cannot think well when you are so hungry that your body keeps reminding you it needs food. To do well in school, have a good breakfast in the morning. Have a good lunch at noon. Both meals will give your body the fuel it needs to get you through the school day.

Your body needs rest, too. You are growing rapidly and your heart, lungs, and blood system need time to take care of your body's needs. Catching up is done when your body is at rest. Doctors recommend eight to ten hours of sleep each night and more if you feel you need it. Less than this will make it difficult for you to keep your mind on your schoolwork. You will feel drowsy, sleepy, and cross. Remember, no one can study and learn unless they are feeling rested and well.

Concentrate! Being in school is important, but it is not enough. Besides being there, you must know what is going on. This means you have to concentrate on what is being studied.

Be attentive to the topic. Think about what is being said. Try to keep your mind from "wandering." The average person talks at about 125 words per minute. A person listening to a speaker can think much faster than that. This means you may have trouble keeping your mind from racing ahead of the speaker you are listening to. To help you concentrate on a speaker's words, here are some suggestions for listening.

1. Take notice of the speaker's most important ideas.
2. Think about the speaker's arguments for these ideas.
3. Think about personal experiences that might relate to the speaker's ideas and topics.
4. Along with the important ideas, note the important details the speaker points out.

When you stop to think that the average person spends

nearly half of his waking hours listening, it seems important to know how to listen well. Try to use the TQLR formula for good listening.

T *Tune in.* Concentrate on the speaker.

Q *Question.* What is the talk going to be about? What will the outcome be?

L *Listen.* Listen for the main points. Think ahead. Try to relate what you are hearing to information you already know.

R *Review.* Think back over the talk. Try to remember as many main points as possible.

For effective listening, the following six ideas will help you.

1. Pick a good seating location.
2. Develop an interest in the topic.
3. Organize your thinking.
4. Expect important points in the talk.
5. Get it now. Get it down in your notes and in your mind, too.
6. Always evaluate your listening habits. How are you doing? How can you do better?

Take notes. Sometimes it is difficult to keep your mind on what is being said. Try to think about the topic. Think about the important ideas and facts you hear. Remember as much as you can. But accept the fact that you cannot remember everything. Writing notes will help you to recall later what was discussed.

Do not try to write down everything the teacher says. Pick out the important ideas and facts that you hear in class lectures and discussions. Write these down in a notebook. Have a notebook for each class or have a large notebook divided into sections, one section for each class. Write the notes as clearly as you can. Remember, you will have to read these notes later. So you will want to be able to read them easily when you review. Sometimes it is a good idea to review and rewrite your notes more carefully at the end of each day. This way you can be sure that the notes are clear and that you understand them.

Much of the information for your classes will come from the lectures. If you are able to take good notes, you will find it easier to learn about the lecture topics. Keep in mind what the purposes of a lecture are.

1. Lectures help to explain difficult or complex subjects so that these can be more easily understood.

2. Often, your textbooks only introduce ideas or topics. Additional information about ideas introduced in your textbook is provided in lectures.
3. Lectures present to the listeners material that is difficult to locate in other resources.

The things that you do most easily are the things you do regularly, by habit. Taking notes should become a habit. If taking class notes becomes a habit, you will find that it will be quite easy for you after a short time.

A way of making certain that your notes are accurate is to compare them with another classmate's notes. You can do this together and talk about any differences there may be. However, you should avoid making this a social situation. Be thorough but be brief!

Have a good location in the classroom. The seat you pick or are assigned to in your classroom is important. Be sure that you can hear the speaker or discussion well from your location in the classroom. If you have trouble hearing everything, ask to have your seat changed to a better location. Be sure that you can see the chalkboard clearly. When films and filmstrips or slides are used, be sure that you have a good view of the screen on which these are shown. If not, a change of seat will help you.

You have many friends in school. However, sometimes friends who sit near you may keep you from concentrating on your studies. Remember that your classwork is important. If you find yourself talking to your friends so much that your work in class suffers, it is time to make a change of location. Save your visiting for free periods or for after school hours!

Always have the tools you need to do a good job. In school this means a notebook, a pen or pencil, and the right textbook. You may even consider keeping a daily checklist of these and other special materials needed for your classes.

Ask for more information. At times, what you are watching or listening to in class will not be clear to you. If you do not understand a point, ask questions or ask to have the point repeated. Do not be afraid to do this! Remember, it is important that you understand what is being studied.

Prepare for your classes. You will learn a great deal more from your class lectures and discussions if you prepare for these in advance. Be sure you are up to date in your reading assignments. This will give you a background of information that will help you to understand the lecture in class. Reading before the lecture will also help you develop your own ideas on the topic your class is studying. And this will make the lecture more understandable.

Vocabulary from your readings will help you get the important ideas your teacher talks about. Get into the habit of looking up the meaning of any word you do not understand.

Some teachers outline the main points of a lecture. Be sure to write these in your notes.

Share your ideas. Being in school, paying attention to the lesson, thinking about the lesson, taking notes, and asking questions are all important. But, besides these, remember that every student has ideas and information on any topic. Be sure to share your ideas with your teacher and your fellow students. Remember that your ideas are just as important as anyone else's. You will feel better about being in a class if you take an active part in the class discussions.

Each student can help to make a lesson more interesting by contributing to the discussion. Remember that the school is there to help *you*! There is no need for you to feel shy about participating. And your ideas on a topic may help to make that topic more understandable for your classmates.

Grouping arrangements in class

Schools carry on learning activities in groups of various sizes. The kind of learning activity planned will usually determine the size of the group. For example, a motion picture film can be shown to 200 students as well as it can to 20 students. The following information discusses some of the more common groupings for activities.

Large group activities. A group of 200 students would be a large group. The school's purpose in arranging for a group of this size is to show a film, present a speaker, or distribute general information of some kind.

Note-taking is usually very important in large group activities or classes. Good listening skills are important, too. Being able to hear the speaker well or to see the film screen clearly are important. Remember what to do if you have trouble hearing the speaker or seeing the screen? Change your seat!

Take notes carefully. With 200 or so students in a large hall, there will be noises to bother you. Try to ignore these. Concentrate on the program. Think about the program. Use your listening skills.

Small group activities. A small group may be made up of as few as 4 to 8 or as many as 12 to 15 students. A group of this size is right for discussion purposes. There are few enough students so that each one has a chance to take an active part in discussions. The exchange of ideas can help to lead to a better understanding of the topic being studied.

In this kind of group, listening skills are important. Note-taking skills are also useful so that important ideas and facts may be recorded for study and review later. But most important of all is participation in the discussion and other activities. Remember, to make a learning activity more valuable, *each* student should contribute to discussions, raise questions, and make comments to increase understanding by *all* students.

Individualized study. Much of the study in schools today is individualized. Each student learns at his or her own rate. How much you learn studying by yourself depends a great deal on how well you use study skills. These are discussed in detail in unit 8 of this book. But the following tips will help you to sharpen your study skills.

1. Plan your work with care.
2. Be sure that you understand your assignment or project.
3. Use a variety of learning materials. Books, tapes, films, slides, filmstrips and other media can be of great help to you.
4. Keep careful notes of the information you find.
5. If you are not certain of some point, ask your teacher to explain it to you.
6. Check with your teacher often to make sure that you are on the right track.

Good planning, concentration, well-written notes, careful reading, and review will all make your classwork more valuable to you and increase your understanding and learning.

3. How can your teachers help you?

You need your teacher

What and how much you learn depends on *you*! You can educate yourself. And some people have done exactly that. But doing it all alone is not the best idea. That is why you are in school. Schools are there to help you learn. And that is why teachers work in schools. The teacher's job is to help you with your learning. With a teacher's help, your learning can be faster, better, and more accurate. So, the first thing to remember is that teachers are working in schools for one reason—to help you and other students do a better job of learning.

Teachers are people

People are all different. And, because they are people, so are teachers. Some teachers like to have their classes very formal, well-organized, and orderly. These teachers may prefer to have students sit in assigned seats every day. They may want written work done and turned-in according to detailed instructions.

These teachers are usually very businesslike. Emphasis will be placed on learning subject matter just as it is presented in readings or in lectures to the class. There may be drill of some type for students.

Activities and assignments will be the same for the whole class. A large part of the time in class will be used for required activities so that each student will know clearly what is expected of him or her. Lectures and tests or written assignments will make up most of the activities carried on in class. Discussion may be limited to the students answering questions that the teacher asks.

Other teachers prefer more informal classes. They may not mind it when students sit in different locations every day. Discussions will be more informal with more give-and-take comments by students. The form for written reports will be left up to the students. These teachers usually only require that the work be done well.

Teachers who prefer informal learning situations may have purposes that are broad and less defined. They may be concerned with the growth and development of students in terms of personality as well as academic growth. Objectives in class may vary from student to student just as assignments may vary, too.

Class control will be informal. And there will be less emphasis on conforming to a set pattern of work in class. Students will often have a role in class planning with the teacher. Activities that permit students some movement and freedom will usually be chosen. Such teachers usually feel that subject matter is important when it contributes to broader goals than simply learning facts.

Matching teachers with students is as important as matching subjects with students. You must study your teachers and decide what kind of person each teacher is. You need to do this all your life with different people. You study your parents and your friends so that you can understand them. Then, the way you behave towards each one is shaped by the nature and personality of that person as well as by your own personality.

In the same way, knowing what each of your teachers is like will help you find out what each expects from you. And that will help you to be more successful in class.

You must learn to get along with your teachers just as you must learn to get along with other people. To help you with this task, let us look at the job of the teacher. What do teachers do for us in school?

A teacher's job

Teachers are leaders. Teachers are responsible for what goes on in the classroom and in the school. Their job is to lead the learning that goes on. They plan with students the kind of activities that will help students grow in understanding and knowledge. They guide the work that is done in the classroom.

Teachers are demonstrators. Teachers are older, have had more experience, and have been trained. They can show students how to avoid mistakes and find better ways of studying and learning. They can demonstrate the way to do various procedures.

Teachers are resource persons. Much learning is the result of questions asked and answers given. To find answers to questions, you need to know where to look for information. Your teacher can help you do this by making you familiar with places where needed information can be found.

Teachers are counselors. There are many problems bothering young people. Some of these are school problems. Others are problems found outside of school. Students are anxious for help with problems and look for advice on how to deal with difficult situations. Your teachers should be people you can turn to for such advice. To do so, you must have confidence in your teachers. You must trust them and respect them.

Find time to talk to a teacher about problems you are having with lessons. You can do this when the class is working on a written assignment. Take a few minutes to ask a teacher for help. Your problem may be one which the teacher can help you with by making suggestions to you on how to do your work more efficiently.

If there is not enough time in class to ask for help, go to the teacher after class or during a free or study period. Most daily programs have several study periods each day when this can be done.

Asking a teacher for help does not mean that you are failing to do your job. In fact, it will tell the teacher that you are serious enough about your work to want to do better.

Getting along with teachers

In the middle school or junior high and high school, you will have an opportunity to select some of your teachers. Before you have to make your selections, you should think not only of what different teachers are like, but also of what kind of person you are.

To get the most out of your education, you must have teachers with whom you can get along. You need to consider the personality of teachers. Are they friendly? Are they cheerful? Do they have a sense of humor? Do they know their subject matter? Are they fair to all students? Is their teaching style like your learning style?

Getting along with your teachers depends on you as much as it does on the teacher. The following are five suggestions that can help you improve your relationship with your teachers.

1. Be friendly. Begin your class and your work with each teacher with an open mind. Do not be deceived by ap-

pearances. Sometimes people are not what they appear to be. A sour-faced teacher may really be a friendly person underneath. After all, are you sure what kind of appearance you make to others? Begin on a friendly basis.

2. Be open-minded. Rumors about teachers may spread rapidly. These rumors are often untrue. Try to be fair about your teachers. Give each one a chance before you make up your mind about him or her.

3. Ask for help. Teachers know a great deal about what is going on in class. They often know which students need help. However, with as many students as some teachers have, it is difficult to know when each and every one needs help. Ask for help. You will be doing both yourself and your teacher a favor. After all, that is what the teacher's job is all about—helping students learn!

4. Check often with your teachers. Of course, it is always a good idea to check with your teachers when you need help or when you do not understand a lesson. But it is also a good idea to check when you think you are doing well. Communication between teacher and students is important so that they understand each other better. And your teacher will be glad to know that you are interested enough in your work to ask about it often!

5. Remember, teachers have feelings, too! Teachers are people and all people have feelings. At different times teachers may be happy, or angry, or sad. You can tell the difference.

If you cannot get along

Sometimes, the teacher to whom you may be assigned may not be the right kind of teacher for you. The teacher may have a personality that does not fit with your personality. You may have trouble getting along with each other. And you may feel that the teacher does not understand you.

At other times, there may be trouble because the teacher's style of teaching does not fit your style of learning. If the teacher is a formal type of person, one who likes order and a systematic way of doing things in class, you may feel that you do not learn best in this kind of learning situation.

Give the teacher a reasonable amount of time. Give yourself a chance to adjust to that teaching style. After a trial period, if there are still problems, it may be best to ask for assignment to another class. This may be best for both teacher and student. Effective learning requires a good teacher-student relationship.

4. What can you do if you fall behind?

Avoid panic

There may be times when you find yourself falling behind in your work. You may still be working to finish one assignment when you are given another—then still another. How can you do all of these assignments when you know that your work will continue to pile up?

When this happens, some students become excited and they panic. They rush to finish the work quickly. And because they hurry, they make mistakes. So, the problem grows worse instead of better.

Fear is one of the worst things that can happen to a student. Your thoughts get all mixed up. You become unsure of yourself. You get nervous and upset just thinking about your problems. You become more and more discouraged. It would be easy at this point to give up and do nothing. This means failure, of course.

But that is not the way to act in an emergency. The worst thing to do is to panic or to give up. Nothing is gained by either of these. Instead, stop and think. What is my problem? Why am I so far behind? What can I do to catch up with my work?

See your teacher

The answers to these and other similar questions are not easy ones. You may need help to find the answers. Who can help you? Why, your teacher, of course!

Your teacher is the first person to turn to when you need help. Remember, the teacher is there to *help you!* Your teachers do not want you to fail. They want you to succeed. They want you to be able to show how much they taught you.

Find a time when you can speak to your teacher. Make an appointment for a conference. Remember that a teacher is a

40

busy person with many students to think about. Therefore, ask for a time when both of you can sit down to carefully talk about your schoolwork problems.

At the conference, have your books, notebooks, and assignments with you. Your teacher and you will have to look at these to find out where your difficulties are. Both of you will want to talk about whether or not you understand your assignments and your study and reading materials.

You will also want to talk about your study schedule. How are you using your time in school? How much time do you spend on your studies at home or at the library? Is this time really used for study or is it used for other purposes? Are there lessons that you do not understand because you are not spending enough time on them? How can you adjust your study schedule?

These questions and the answers to them can help change your work and study habits. They can help you do a better job of keeping up with your schoolwork.

Try to help yourself

Talking to your teacher about your study problems is a good idea. But along with this, you should look carefully at your own study schedule and practices. Think about how you are budgeting your time for study at school and at home.

Study the suggestions given in unit 8 of this book. Are you using these suggestions? If not, try them out. They have worked for many students and will work for you if you give them a fair chance.

Make a list of the points made in unit 8. Think about each point, one at a time. Think about how you are using each point in your own work. How can you make better use of it? Write down your study habits as they relate to each point. Then decide which of your study habits may need improvement.

Check yourself regularly to make sure you are on the right track. Your work should begin to show improvement as you work your way into an organized program of study.

Keep in mind that you are not the only one who has problems with his or her schoolwork. There are other students who also have problems and they are just as worried as you are. But if you are willing to ask for help and then to make an honest effort to do better, you can improve your schoolwork, learn more, and be more satisfied with yourself.

Activities

The unit-end activities have been designed to help you to practice and gain the ability to use the various classroom skills discussed in this unit. Please do not write in this book, but place your answers on a separate sheet of paper. Where appropriate, answers to the activities can be found in the **Answer Key** that begins on page 290.

Readiness checklist

A classroom problem shared by many students is lack of preparation for classwork. This problem includes not only failure to complete required out-of-class assignments, but also involves failure to have all the tools needed to do the classroom job. In order to avoid this problem, some students have begun to use a daily checklist similar to the following. You may find such a checklist to be a handy classroom aid.

Date:_____   O.K.

  1. Assignments completed   _____
  2. Textbooks packed   _____
  3. Workbooks packed   _____
  4. Notebook packed   _____
  5. Dictionary packed   _____
  6. Ruled paper   _____
  7. Scratch pad   _____
  8. Pencils (sharpened)   _____
  9. Pen (filled)   _____
10. Eraser   _____
11. Ruler   _____
12. Other supplies
    a._____   _____
    b._____   _____

Improving participation

A large percentage of the grade you will receive in a class will depend upon your classroom behavior and the degree to which you participate in class activities. Complete the following questionnaire, answering the questions as honestly as you can. If most of your responses fall into the "Sometimes" or "Never" column, this may indicate a deficiency in classroom behavior and participation that could affect your success in class.

	Always	Sometimes	Never
1. Do I avoid cutting classes?	___	___	___
2. Am I on time for the beginning of the class period?	___	___	___
3. Do I avoid talking to classmates, passing notes, and/or making unnecessary remarks once the class period begins?	___	___	___
4. Do I have all of the books, tools, and supplies on hand required by each class?	___	___	___
5. Do I concentrate on the work that must be completed during classtime?	___	___	___
6. Do I concentrate on taking notes during lecture sessions?	___	___	___
7. Am I careful to choose a seat located where I can hear and see all important class activities?	___	___	___
8. Do I ask questions, participate in discussions, and otherwise make myself visible in a positive way?	___	___	___

A guide to reading skills

3

What do you think is the most serious problem students have? What is the area in which you feel the greatest need for improvement? Chances are the answer to both of these questions is the same, reading skills. Many students are unable to keep up with the amount of material they must read. And they are not able to fully comprehend the material they do read.

This unit discusses the subject of reading skills. It explains to you some procedures that will help you to more fully understand what you read. And it presents a program that could help you improve your reading speed.

The contributor of this unit is Margaret Jane Bicek, Secondary Reading Specialist, Forest Lake Area Schools, Minneapolis, Minnesota.

1. Why is reading important?

Reading and schoolwork

How often must you use reading skills during a school day? When is the last time you were able to complete a homework assignment without doing some reading? It is obvious that reading is the key to success in school.

Not too long ago, a group of teachers made a study of students and learning problems in schools around the world. A curious fact came out of this study. The teachers discovered that a student who did poorly in subjects such as math or art could still do very well in his or her other studies. But a student who did poorly in reading almost always did poorly in all his or her other studies.

For awhile, the teachers who made the study were puzzled by this. But they soon had an answer to their puzzle. The teachers examined the subjects that pupils were taking and discovered that even subjects like math or science were based on reading.

Of course, there were also other skills involved, such as learning to add and subtract in math. But most of the explanations of how to do things had to be read by the student. Many of the homework assignments required students to read long sets of directions. And tests and problems in class often involved "story problems," problems that were explained in words and had to be read and understood to be solved.

What was true for the pupils who were studied is also true for you. Do you have textbooks for most of your courses? You may use textbooks more in some classes than in others. But for almost any class you will take there will be some items that you will have to read. Even in classes that do not use a textbook, there will usually be mimeographed handouts, instruction sheets, or pamphlets. Your success or failure in these classes will depend on your ability to read the required materials.

The longer you stay in school, the more reading you will have to do. But many schools only teach reading until about the fifth or sixth grade. This means if you are a poor reader by the time you enter junior high or high school, you are in deep trouble. And the farther along you move into the educational system, the further behind you will fall.

As you move from grade to grade, your teachers expect you to build your knowledge of each subject area. An important way to build knowledge is through reading books. You are probably asked to write term papers or research papers. A lot of the information you present in such papers comes from reading you do on your own in a wide variety of sources. And finally if you go to college, almost all your study time will be spent reading. You need more and more information. And most of this information comes from printed materials you have to read.

Even if you could get tapes or movies containing all the information you need to know, these would not be much help. Your normal listening rate is about 150 words per minute. Yet almost anyone can be taught to read twice as fast as that. And you can learn to skim or scan read for information at nearly 10 times that speed. With the amount of information you have to learn, there is simply not enough time for you to use only audio visual materials.

Magazines and books may all be on microfilm in the next few years. But they will still have to be read. The same is true of most of what you have to learn in school. Your school is probably not going to throw all printed materials out the windows very soon.

A problem that keeps growing

You are moving into a world where every day more and more technical reading is required of people. Instructions for using appliances are becoming more complex. There are written instructions to follow for food preparation. Traffic signs, instructions giving travel directions, and safety information all require the ability to read.

Yet a recent government study shows that 4 out of every 10 Americans cannot read most government forms. For example, every year millions of Americans give up trying to prepare their income tax because they are unable to read the instructions. This is one of many examples where poor reading ability or the inability to read costs people time, money, and some control over their own life.

Also, your ability to get and keep a job is directly related to your ability to read. The simplest jobs require some reading

And outside of school

ability. And the more specialized the job, the greater the need to be able to read confidently, quickly, and efficiently.

Ask yourself this question: "Can I survive *on my own* in the world outside my school if I am unable to read well?" If you answer this question honestly, you will know that you cannot. Whatever you will have to do to live your life and especially to improve the conditions of your life will involve your ability to read.

Improve your reading skills

Since the ability to read is so important, you should work as hard as you can to improve your reading skills. Improvement of reading skills will pay you many dividends now and later.

Most importantly, top performance in reading is going to save you time. You will remember more of what you read the first time you read it. You will be able to decide quickly what is the best way to read the different kinds of materials you have to read. You will be able to choose a reading rate that will get the job done most quickly and efficiently.

If you have been able to read this book, you have the *basic skill* in reading you need to succeed in school and after. But there are probably some skill areas in which you need practice or improvement. If you practice and use some of the ideas presented in the following sections, you will find that reading can be made to work for you with less frustration and wasted effort.

The sections that follow will enable you to pinpoint those areas in which your reading skills need improvement. You will draw up your own reading skills profile that will make obvious both your strengths and weaknesses. This reading skills profile will help you to do three things.

1. You will get a chance to judge how well you read now.
2. You will be shown how to use this information to correct weaknesses and maintain strengths.
3. You will be given practice designed to improve your reading speed, and to help you learn how to vary your reading rate.

Stick with it. Read on for a few more pages. The next sections of this unit can send you on your way to stronger reading habits for life.

2. How well can you read?

Are you a reader who zooms at 90 miles per hour, then cannot tell where you have been? Are you a slow reader who forgets the beginning of an assignment before you make it to the end? Or are you a reader who needs three trips to the refrigerator and a run with your dog every time you have a chapter of history to be read?

There are as many kinds of readers—good and bad—as there are people in the world. You can get a general idea of what kind of reader you are by constantly checking your reading habits.

People usually discuss two things when they talk about reading. One is how fast they can read, or *reading rate*. The other is how much they understand, or *comprehension*. But within these two areas there is a great range of other things that make up reading. You will have the chance to find out what these "other things" are as you work through this section. And you will have the chance to "check" yourself out, judge your own skill level, on a number of these "other things."

In fact, this is a good time to try out something for yourself. Why not make a "picture" of yourself reading? Not a photograph or drawing, of course, but a written profile or sketch of the things you do well or not so well that make up your whole "reading act." Such a profile will help you judge your present level of reading proficiency.

Set aside a notebook or a section of a binder you already use for making up just such a profile. You can then use your reading profile as a guide to setting up a reading improvement program that is just for you. What you work on now can be the starting point. You can keep track of your progress as you try to improve your reading skills through a program of practice.

A mysterious skill

An important step you will have to take in this section is to think about reading in a way you probably never have before. Even if you think you are not a good reader, you still read as automatically as you tie your gym shoes. In order to read at all, you must depend on your mind to work unconsciously or it would take you forever to figure out the words in a short paragraph. Your mind cannot pause to relearn or interpret a word every time you see it.

In fact, did you know that reading the way good readers do could be called physically impossible? It is impossible, that is, when you think of reading as sounding out each letter in your mind or looking at each word on a page.

No one knows how your mind makes certain black marks (letters) on a page suddenly mean something to you. All that can be said for sure is that most people do get past the beginning reader's stage of consciously sounding out every letter of every word. Once past this beginning stage, your mind does an amazing and mysterious thing. Dozens of different messages travel to your brain at once. Dozens of different skills and habits go to work at the same time. In just a split second, your mind grasps the meaning of whole words, phrases, even sentences.

This section is designed to help you become more aware of some of the reading skills and habits *you* use. It will help you get rid of some habits that hold your mind back from making those quick decisions about meaning. And it will help you learn some new ways of doing things that will alert you to make decisions about meaning in quick, direct ways.

Check your reading level

You may begin checking out your present level of reading performance by using the selection that follows. The exercise will help you to judge both your present reading rate and your present level of comprehension. Read the selection at your normal rate of reading speed. But keep track of how long it takes you to finish reading the selection. Then answer the questions.

The easiest way to time yourself is to use an automatic timer or to have someone else keep time for you. However, a clock or watch with a second hand may also be used to time your rate of reading speed.

Write down the time when you start. Read at your normal rate for one minute. Mark the spot at which you are reading at the end of one minute, and write down the time when you stop. Do not count the time it takes you to answer the questions.

Karate

Even though it took movies and TV shows to bring karate to the American public, it is a very old art.

Karate began around 400 B.C. when religious leaders in India used it as protection against wild animals. From there it spread to Korea, then to Japan and China. This journey took nearly 2,000 years, but its spread to America took only about 25 years. A different kind of fighting—World War II, the Korean War, and the Vietnam War—exposed U.S. soldiers to karate when they were in Asia. They brought it back with them after each of the wars, and many of the schools teaching karate are run by former soldiers.

Karate is the name for unarmed combat which relies on kicks or hits with the hands, elbows, knees, and feet. The name itself is Japanese for "empty hand" since no weapons are used. Students must learn the forms of different kicks and strikes, of course. But they also spend much time on stances, which are correct ways of standing for different purposes. Blocking an opponent's blows is also important.

Students also learn different styles and movements depending on the type his teacher knows. *Tae kwon do* is the style which comes from Korea. It emphasizes kicks. The *kung fu* style, made popular by Bruce Lee movies in the early 1970's, originated in China and demands flowing, circular movements instead of the hard, chopping approach of the other styles. American karate is usually an international mix.

One aspect of karate that is often forgotten is that its purpose is self-defense. Since blows delivered with full force can kill or cripple, students are trained to control and stop their movements with only fractions of an inch to spare. All competitions rely on the quality of the movements, not hurting or knocking out the opponent.

1. How did karate come to the U.S.?
2. How old is karate?
3. What does the word *stance* mean?
4. Why would it be difficult to combine *tae kwon do* with *kung fu* if you were learning karate?

OK. You now have read a 300-word passage, timed yourself, and answered some questions. From that you can start to get a lot of information about how good a reader you are.

Rate your WPM

First, figure out your reading rate in words per minute (WPM). If you marked the spot where you were after one minute, you can just count the words up to the mark. That is your WPM reading rate. If you read the whole passage, follow these steps:

1. To figure out your WPM reading rate, use the time in minutes and seconds you wrote down at the beginning and the end. Subtract your starting time from stopping time. For example, say you started to read at 7:35 and ended at 7:37 and 5 seconds. It took you 2 minutes and 5 seconds to read the whole passage.

2. Now, change the time completely to seconds. Multiply the number of minutes by 60. Then add the extra seconds to that number. Using the time of 2 minutes, 5 seconds from the example, you get $2 \times 60 + 5 = 125$. So, it took a total of 125 seconds to read the passage.

3. You now will want to know how many words per second you read. There are 300 words in the passage. If you take the time of 125 seconds and divide it into 300 words, you get $2^2/_5$ words per second.

4. Now, change the words per second to words per minute by multiplying by 60. The figure $2^2/_5$ words per second multiplied by 60 is 144 words per minute.

Now, try your own time and go through the steps. If you want to put the formula in your notebook, it is

$$\frac{\text{number of words read}}{\text{time in seconds}} \times 60 = \text{WPM}.$$

An example of the use of this formula to find a WPM rate would be

$$\frac{300 \text{ (words)}}{60 \text{ (seconds)}} \times 60 = 300 \text{ WPM}.$$

Figuring out your reading rate is the first step in making up your reading profile.

Check your comprehension

It is not as easy to measure your comprehension and understanding of what you read as it is to do the math that shows you WPM. However, the questions that follow the passage will be able to give you an idea of how much you understood. If you can answer three of the four questions easily, your level of comprehension and understanding is adequate.

These questions will also give you an idea of what some of your specific strengths and weaknesses are in comprehension and understanding. Each question tests a different area of comprehension and understanding. Question one tests the ability to identify the main idea in a passage. Question two is a fact or detail question. Question three is a vocabulary question. Question four asks for an evaluation or judgment of the article. These four kinds of questions will be asked at the conclusion of each reading exercise in this section.

Of course, there are many other things involved in reading comprehension and understanding. But these four areas are ones that you are commonly tested on in school.

There will be suggestions later in this section as to how you might improve both your WPM reading rate and your level of reading comprehension. For now, use the three exercises that follow to get a picture of your present reading level.

Some additional readings

Each of the three readings that follow is about 300 words long. Record in your notebook your rate, your answers to the questions, and which of your answers is right and which is wrong. Correct answers to the questions can be found in the readings. As you do these exercises, keep the following nine key questions in mind:

1. Do you really understand what you read?
2. Do you change your WPM rate as you switch from one kind of material to another?
3. Are you reading out loud to yourself?
4. Do you find yourself rereading often?
5. Are you reading word by word?
6. What do you do when you come to unfamiliar words?
7. At what time of day and in what kinds of physical surroundings do you do most of your reading?
8. Do your eyes get tired or blurry as you read?
9. How often do you read?

Your answers to these questions will begin to give you information as to what your reading habits are. In working on your reading skills profile, you will find that improvement in your rate and comprehension is closely tied to identification and improvement of your reading habits.

Completion of the three exercises below will give you a more complete idea of where you stand in reading skills. Each exercise is about the same general topic. Each is about 300 words long and is followed by four questions. Each exercise has been written at a different level of reading difficulty. The first exercise is written at an upper elementary school level. The second exercise is at about the junior high level. The third exercise is at a high school reading level.

History of Television (first level)

Almost everybody watches TV today. This may seem funny to people who are the same age as your parents or grandparents. That's because TV didn't even start until after they were born or grown up.

Now almost every house has a TV set in it. One-third of all the families have two TV sets. Some people have more than two TV's. More and more people have color sets every day.

All of this started in the 1920's with experiments. They were tried out with all sorts of different machines. Finally one company decided to put TV's in 150 houses around New York City. They made up programs just for those people. The first one was a cartoon of Felix the Cat. This started in 1936.

The companies had to stop doing these programs after five years. That's because the United States started fighting World War II. The TV companies had to work on other machines that were used in the war instead of just for fun.

Once the war was over, though, TV came back. At first, you could only watch TV if you lived on the East Coast of America. Soon the programs were sent all over the country.

In the 1950's, people got interested in a big way. They would stand on sidewalks to watch TV's in store windows. They would go over to friends' houses to see a show. Sometimes the first family to get a TV was sorry. Their house would be full of friends all day long. They would hardly get to watch the set themselves.

The first color shows were tried in 1953. Almost nobody had a color set. After 10 years, lots of people had bought them even though they cost a lot more. Almost all the shows now are in color.

(Note: This selection is written at an upper elementary school readability level.)

1. Where did people go to watch TV when it first became popular?
2. Why did companies have to stop sending TV shows in 1941?
3. What does the word *programs* mean in this story?
4. How can you describe the way Americans got interested in TV in the 1950's?

Programs on Television (second level)

Programming on television has changed a lot over the years.

The first shows were mostly entertainment. Cartoons, comedy, and variety shows took most of the time. Quiz shows were very popular. They were a little different from the game shows of today because big money went for straight questions and answers. There was a big scandal, though, when people heard that the answers to very hard questions had been given to the winners before the shows.

Public affairs and news programs started early in TV history. The groundwork for this was laid when the first coast-to-coast broadcast showed President Harry Truman beginning the peace treaty meetings with Japan in 1951. The U.S. Senate allowed TV cameras to film its investigations, too. The public was able to see one committee question mobsters about crime and the Mafia. Later, they could see very emotional meetings when one senator, Joe McCarthy, accused thousands of people of being Communists. This kind of coverage was continued in the famous Watergate hearings that investigated President Nixon and his staff.

One thing that many critics point out is that TV has brought a lot of violence into homes. They say that early morning cartoons and nighttime dramas show too many fights and killings. It is true that TV news programs have shown more real-life violence than ever before. Millions of Americans saw Jack Ruby shoot the man accused of killing President Kennedy, for example. Millions also saw the war in Vietnam on TV every day. Some people think this should be controlled, but others do not.

One kind of show that has remained popular and almost unchanged since the beginning is the soap opera. Once soap companies did sponsor them to reach housewives during the day. Now they are popular with many different audiences and have a wide range of sponsors.

(Note: This selection is written at a junior high readability level.)

1. What is one thing critics say TV should not have brought to American homes?
2. Why was there a scandal about the early quiz shows?

3. What does the term *public affairs* mean?
4. Why do you think soap operas are not just for house-wives any more?

Light Splitting in Color TV Cameras (third level)

The color TV camera performs a whole range of complex tasks so that the image before it will reappear before your eyes on a TV set. Most TV transmissions now are in what is termed *compatible color*. This means that the signals may be received on a color set and result in a color image or they may be translated into a black and white image if the receiver is not a color producer.

The spectrum of color is produced by mixing the three primary colors just as an artist does. Yellow and blue mixed result in green, and so forth.

The job of a TV camera begins when its lens captures light from the scene in front of it. It must split this into three images, one for each primary color. *Dichronic*, or two-color, mirrors are used for this process as blue light is bounced from the first mirror, allowing red and green to continue. Then the red elements are reflected and green is allowed to pass through. The three separate light beams are then processed independently by the camera until your eye reassembles them on the TV screen.

A pattern of electric charges is created by the light striking a target area. As electrons flow from the area, they become the signal to your TV set to show that color in a glowing dot in a tiny area.

Because the signals are separated by color, TV cameras can be made to block out anything that's just one color. This device is used to insert weather maps or scenes from other places. One area in the main scene is painted all blue, for example, then at the desired time all the blue light signals are blocked. A second camera can then fill in the "hole" with the desired picture.

(Note: This selection is written at a high school readability level.)

1. What is the primary function of the TV camera?
2. Why can TV cameras be made to block out anything that's just one color?
3. What does the term *compatible color* mean?
4. In what form is light transmitted from the TV camera?

Look over the rates and answers to the questions you have recorded for the practice readings. Do you notice any patterns in your reading? What habits did you rely on as you read? Did your rate surprise you for any of the passages? Where did you miss more than one question?

To help you pinpoint reading strengths and weaknesses, look again at the nine key questions that were discussed earlier. Be honest with yourself as you study these questions. Remember, you are the only one who can really know what is going on inside your head. You are the only one who can tell how good or how poor your reading habits are.

1. *Do you really understand what you read?* Do you get the feeling that your eyes are moving over the words but that nothing is making any sense? Do you almost always get one kind of question right or wrong? You should be able to tell at what level you read most comfortably by how many questions you can answer. If you are able to answer three out of four questions for a given level, you probably comprehend most things written at that level. But this does not mean that you are comprehending as well as you *could*. You should still work to learn new ways to improve your reading comprehension and understanding.

2. *Do you change your WPM rate as you switch from one kind of material to another?* Have you ever noticed that you slow down when you come to a new or hard part of a reading? Or are you stuck in one gear and never change?

It might surprise you to know that the fastest readers are not always the best readers. Neither are the slowest. The best readers are the people who can change speed to suit the difficulty of the material they are reading.

No one agrees on what the perfect WPM rate is. But people can read easy or light material at 600 words or more per minute and still understand most of what they read. The more usual rate is between 200 and 300 words per minute. Most high school and college students read at about 200 words per minute for writing that is at an average or middle level. Even the best readers should and do slow down to 100 words per minute or less when they are studying very difficult material.

What you have to do is gain the ability to choose a WPM rate that will get you through your reading quickly, but still lets you understand as much as you need to. Reading at 800 words a minute does you no good if you have to reread passages to comprehend them.

3. *Are you reading out loud to yourself?* Many people whisper words under their breath as they read. Other

people move their lips for some or all of the words they come to. Some people also notice that they somehow "hear" each word inside their head as they go along.

All of these habits are called *subvocalization*. Some experts say we all subvocalize. But good readers hardly do it at all and have to be specially tested to record subvocalizations. Many reading experts believe that any subvocalization slows down WPM rates and keeps everyone from reading as well as they could.

You should concentrate to minimize subvocalization in your reading habits. You should have someone watch your lips as you read. Or you should put your fingers lightly on your voice box as you read. You will give yourself away with some vibrations and movement in your throat even when you are not consciously aware that you are subvocalizing.

4. Do you find yourself rereading often? Some people have fallen into the habit of rereading groups of two or three sentences as they work through a passage. They keep losing their place or forgetting the content of the passage. Be honest with yourself! If *you* do this, you are wasting valuable time.

Even though you will want to vary your WPM rate, you should also try to set a smooth pace. Rereading is a hard habit to break. But in the long run such rereading is a waste of time.

5. Are you reading word by word? Anyone who looks at each word separately as he or she reads is reading much too slowly. If you are doing this, you are probably also hurting your comprehension.

Reading in phrases or in groups of words helps you in two ways. You can read much more quickly because with practice you can learn to see groups of words as quickly as you can see one word. And you will help your comprehension because word groups often contain more precise meanings than a single word can.

6. What do you do when you come to unfamiliar words? There will always be times when you have to stop reading and think about the meaning of a word. But if that happens to you a lot, you need to change some of your reading habits. When you have to stop too often, you forget your line of thought. Your comprehension of the content begins to fall. And your WPM rate also begins to suffer.

You may need to organize a vocabulary building program. While the next section of this unit will give you some tips to aid vocabulary building, keep the following points in mind.

You should continuously be trying to increase the number

of words you know. The more words you know and are sure of, the greater will be your WPM rate and your level of comprehension.

You may also try to guess word meanings if you have enough context clues. Then you can read on and check your guess after you have completed your reading.

7. At what time of day and in what kinds of physical surroundings do you do most of your reading? You might surprise yourself with at least part of a miracle cure for reading difficulties if you just look around you.

You have probably been told that it is a mistake to try to read while watching TV or listening to a radio. But you probably try to do it anyway. Almost everyone does.

In fact, this is true. You may *believe* you read better with some background noise. But you do not. Just by eliminating background noise, you will almost guarantee an increase in your WPM rate and in your level of comprehension.

Some people can read with great comprehension propped up in bed or stretched out sunbathing. But most people cannot. Physical position or physical location can be as distracting as background noise. You would be better off to set aside a spot for your reading that is not a sleeping or a recreational area.

Neither is it a good idea to wait until you are tired to read. And reading in dim light is not only bad for your eyesight, it also invites your body to say it would rather sleep.

8. Do your eyes get tired or blurry as you read? If it has been some time since your last eye test, you should make sure that your eyes are not signaling that you may have some problem. Your eyes might itch or you may begin to have trouble focusing. Eye conditions change more quickly than you realize. Such conditions can be the cause of reading problems.

9. How often do you read? Honestly now, do you read something every day? How much time do you spend reading daily?

If you hardly read at all, it is unlikely that you will ever be a good reader. As with other things, you have to practice if you want to be good at reading. Your efforts will be rewarded by a gradually increasing WPM rate, and a rising level of comprehension.

3. Do you understand what you read?

One of the worst feelings in the world has got to be that sinking moment when you realize you have moved your eyes over an entire page or chapter and do not remember a word. You have spent time that you cannot afford to waste. And you begin to dread reading assignments as the results of your efforts seem worth less and less.

Fortunately there are some things you can do to keep this from happening to you very often. Suggestions that might help you are presented in this section. Some of these things will take time to get used to. Others may seem like they keep you from getting down to reading for much longer than you would like. But if you try these ideas out and can stick with them for awhile, you are guaranteed some improvement of reading comprehension.

Take a look at the reading profile you started in the preceding section. Have you written down that you sometimes do not understand what you have read? Or that one area you want to work on is reading to remember information?

This section will give you some hints on things to do *before* you start reading. And you will get some suggestions for things to do while you read, followed by some techniques for vocabulary improvement.

Learn to read backwards

Reading backwards is one of the more useful skills you can acquire. This may not sound very logical. But it does not mean what you think it means. Reading backwards for this purpose is deciding what information you need to get out of a book *before* you start reading.

You may still think this is impossible. How can you tell what you will need to know until you have read it? There are two main ways of doing this. One is surveying every book,

especially a textbook, before you ever read a word. The other
is to set a purpose for everything you read.

Survey a textbook. *Surveying* means taking advantage of all
the landmarks a book gives you so that you have an idea of
its shape and contents before you begin to study. Some of
the steps in surveying a textbook are outlined below. If you
have a book with you to study, try the steps out on it. If not,
use this book, looking for the same kinds of clues.

1. *Start with the table of contents, looking over the chapter
titles.* Sometimes the list will also include the subheadings
for each chapter. You will then have an idea of the topics
covered in the book and which of these topics will help you
to get the information you want from the reading.

2. *Flip to the back of the book and see what helps may be
there.* The index, of course, can be useful if you need to find
certain pieces of information. But often a book also has a
glossary of terms, a list of dates or names that are important,
or even a summary or outline of the whole book. Answers
to questions and exercises may also appear at the back of
a book.

3. *Look at some of the publishing information on or before
the title page.* You should know how old the book you are
using is. Just think of what information would be left out of a
history book that was published in 1970, before Watergate or
the energy shortage. You can avoid confusion and waste of
time by checking the publication date.

4. *Take a look at the introduction and preface.* Sometimes
the introduction and preface tell you nothing about the
book. But other times they will guide you to good ways of
studying the book or tell you things that were left out of
the book.

5. *Look for signals that direct you to what is important in
the material you are reading.* Any textbook and most information books have ways of showing you what is important.
Look for the use of a different kind of printing to show main
headings. Sometimes the words are darker, or in colored ink.
Special headings may be centered or out in the margin of a
page. Often new words or important words are printed in
darker type. There may be definitions of important words
given at the bottom of the page.

6. *Check to see if there is an introductory section or summary paragraph.* If there are, read *both* sections right away.
You will then have the best possible overview of the information that you need.

7. *Look to the end of sections for study questions.* If the

material you are reading has study questions, read this *before* you read the assignment. These questions will give you a good idea of what points are covered in the material you are going to read.

8. *Find the topic sentence.* You probably have been taught to write paragraphs around a topic sentence. Most of the people who write textbooks and other reading materials have been taught the same thing. Try this experiment. Pick a chapter or section from any book. Read through it quickly, forcing yourself to look only at the first sentence in each paragraph. This will usually be the topic sentence. By the time you have finished the reading, you will have created a summarized version of the chapter or section.

9. *Study the maps, graphs, pictures, captions, and other illustrations.* You will need to look at the illustrations when you come to them during detailed reading later on. But a quick look beforehand will give you a hint of what kinds of things are emphasized in the reading material. In a math or science book, the graphs and illustrations may sum up the main ideas better than the words can.

10. *Change the information from your survey into questions to answer as you read.* You can change subheadings into questions by rearranging words. For example, if one sub-head is "Contributions of Italian Americans," you can turn that into "What did Italian Americans contribute?" You should write some of these questions out for yourself to make sure you are paying attention to the right things. You can also use your questions and answers to review for tests later.

Set your purpose. Once you have some idea of what your reading is going to contain, you can begin to set your purpose. You may want to write down your purpose before you begin reading. In this way you will be sure to think about it as you do your reading.

One of the best ways to set a purpose is to decide what your end product needs to be. If you are reading for pleasure or to fill time, you can set a purpose of practicing reading techniques.

If you are reading for a test that you know will have lots of names and dates, you will have to read slowly and concentrate on facts and details. This is also true if your survey of the book shows that it is detailed and emphasizes many facts.

When you know you are going to have an essay test or will need to write a paper, you will have to look for main ideas. You will note only the most important facts.

Your purpose will be one thing if the novel you read is part of a unit where you are expected to compare certain characters. It will be very different if you know the novel is an example of a certain kind of writing and you are supposed to be able to show how it fits into that mold.

Other kinds of reading, perhaps in a science or industrial arts course, will require you to identify certain principles and then know how to apply them or make them work. When that is true, your purpose again is different.

Think of everything you have to get out of the material you are going to read. This will help you decide what it is you are going to emphasize as you read.

Once you have done a survey and set your purpose you are ready to read. However, your efforts to get ready to read will be wasted if you fail to concentrate on being an active reader. There is no easy way around this point. You must keep your mind active and involved if you are going to understand and remember what you are reading.

Be an active reader

There are some tricks and tasks you can set yourself that will help you to become an active reader. They are listed below. Try some of them. Please note that you will have to read with a pencil in your hand to do them.

1. Underline the main ideas. Even if you rent your textbooks, you can usually make light pencil marks which you can erase later. If you are really having trouble in a class, it may be worthwhile to find out if you can buy your textbooks. You can then mark your books in whatever way seems best for your purposes.

Force yourself to think as you read, sifting out the details and concentrating on topic sentences and main ideas. Underline the sentences or parts of sentences that include those main ideas. This will be useful later for reviewing the material. It will also force you to decide what is important as you go along.

If you find it hard to pick out the main ideas, look at the clues and questions you developed in your initial survey. Try out the first sentence of a paragraph to see if it summarizes most of the information in the paragraph. Look at the last paragraph in each section, checking for clue words like *therefore, overall, we can see,* and so forth.

2. Invent a code. You should avoid underlining details. But you should identify them and pay attention to the important ones. So, develop your own code to give yourself clues. You can use your code, then, to identify different kinds of details.

You can make notes so that later you will be able to find information that was confusing or seemed especially important.

Some codes you might want to try are:

a. Putting a circle around key words or unfamiliar words.

b. Putting a single line in the margin for a paragraph that summarizes a section.

c. Putting a double line for a major summary.

d. Putting a star beside each application of or experiment with the main ideas you have underlined.

You may want to put letters in the margin to stand for different things, like a character's initials when he makes a major speech or does something important in a novel. Or, if you find certain themes or ideas coming up again and again, you might pick a letter to stand for them. That way, if you need to write about a certain aspect of what you have read, or talk about it in class, or review it for an exam, you can just run your eye down the margin and find the right sections.

You should also use brief notes. Just a word or two, like *causes of war*, will summarize some details and action so you can find them quickly.

3. Write a summary. You need not write in complete sentences or paragraphs, but jot down a summary of each section or chapter as you complete it. This summary may be placed either in the blank space that usually comes at the beginning of a chapter or in a separate notebook. If you have a good summary of each assignment it will be easier for you to review your reading assignments. However, the most important payoff again is to make yourself think about what you are reading and to practice picking out what is important as you read.

4. Tie information together. Keep in mind that the only way to remember facts is to tie them to something you already know. It also helps to try to think of ways your own life might relate to the things you study in school, or ways you might be able to use any of the information. You should also note any connection you find between one chapter and another or between subjects, like American history and American literature.

Review and test yourself

Think of what main ideas you have been able to identify. Try to summarize the chapter in a few words. List details under the main headings in the book or in your notes. Answer the questions you asked yourself when you surveyed the book or background material.

Keep pushing yourself to remember what you have read.

No matter how thorough you think your job of reading was, it is worthless if you cannot remember what you read.

Keep trying to fit information into an outline so you have fewer details to remember. If you can think of the main topic, then an outline, you will have less to recall than if each bit of information has to be remembered separately.

In addition to the suggestions made above, there is one other thing that can contribute to improved reading comprehension. You should try to keep expanding your vocabulary. The number of words you know and are comfortable using is important for several reasons.

For one thing, you will understand what you read much better if the terms and words have a clear meaning to you as you read. Usually, if you know the meaning of certain key words, you can get a grip on the main idea.

You need to have the words available to you for tests and writing, too. You show how much you know by the kind of words you use. There is proof, too, that the number of words you know has a lot to do with how clear your thinking is. Your mind depends on words to label complicated ideas and important concepts.

It also slows your reading rate when you have to keep stopping at each new word. You want to be able to quickly understand the meaning of what you read. You should try to avoid having to stop and figure out the meaning of words.

Vocabulary adds to understanding

While vocabulary building techniques are covered in great detail in unit 6 of this book, here are a few tips you may find useful. You may think the only way to learn more words is to keep looking them up in the dictionary. Actually, the best way to learn words you need to know is to watch for them as you read, perhaps circle them to draw your attention to them, and go on. Use the context in which a word is used to make a guess as to the word's meaning. See if the sentence in which the word is used explains or defines it. Look at what is given as an opposite word or concept.

You may have to refer to a glossary or dictionary for some words. If you do, be sure you choose the right meaning. Remember that the same word can have different meanings for different subjects. For example, the word *plane* has a different meaning in math, in woodworking, and in history. Write down the meaning of any unfamiliar word. Refer to the meaning as you need it.

Work to add words

Just getting the meaning of unfamiliar words, though, will not do you much good. You must use the words as you read.

It may be helpful to make a list of key words as you go. You can then glance over your list to be sure of the words you need. And the list can also be used as a study and review aid.

If you find that you are stopping for many ordinary words as well as words that are new in each subject, you should start a campaign of vocabulary building. A good way to do this is to make a list of words you keep seeing but do not know. These are words you should learn. There are also study aid books that will give you lists of words or word parts to work on. Knowing these parts is a shortcut to a good vocabulary. Remember, though, it is usually best to concentrate on those words that have meaning and real use to you. Set yourself a goal. Decide you will learn at least five or six new words each week. Make yourself use these new words in writing or speaking. You cannot really say you know the meaning of a word unless you are able to use it.

Vocabulary building is a slow process. But *building* is the main idea. Adding new words will help your reading to become smoother and more meaningful.

Summing up

The best way to improve your comprehension and understanding is to become an active reader. You must prepare so you know what the main ideas are in the material you are going to read. You should mark and organize main ideas and details. Then, you should try to fit what you learn into your past knowledge and review to keep what you have learned in your memory. Vocabulary work will also help you to comprehend and remember what you read. All of these suggestions taken together will help you to become a smoother, more efficent reader.

4. Can you increase your reading speed?

"I read OK. It's just that it takes so long." This is a common complaint students make. Everyone would probably like to be able to read faster.

For one thing, advertisements for speed-reading courses make it look so easy. You see people who are hardly able to turn the pages fast enough to keep up with their WPM rate. And there you sit, taking what seems like hours to read one chapter.

And, it seems to get worse for most students. As you move to higher grade levels, there is more to read. Some classes require as much as a chapter to be read every night. Some teachers act as if their class is the only one you are taking. These teachers make what seem to be endless reading assignments.

There is good news for you, though. It is just about a sure thing that you can learn to read faster than you now read.

Almost everyone reads more slowly than his or her potential. Reading rate is one thing that is almost never taught in school. And tests show that many adults actually read more slowly than they did when they were in school.

Systematic practice to increase reading speed will work for most people. The real problem most people have with their reading rate is in not trying to improve it.

As was mentioned earlier, most school systems do not teach reading skills after elementary school. And yet growth in reading skills is necessary even for older students. It is also true that you cannot work on increasing your reading rate unless you already are a pretty skillful reader. This means that junior high or high school is the time and place to work on your WPM rate. Yet very few schools offer students the chance to do this. And most people feel they do not have the skill to increase their WPM rate.

More things to read

Understanding comes first

So, most attention in school and at home is given to increasing comprehension skills. And these are *very important.*

In fact, comprehension skills are the most important of the reading skills. If you have to choose between working to improve your WPM rate and working to improve your understanding, choose to concentrate on understanding.

It makes no difference how fast you read if you are not soaking up the information you need as you go. *This chapter is not for you unless you have your comprehension up to where you understand most of what you are reading.* You will hurt your overall reading effectiveness if you concentrate on rate before comprehension.

Once you are at a comprehension level where you are confident, though, reading faster certainly has advantages. If done right, a reading speed program should also be a program for improving your understanding of what you read. Some people who read very slowly may actually be hurting their ability to understand what they have read. Their slow WPM rate interferes with their understanding.

Improving your WPM rate also has the advantage of letting you use your reading time more efficiently. And it may also help to make reading less of a boring job or something you hate and dread. An improved WPM rate can let you enjoy reading more and get more practice out of it. But keep in mind that both a good level of comprehension *and* a good WPM rate are necessary for effective reading.

Practice slower reading too

Would it surprise you to learn that reading *slower* should be part of your WPM rate program? You might remember that when you were developing your reading profile, one of the questions asked you was about reading rate. You were supposed to check if you changed your reading rate as material got harder. Flexibility of reading rate is the mark of a good reader. It is also something that takes thinking and practice.

In the previous section, it was suggested that you set a purpose for yourself each time you read. You might remember that part of setting a purpose involved deciding what WPM rate would be best for understanding the passage being read.

Much of what this section will tell you is directed toward simply reading faster. That is because most people need to have a program of rate improvement to add faster reading to their reading habits. But, remember that slowing down when it fits your purpose is also part of your whole rate picture.

Take a look again at the reading rates you figured out for yourself in doing your reading profile. Compare them to this breakdown of reading rates.

Suggested rates used for different purposes

Words per minute	Purpose
150 or less	hard, very technical, poetic or unfamiliar material
200-300	normal studying, average material
350-600	light reading, newspapers, magazines
up to 1,000	skimming and scanning

The numbers suggested on this chart are not magic or absolute. They just give you a general idea of how much variation there can be in the WPM rate for different kinds of reading material. No matter what your current rate is, you can see that it will be too fast for some purposes and too slow for others. What you want to be able to do is to get a "feel" for what you can do at each different rate. Then, you can choose the rate that will be best for each purpose as it comes up.

This section can add three important things to your reading profile notebook.

1. It will give you a list of reading habits that hold you back from reading better and faster. Along with each habit on the list is a set of suggestions for overcoming it. You should add those habits you want to change to the section you already started in your reading profile.

2. You will get the outline of a system for learning to read faster. You have to make yourself practice, though, and keep track of your progress if you want it to work. Adding an outline of your WPM rate program and charting your progress should also be part of your personal reading notebook.

3. You will be introduced to two kinds of high speed reading that should be used in connection with studying and looking for information. Knowing when to use these techniques should be part of your plan when you are setting your purpose for reading.

Choosing to read more slowly is one thing. But reading slowly because of bad reading habits is another.

Study the list that follows. It is a list of things people do

Habits that slow you down

when they read. You may find that some of the habits on this list are ones you wrote down in your reading profile as reading habits you would like to change. This time you will get some suggestions on how to eliminate the habits that may be slowing you down.

After you have had a chance to try some of these suggestions, you will be given a plan for increasing your WPM rate through practice. Remember, though, the habits on the list that follows will hold back any attempt to increase your WPM rate. So it will be necessary for you to get rid of any of the habits you might have that are on this list.

Stop subvocalizing or reading aloud to yourself. Not everyone who subvocalizes realizes it. You may only whisper or move your lips slightly. But any movement that can be noticed will hurt your WPM rate. Try putting your fingers lightly on your voice box again as you read this. Also ask yourself if you are forming the words in your mind as you read.

The best cure is to keep yourself paced smoothly. You cannot talk, even under your breath, nearly as fast as your eyes can move. So, if your eyes are sending information faster than your voice can keep up, you should find yourself subvocalizing less and less.

Change word-by-word reading habits. Some people look at every word by itself just because they read so slowly. Other people run their fingers under each line, or point to words to keep their place. For whatever reason, reading one word at a time hurts you in two ways. First, you cannot read very fast if you spend time on each word in turn. Second, it is hard for your mind to make sense of a lot of single words being sent to it in a row. It is much easier to understand things you read if you are automatically putting them into idea groups as you go.

Read sentence number one, and sentence number two. Notice the difference in the way these two sentences have been arranged.

1. Being   able   to   get   a   tan   and   build muscles   is   part   of   why   city   life- guards   want   their   underpaid   jobs.

2. Being able   to get a tan   and build muscles is part of why   city lifeguards want   their underpaid jobs.

70

In sentence number one, your eye probably had to stop on each word, maybe even go back a time or two to get the ideas right. You can read sentence number two by stopping your eyes only once for each word group. The first version requires *three times* as many stops as the second one. This means it takes you much longer to read sentence number one than it takes to read sentence number two.

Look at the dot in the middle of the row of numerals and letters below. Keep your eyes on that dot and notice how many numerals and letters you can see.

09876543210987654321 • abcdefghijklmnopqrstuvwxyz

This is called your "visual span," or how many printed characters you can see at each stop. The best way to increase what you are taking in each time your eyes stop is to move at a fast enough pace so that you are forced to stop reading word by word. Try going through a magazine article and marking word groups.

This season/of college basketball/promises/to keep fans/ buying tickets/to see/their favorite teams/in action.

If it is hard for you to break the word-by-word habit, try cutting up a newspaper and using it as an aid. You can also use a magazine with narrow columns of writing. Tape one story onto a piece of paper and draw a line down the middle. Move your eyes down the line and force yourself to read the story without moving your eyes to the right or left.

This is hard to keep up for very long unless it becomes a natural procedure. But it will show you how much your eyes can take in at once. Try the procedure on this example:

Did you know that you
are doing things all the
time because of tiny changes
in your body? Nerves
send messages from little
bits of information that
can affect what you do.
      For one thing, you
feel thirsty when you
have lost only one
percent of your body's
water. Or, one nerve
on the bridge of your
nose can stop a
sneeze.

Keep a smooth even pace. Remember that stopping for every word you do not know or to reread sentences will hurt both your WPM rate and your understanding. You have to be an active reader to improve both your WPM rate as well as your understanding.

If you let your mind wander or if you stop fitting the sentences together in your mind as you go, you will have to reread. Of course, rereading is fine if you have to work on very hard material or want to review. But most of the time a lot of stopping and going back is not good.

Read to the end of the page or section, keeping up a good, solid pace. *Then* go back. You may want to keep a pencil in your hand to put a dot or check by lines you want to review or that have words that need to be looked up. That way you will be sure you can find the spots where you stopped.

Arrange your time for top performance. You will not be reading efficiently if you leave your studying until late at night when you are tired. If you keep putting it off until you are hours behind, you will also be unable to keep up a steady pace.

Trying to read at a very high speeds in short bursts is not very useful. You will probably break up your concentration and line of thought so much that any gain in words per minute will be lost by poor comprehension. Reading when you are rested and can plan reasonable breaks will pay off in increased efficiency.

Ask yourself what your purpose is each time you sit down to read. You may be missing chances to use a higher speed because you are not thinking of how much you need to get out of things you read. If you have decided that something is going to be hard to understand, use your previewing skills. Then try to make your second reading go faster. Using rapid reading when you sit down with a magazine will give you a chance to practice with easy material.

Put yourself in training. It is a good idea to put yourself on a training program that is separate from the reading you normally do. Try these steps to put together a plan for yourself. You can choose to read just about anything that interests you. You can do it without paying the high charges of speed reading classes. But, you do have to make yourself practice regularly. If you think you cannot do it, you may want to ask for help from your family or promise yourself a reward every time you stick to the plan.

Before you even start, though, review the steps for calculating words per minute. Remember, the formula is

$$\frac{\text{number of words read}}{\text{total time in seconds}} \times 60 = \text{Words Per Minute (WPM)}$$

You should also figure out the average number of words per line of what you are reading. That way you can get a fast total on the amount read by counting just the lines or pages.

Also, choose a book or magazine that is easy and enjoyable. The best thing is usually a light novel or a magazine with narrow columns and not too many pictures. Then, transfer your plan to your notebook, along with your information on how many words per line and lines per page you will read on the average.

There are many different plans for building reading speed. Each plan may work better for some people than it will for others.

What follows is a plan that has worked for many people. The plan is simple to understand and can be followed without special help or equipment. The most important requirement is consistent practice. Reading rate does not increase naturally. You must work at it.

1. Decide on a set amount of reading to work with. Usually a page or two of a paperback is good. Read it at your usual pace. Figure out your WPM rate.

2. Take an index card or folded piece of paper. You will be using it to pace yourself down the page. If you have had problems with going back to lines you already read or with reading word by word, use of the card can help you with these problems, too. You should try to look at the middle of each line or make only two or three stops at the most in each line.

3. Now, concentrate on speeding up. Try to read the next set of pages at a steady but faster pace. Keep your card moving smoothly—and do not expect to recall everything on the page.

4. Pause and be sure you are understanding *most* of what you have read. Then keep up the pace with only brief stops in between your sets of pages.

5. Keep reading for at least ten minutes, longer if you can. You can finish your practice period by reading a couple of pages without pushing yourself so much.

6. Practice every day if you can, and figure out your WPM rate at the end of each week. Try to increase your WPM rate from week to week. As you continue with the plan, improvement will be obvious.

7. Add a chart of your progress to your notebook. You can also keep track of how many pages you are reading each day in the same way. Use graph paper or draw your own lines. A sample of one student's progress might be:

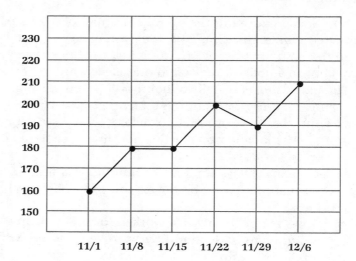

Avoid letting your understanding slip when you are reading. And keep in mind that you have to read *more slowly* sometimes to be a good, flexible reader.

Two higher speeds

In addition to reading faster overall, you should add two kinds of very high speed reading to your total plan. These are called *skimming* and *scanning*. Any reading class that claims to teach you to read 1,000 words per minute or a textbook in an hour is really teaching skimming and scanning.

Skimming is usually described as a very high rate of eye movement used for a general overview. Skimming consists of going over the surface of something, usually by looking at topic sentences, names, and other highlights.

Scanning is also a very high rate of eye movement. The purpose is the opposite of skimming, though. When you scan, you are searching for just one thing and ignoring all the other words. For example, you would use the skill of scanning if you were trying to find where a person's name was on a list.

These are very useful kinds of reading skills. Skimming is great for a first look at a book to see if it seems interesting or has information you need. It can help you to see if two books are pretty much the same or if they have important differences.

Scanning is a skill you have to use every day to read time-tables or the phone book. If you had to look at every word and decide which was the entry you needed, ordinary searches could take forever. Scanning skills are very helpful if you are doing research and must look through many books to find a few sections that have information you need.

Both skimming and scanning help in reviewing books and notes for tests. And they will help you to get an idea of which books will be the ones you want to look at further.

But, you have to be sure you know that skimming and scanning are not what is usually meant by reading. Remember that you can read one word when it is flashed at you for 1/1000 of a second, but you cannot read 1,000 words per second no matter what. The same is true of skimming and scanning. These skills rely on your picking out just a few bits of information you can use later, not really seeing everything on all pages.

Skimming, scanning, and any other similar methods cannot give you 100 per cent recall, and probably cannot even give you 50 per cent. For one thing, your mind is unable to hold that many words in your memory all at once. For another, it is common sense that you cannot remember something you never saw. If you look only at the words in an *S* pattern down the page, those are the only words you can expect to remember.

You should probably practice all the skimming and scanning you can when you are studying your textbooks. For example, set yourself names and dates to look for in your history assignments. Scan the index of a book on purpose to see how quickly you can find the page where a homework question might be answered. Skim some of your assignments before you go back to read them closely.

Try to add skimming and scanning to the options you think about before you begin any reading. You may find you can use the techniques for many purposes as you go along.

And finally

By now you should have your notebook filled with an outline of what kind of reader you are. You should have some ideas for understanding more of what you read. And you should have a plan to improve your reading rate. Do not waste the effort you have put in up to now. Use the skills that have been discussed. Practice, concentrate—and keep growing as a reader.

Activities

The unit-end activities have been designed to help you to practice and gain the ability to use the various classroom and study skills described in this unit. Please do not write in this book, but place your answers on a separate sheet of paper. Answers to the activities can be found in the **Answer Key** that begins on page 290.

Understanding the unit

Review your understanding of important points in this unit by answering the following questions.

1. What is one way that subvocalization can limit the level of your reading performance?
2. What are some situations in which you might survey a book?
3. What is the formula you can use to compute your WPM reading rate?
4. How do you go about setting a purpose for your reading?
5. How can the practice of underlining help you to improve reading efficiency?
6. What should you do if you come to a word you do not know in a reading assignment?
7. When should you read slower?
8. When should you use the skills of skimming and scanning?

Find the main idea

Being able to find the main idea in a paragraph is an important skill that will help you to become a more efficient reader. Read the following paragraphs and decide which is the main idea in each. Write down the number of each sentence you believe contains a paragraph's main idea.

Yogurt

(1) Yogurt is a food product that belongs to the same food group as milk, eggs, and cheese. (2) Yogurt has the same nutritional value as these other dairy foods. (3) Another food in this group would be cottage cheese.

(4) Yogurt is made by the process of fermentation. (5) Two different kinds of bacteria are added to milk, and then the milk is kept at a warm temperature. (6) This lets the milk ferment in a controlled way. (7) The sugars in the milk are changed to lactic acid. (8) This lactic acid then thickens and sours the milk.

(9) Some yogurt is sold plain and unflavored. (10) Other yogurt has fruit or flavorings added to it. (11) A new favorite is frozen yogurt, which is very much like ice cream. (12) Some cooks add yogurt to their recipes, while others choose to serve it as is. (13) All these additions, changes, and uses show that yogurt is a very versatile product.

(14) Some dieters rely on yogurt as a low calorie meal. (15) While it is true that plain yogurt is low in calories and high in protein, many people do not realize that the flavored and frozen yogurts can be very fattening. (16) Yogurt has all the nutritional value of milk. (17) While low-fat milk is often used to make yogurt, the flavorings can be high in sugar. (18) And sugar is a substance many people are anxious to keep out of their diet.

Using context clues

Read each of the following entries. Each entry contains a word that is printed in italics. Look for context clues in each entry that will help you to understand the meaning of the italicized word.

1. At one time, an actor used only the *domino*, or half-mask, to cover his or her face.
2. Her car's *dieseling* began to drive Judy crazy. Then her mechanic told her she could keep the car from running on after the ignition was turned off by filling it with premium gas occasionally.

3. My father was really angry when his partner sued him for making *defamatory* remarks. Father said he would never make remarks that would hurt his partner's reputation.
4. The hero dashed to the edge of the *precipice*, only to see his brother lose hold of the edge of the cliff and fall to the valley below.

Reading for details

Copy this passage onto a sheet of paper. Then read and mark the passage as you would if it was a class assignment. After you have completed reading and marking the passage, answer the questions which follow it.

Atomic clocks

People have always wanted to know what time it is. They may not have had the mania for clock watching that many people have today. But as far back as the beginning of recorded history people seem to have made use of movement of some kind to mark the passage of time.

Shadows of trees moved as the sun passed through the sky, and so ancient people made sundials to chart that movement. The *clepsydra,* or water clock, relied on the regular flow of water from one vessel to another to mark the passage of time. Mechanical clocks relied on the movement of gears and wheels to show the changing of minutes and hours.

These clocks all used observable movements as the basis of their timekeeping. Accuracy was good, but not precise. It was only with the advent of the atomic clock that accuracy became almost unbelievable.

The atomic clock is actually tuned to the movement of molecules and atoms. These movements cause vibrations. The vibrations are just a tiny fraction of the movement used in the past to judge the passage of time.

The accuracy of atomic clocks can be set to within a few seconds in 100,000 years. It is rare that such accuracy is needed—certainly we can make do with much greater margins for error in our wristwatches. But for scientific work, where time is measured in the tiniest segments and the smallest change is critical, atomic clocks are necessary.

There is another kind of atomic clock that is always ticking away around us. It involves a process that is called *carbon dating*.

Carbon 14 atoms in organic material decay at a regular, known rate. So, it is possible to determine how much decay has taken place and to estimate the age of an organic material by gauging its level of carbon 14.

Unlike the kind of atomic clock that was mentioned first, carbon 14 timing is not accurate to within thousandths of a second. In fact, scientists usually hope carbon 14 timing is accurate to within hundreds of years.

1. What kinds of marking or coding did you use when studying this passage?
2. What is a *clepsydra?*
3. What kind of movement is used to tune an atomic clock?
4. How accurate can an atomic clock be?
5. In what other way can atoms be used to mark the passage of time?
6. How accurate is this second system?

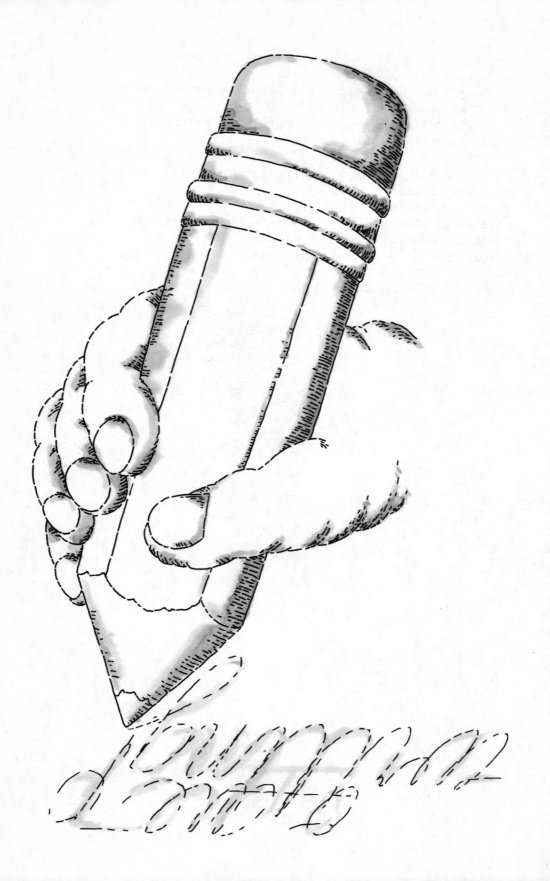

A guide to
writing skills

Are you able to write well? Can you explain ideas and opinions clearly and concisely on paper? If you cannot, you are not alone. The ability to write well is a skill that is developed only after many tries and serious practice. But most people are unwilling to make the effort needed to become a good writer.

The subject of this unit is writing skills. You will be shown organizational techniques that are used by effective writers. And you will be taken step-by-step through the procedures used to prepare and write a short report and a term paper.

The contributor of this unit is Betty Jane Wagner, Chairperson of the English-Philosophy Department, National College of Education, Evanston, Illinois.

1. Need some help?

**A message
to deliver**

What is writing? It is simply a message on paper from someone to someone else. The test of good writing is how well
it comes across to the reader. If it is clear, direct, unclut-
tered, and fully developed, the reader will know what the
writer wants to share with him or her. If the reader is confused, either the writer has not done a good job, or the reader is not paying attention or is not ready for the message.

To write effectively, you need a clear image of the person
to whom you are writing—the "intended receiver." You
write best when you write for someone who needs to know
what you are saying. Because in school you are usually writing for a teacher, you may have a problem. The teacher may
already know more about the subject of your writing than
you. In addition, the teacher may write better.

If this worries you, forget your teacher as the "intended
receiver" and instead imagine you are writing for a person
younger than you, or someone who has never read what you
have, or has not thought as much as you have about your
subject. This way you will think about the important thing in
writing: How can I get my message across to the reader?

Write a first draft

You cannot write well if you worry about making mistakes in
spelling, grammar, and so on. Forget errors until after you
have spun out a *first draft*. Do not stop to look up the spelling of words, to worry about correct punctuation, or to decide where new paragraphs should begin. Instead, think
only about what you want to say.

While writing this first version, pretend you are talking
with an interested friend. What does that person need to
know? How can you ease him or her into knowing what you
know? What details or descriptions can you give to make the

reader become aware of what you want to say? Once you have thought about this a bit, quickly write out a draft of your message for this reader.

Do not give up. Keep writing even when you think what is coming out sounds stupid. You can always cut out the weak parts later. Just keep your eye on that ball—that curious, interested, uninformed reader—and keep swinging toward him or her. As with anything else, you get better with practice. If what you first write does not suit you, change it later.

Good athletes know their best performances come after warming up. Good bits of writing come after a period of free writing—warming up by babbling on without stopping to worry about the quality of the writing. Talk to yourself on paper. Write anything while you are warming up. How do you feel about the writing assignment you are starting? What are the various ways you might begin this paper? What problems do you see looming before you?

Practice your writing

Many authors and some students keep journals—collections of random sketches, descriptions of experiences, on-paper ramblings about their moods or problems, about decisions to make, or about wishes and dreams. This writing by *self* for *self* provides an excellent source of ideas for later writing. You can go back and look at your journal and pick out good parts. A journal is merely a place to keep all your writing warm ups together.

If you have a writing assignment, jot down in your journal any ideas you have for it. If you are not ready to put these ideas into sentences, then just list them.

Even if you do not have a writing assignment due, jot down ideas that you would someday like to put into a story, poem, or essay. They will be good reminders when the time comes.

Much of the material in your journal will not be useful to you as a source for later writings. Do not worry. The process of getting the writing flow going is valuable in itself. Once you have established the flow, however, you need to select only the best and to reject wagonloads of words. There is no other way to become a good writer.

The puzzling truth about writing is that you should not try to be a good writer all the time. But write anyway. You gradually do get better. If you stop writing because you are convinced you are not doing well or if you put off starting at all, then there is no hope for improvement. Thinking about writing does little good.

Starting in

There is no magic to writing. Even if you keep your eye on the reader and spend time with a journal, you still have to decide what you want to say to your reader. Sometimes the whole point of a piece seems clear. All you have to do is sit down and write it out. But most of the time you have to write, not because you have been inspired, but simply because an assignment is due. So you have to set aside the time to write whether you are in the mood or not.

The time to begin working on an assignment is the day you get it. Take your first free 10 minutes and force yourself to write about the assignment for at least that long. Of course you are not ready. So what should you write? Anything. If worse comes to worse, write about why you wish you did not have this assignment. Make a list of everything you would like to include in this paper. Do not rely on your memory. Whenever you have an idea, write it down. Thinking about an assignment right away gives you time to work on the problem as you go about your daily affairs. Keep a notepad handy for jottings. Brainstorm with yourself.

Start writing immediately. It does not matter what you write now. What matters is that you do write. Postponement often creates anxiety problems. And your nervousness will inhibit clear thinking. Get on with it. Write! Writing something will make you feel less anxious.

Once you start thinking about a problem, your whole self—the unconscious as well as the conscious part of you —goes to work on it. If you are determined to do well, and if you start early putting down on paper all your ideas at the moment, you may be surprised at the new insights that come when you least expect them. You may find yourself getting ideas right before you go to sleep at night, or before you get up in the morning, or while you are waiting your turn at bat.

Another good thing to do right after you have gotten an assignment is to talk it over with a group of friends. You may do this anyway. You thought it was just grumbling together, but you were really beginning to write your paper. How? By sorting out your feelings about the assignment and by clarifying with each other just what the assignment calls for. If you are confused about an assignment, especially after a discussion, by all means go back to the teacher. There is no point in getting off on the wrong track.

Write down everything you can remember about the assignment. This may merely be a set of notes or a list of ideas. Add it to the list you made for yourself earlier. Anything you put down helps later.

Now wait at least a couple of hours. Look back over the first 10 minutes of writing you did and the notes you wrote after talking with your friends. Put a plus mark (+) beside the good ideas and a minus (−) beside those you would just as soon forget. If something strikes you as really good, give it an exclamation point (!) and begin thinking how you would write a paper with that idea as the main point. It may be the first 10 minutes of writing you did is good enough for the beginning of your first draft. Ask yourself, what does the reader need to know? If that person was sitting in front of you, how would you begin? You might wander a bit if you were speaking, so do so on paper. Try to guess what another person does not know about your experience. After all, he or she is not you and cannot read your mind. Write what you are thinking. If you prefer, draw diagrams or sketches to remind you of what you want to put into words later. Now take these words or sketches and put them into sentences. Do your words seem no good or, at best, weak and ordinary? Do not worry. Just keep going. Write as long as you can—for at least 10 minutes without stopping. Write on only one side of the paper so you can later cut out parts and rearrange others. Leave wide margins for notes to yourself.

Summarizing

Stop and read what you have written. See if there seems to be one main idea—something important you are trying to say. Summarize it! Is there a place early in the paper where you might put that summary? Maybe you have already summarized your main idea in another part of your paper. If so, do you like your new summary better? Then substitute it. Now see if there is a way to shorten the summary into a title. If so, do it. So far, so good.

Now you have a summary statement that ties together what you have already written, and you have a title. From here on, you need to fit everything around that summary statement.

Think about the summary statement and the reader. Is that person going to be able to follow what you are saying? How are you going to make him or her believe that summary statement? What else do you need to tell? Writers who fail to take account of their readers make bad writers. It is the writer's job to help the reader get the message. To do this well, you need examples, definitions, comparisons or contrasts, descriptive detail—any kind of extensions or expansions of the summary idea.

This advice may seem to apply only to the writing of reports or themes, and not to stories or poems. Not so. In any kind of composing, it is useful to begin writing and then to stop and summarize in a short sentence. Your summary for a poem or a story is your guide, though you seldom put it directly into the writing. In nonfiction, the summary is both your guide and the reader's. You write it out for both of you.

<table>
<tr><td>

**Finishing a
first draft**

</td><td>

Once you have your summary statement and you feel that it says what you intend, then finishing the piece is comparatively easy. Now you have two guides to writing: the reader and what he or she needs to know, and your own summary statement of what you have started to tell this reader. If you are writing a report or theme, decide which facts and illustrations make your point most convincingly. You may decide to contrast your idea with one that challenges it. For example, if you are arguing that handguns should not be owned by private citizens, you could present the arguments for ownership of handguns and then show why you take issue with them.

</td></tr>
</table>

You are still working on a first draft. Now is the time to be a big spender of words. Later, you can cut down excessive words. If later you are afraid to get rid of any of your hard-won prose, then you will be in trouble, no doubt about it. For now, write down all the ideas you can think of.

Remember, while doing your first draft, forget about grammar or rules. At this point, it would only tend to slow you down, make you less sure of yourself, clutter your mind, and make your writing come out unclear. The great advantage of writing as fast as possible is the likelihood of capturing the intensity that comes in expressing yourself with abandon and energy. Get in the habit of writing without stopping. Circle words to check later for spelling. Note in the margin places to come back to for checking on paragraphing, punctuation, or wording.

While writing a first draft, it helps to think someone else is going to go through and correct all the errors later. Your job for now is only to get down what you want to say.

<table>
<tr><td>

**Get other
people's ideas**

</td><td>

The best way to test something you have written is to read it aloud to other people, preferably your own age. If your friends like parts of your writing and are confused by other parts, this will help you decide which parts to cut out or rewrite and which to add to and make more important.

Some students who want to develop their writing skills

</td></tr>
</table>

meet regularly to read drafts of their writing to each other and to talk together about the writings. They may call themselves a "Writing Workshop." Each person agrees to bring a draft to read aloud at each meeting and to respond to everyone else's paper.

Start by propping up your summary statement where you can see it. Go through your paper and take out all the parts that do not pertain to that summary. Use a copy editor's shorthand for delete. Your edited first draft may look like this:

How to revise

Therefore, the major causes of the conflict could
be resolved down to these: the inability of both
sides to compromise; a tradition of conflict between the two groups; the need of both groups to
expand economically; the absence of a clearly
defined political border between the two groups.

If you delete this way you do not run the risk of crossing out material you may later decide belongs either elsewhere in this paper or in another paper you find yourself writing.

Reread the part or parts your listeners liked. How can you make this part more important? Should it be at the beginning? Should it be longer?

Now go through your paper and reread the part or parts where your listeners were confused or uninterested. See if you can find a way to improve the writing. Rewrite.

Finally, reread the entire paper, leaving out the deleted portions and reading the revised wordings of sections you improved. This time pay attention to the order of the various paragraphs. See if another arrangement would work better. Are all the paragraphs on the same idea in the same place? When you deleted portions or rearranged them, did it make the paper choppy? Ease into each rough part with an introductory sentence of some kind, what writers often call a "transition."

After you are satisfied that you have done all that you can, rewrite or retype a clean copy of your paper. Read the clean copy for typographical errors. Your paper should now be ready to submit.

2. Can you write a short report?

Why teachers assign reports

Most teachers, especially social studies and English teachers, require reports. Why? Is it because they need evidence that you read the assignments? Do they want to grade you on how well you read? Are they trying to keep you out of trouble? Or are they just ornery?

Most teachers do not assign written reports for any of these reasons. They have a reason that is far more important. Teachers know that you are likely to read more carefully if you realize you will have to respond in some way. One way teachers have found to jog students into paying attention to what they read is to ask them to write about it.

Some reports are summaries, or shortened versions, of what was read. Others are critiques, or evaluations. Book reports may be either summaries or critiques. Still other reports are research studies, that call for reading more than one source and pulling information from several sources together into a well-organized paper.

When you are putting together information about a subject to help a reader understand it, you are doing a kind of writing called expository prose or exposition. This need not be information you have learned from reading. It might be from your own experience.

For example, you might decide to write an informative article on how to repair a bicycle. You might base this article on your experiences repairing bicycles. Or you might decide to write your ideas on a subject, such as professional sports or the value of camping. This kind of exposition is called a theme or essay.

In a report, you are primarily summarizing reading or research you have done. In an informative article, you may be either reporting on something you read or on your own experience. In a theme or essay, you are presenting your views.

In this section, we will be looking at reports. A report is usually shorter than a term paper. Often, like a book report, it is a summary or critique of a single piece of reading matter.

When writing a report, begin by concentrating on what you are reading for the report. Think first about the writer who wrote what you are reading. That person is sending you a message. Try to figure out what it is. Your job will be to send this message on to your reader. This you can do only when you read with understanding.

Choosing a
suitable topic

You may either be assigned a topic or encouraged to pick one connected with a subject you are studying. For a social studies or history class, you may be asked to do a report on "Events Leading to the Revolutionary War"; or for health class, one on "Organic Gardening"; or for science class, one on "Animals Used for Clothing." Or you may choose one of these yourself. In either case, you have to decide whether your topic is too broad or narrow. For a good short report of 300 to 500 words, any of these three examples would be too broad. You first need to limit the topic to something more manageable.

Many students get nervous about choosing a narrow topic. They worry that they may not be able to find enough material to fill up the number of pages the teacher wants. Because of this anxiety they choose too wide a topic. Then they waste time pulling in useless information or writing in such a shallow and superficial way that the result is bad.

Just as a lobster trapper would have a problem if he built a trap with a door large enough to let in a shark, so you would be in trouble if your topic was too wide. Your topic is your trap door to let in information. If you keep your topic narrow enough, you will be less likely to gather information you do not need. It is more efficient to narrow your topic in the beginning so you read only material you can use in your report.

You cannot always be efficient. Sometimes, because you do not yet know much about your topic, you gradually discover it is wider than you thought. When that happens, stop right then and trim it down. Whenever you find plenty of material—even whole books—on your topic, it is time to narrow down. It is much better to flesh out a thin topic than to present a broad one. You want a report full of relevant, interesting information.

Look again at the sample topics mentioned earlier: "Events Leading to the Revolutionary War," "Organic Gardening," and "Animals Used for Clothing." In the list below, each of these has been appropriately narrowed down to a topic suitable for a short report.

> The Boston Tea Party
> Growing Tomatoes Without Pesticides
> How Silkworms Make Silk

Deciding what to read

Once your topic is sufficiently narrow, it is time to start reading. Go to sources in your classroom or the library for information. Get some 3" by 5" cards, or a 3" by 5" scratch pad. Use these as placemarkers now and as bibliography cards later. Start piling up all the books, periodicals, or other materials you can find on your topic. Put a placemarker in each source to mark where you will start reading. Do not take time to read yet.

How can you know if your sources are good? There is no way. All you know is that the titles or headings of sections look as if they might be useful. Glance through the indexes of books that have them. Do not worry that you may pile up more reading than you can do. Some of it is bound to be better or more interesting than the rest. If you reject something now, you will not be able to compare your sources of information.

Look for your subject in the card catalog in the library. Ask the librarian to help if you cannot find material. (See unit 7 of this book for other resources.) When you have a hefty stack of reading matter, you are ready to start skimming.

Go through and select the best sources, the ones that seem the most complete or interesting. Set these aside to read first.

Pick out your two or three best looking sources and start reading. Read quickly, but do not take any notes yet. Just get informed. Skip over parts you do not understand. If you find a source tough or confusing, leave it and go on to the next one.

Listing what is most important

After you have read two or three informative sources, close your books and think about what you have just read. What stands out in your mind? What two to five events or ideas are the most important? Write these down in a list on a sheet of notebook paper. Is there any other essential information you read? Add it.

Look at the whole list. Do some topics logically belong together? If so, put them one after the other. Is one of the topics you listed actually a part of another one? Then put it under the topic where it belongs, indenting it like this:

    The colonists' first reactions
     The Boston Town Meeting

The Boston Town Meeting was actually one of the colonists' first reactions, so it belongs under that more inclusive heading. You may then decide that the heading "The colonists' first reactions," is a big one. Number it with a Roman numeral I. Are any other of your topics listed actually first reactions of the colonists? Look back at your sources to see if there are others you did not list. After deciding what belongs under the big heading, your listing might look like this:

    I. The colonists' first reactions
     A. Mobs at the harbor
     B. Samuel Adams' proposals
     C. The Boston Town Meeting

The colonists' first reactions is a main heading. The others are subheadings that belong under it. Each has a capital letter in front.

Now decide if the rest of the items in your list are main headings or subheadings. Put a Roman numeral in front of each main heading and a capital letter in front of each subheading. The main headings for a report on "The Boston Tea Party" might look like this:

    I. Parliamentary Acts
    II. The colonists' first reactions
    III. Dumping the tea in the harbor

You may or may not have subheadings under the other main headings as you did under heading number II. Just be sure everything you have in your list of most important events is listed somewhere. What you now have is an outline. You may want to go back to your sources to see if there are other subheadings you should add. Remember, never have just one subheading under any major heading. If, for example, The Boston Town Meeting was the only subheading you could find to put under the colonists' first reactions, then you should have reworded heading number II to read:

    II. First reaction: The Boston Town Meeting

or simply:

    II. The Boston Town Meeting

Whenever you find you have only enough material for just

one subheading, go back and reword the main heading to include it. See the next section for more on outlining.

If you have more than five main headings, your topic may still be too broad. Decide which part of your subject you want to focus on and narrow your topic to that. You may decide, for example, that you want to report only on the various ways different historians describe the scene of dumping the tea into Boston Harbor.

You may have another problem. You may not understand your topic well enough to know which ideas are the main ones. If so, read more. Go on to that stack of materials you rejected first. One of them might have material that is easier to understand. You still may not have enough good material on your topic. If so, get help in finding something better.

When you have enough good material and an outline with headings and subheadings, go back and do a more careful reading. For each source you decide to use, take the 3" by 5" placemarker you used for it and write on it all the information you will need later for your bibliography. A *bibliography* is a list of sources attached to the back of a report or term paper. Most teachers require a bibliography for a report, one that lists the following information: the author, the title, the place of publication, the publisher, the date of publication, and the pages you used for every source you read for your report. The time to collect this information is now. See the next section for sample bibliography cards.

<table>
<tr><td>**Reading for a report**</td><td>Whether you are reading a single work, such as a novel, or several sources, you need to read alertly. You might be tempted to read slowly to be sure to get everything, but that is never wise. You give your mind time to drift off the subject and daydream. Bored readers read badly.</td></tr>
</table>

Remind yourself: this writer wants to get a message to me. I must stay as open to that message as possible. You want to take in not only what all the words actually mean but all they *might* mean as well. If everything does not make complete sense, keep on anyway. No book or article makes absolute, unambiguous sense to every reader at the beginning.

If your confusion continues, you have at least three choices.

1. You can write a question mark "?" in the margin, if you own the book, or on a 5"x 8" notepad if you do not. List the page number where you were confused. Then go on reading, hoping to get the drift later and come back to figure out this part. Often, confusing passages make

sense only after you have read a whole piece.

2. You can talk with another person who has read the troublesome passage.

3. You can look up in the dictionary all the words you do not understand and try to figure out what each sentence means.

Confused or not, keep a pen or pencil handy when reading for a report. That way you can catch your first reactions as they flash through your mind and write them down while they are hot. Whenever you get an idea for your report, write it down. While your interest is high you are going to do your best writing. Bored writers write boring stuff.

On your notepad put the name of the author and the number of the page you are reading. Unless you write many long reactions, one notepad sheet will do for three or four pages of print you read. For a long book you probably will not need to make notes except once every few pages. For tough or new material, you may make notes nearly every page. In addition to notes, you can list words you need to look up in the dictionary. You may also want to remind yourself where information on certain topics is found. This list can be your personal index to the reading material. Line up your notepad next to your book so your note is directly opposite the print it refers to. This will help you find a particular passage later.

Write quick notes so you do not interrupt your reading too much. Try a shorthand system of some sort. You might use symbols like the ones shown below.

—	anything you do not agree with or would like to take issue with
+	anything you agree with or think is interesting
!	an unusual or outstanding part
?	anything puzzling or confusing

List events or topics you want to remember. This makes your notepad a personal index for later use.

Using your notes

Your notes are a guide to the progression of thoughts you have had as you read. In the course of the notetaking process you may have changed your mind. In that case, go back and cross out the notes you no longer agree with. Read through the messages to yourself and see if they give you a notion of how your final report might look.

Now look at your other notes. If you have a lot of minus signs you may have the beginning of a good persuasive report, one in which you may take issue with an author or authors. Readers who make judgments, favorable or unfavorable, about what they read tend to make good report writers. Ask yourself why you disagreed. For example, do you think the author failed to be fair to the British in his or her account of the Boston Tea Party? Is the account of this event written from a purely American position?

If you decide to organize your report around your response to those passages where you put a minus sign in the margin, your problem will be to figure out a way to convince your reader that you are right. You must show that you have good reason to take issue with what you have read. You will need to pull out of your own experience and other reading you have done all the arguments or illustrations you can think of that might convince your reader to take your side. Now is the time to keep your eye on your reader.

If you have a great many pluses and exclamation points in the margin, you have a problem of a different kind. This time you must show your reader why you are not just gullible and agreeable. You must show why your own experience has borne out the truth of what you have read. You will also need to show why those parts where you put an "!" may have caught you by surprise. Analyze what really attracted your attention. If something you have experienced made this part stand out explain that experience in detail. Show your reader something about you.

At this point check with your teacher to find out what kind of report he or she expects. There are at least two different kinds of reports: summary and critical. A *summary* is a shortened version, in your words, of what you have read. A *critical report* is an evaluation of what you have read. Either kind of writing is valid. You need to know which kind is expected for this assignment. If you do a summary, you will leave out how you responded to the reading and concentrate only on what you have read. For a summary, your "−" 's, "+" 's, and "!" 's will not be a useful beginning point. Instead, you will want to look at the notes you made that listed the topics or events you want to remember. These will remind you of the main ideas you want to summarize.

After you have finished reading all of your notes and have looked up all unfamiliar words, go back and reread the passages you have marked with a question mark. In the process of completing the reading and working on other parts, you may have learned enough about the whole piece to make sense of the parts that were confusing before. If not, ask your teacher to help you before you go on to writing your first draft.

Now look again at your original outline. You may see problems in it now. It may not reflect the main ideas of what you have read. This is not a bad state of affairs. It may be a clue that you have learned something in the process of reading and taking notes. You have been thinking hard about your subject. And thinking changes a person. Your ideas about the organization of this report may be different now. If so, revise your outline to reflect this.

The first draft of a report

Put your outline in front of you. Keep your notepad handy. Close all your sources. Rely now on your memory of what you have read. Resist the temptation to go back to your sources now as you write your first draft. If you go back, you might be tempted to copy from your sources, and this is the one thing that will ruin your report. Your teacher is interested in you and what you have learned, not in the ideas of the writers of your sources. If you go back and use their words and phrases, your teacher will know it and probably make you do the report over again. A good student report has to be in the student's own words. Keep your eye on your reader and put down what you would tell this reader about what you have learned about this subject.

If you are writing a summary, follow your outline and put down everything you remember about each heading in turn. You can trust your memory to sort out the significant material. Unimportant details will be forgotten. This is another advantage of relying on your memory. You are not tempted to get bogged down in writing unnecessary details. Remember, your report is to be a shortened, capsule version of what you have read.

If you are writing a critical report, be honest. The best critiques are those that reveal you. Whether you agree or disagree with your sources does not matter. It matters that you do not pretend. Your teacher wants to know what and how *you* think. Besides, honest writing is better writing. Weak composition is born out of a decision to write what you think someone else, such as your teacher, would say. It comes off sounding phony—which it is.

Revising

After you write your first draft of your report, wait a day, if possible, before you look at it again. To revise literally means "to look again." If you wait a bit for this second look, you gain a perspective on your paper that helps you rewrite it. It helps to pretend that someone else wrote it so you can be objective about its faults.

In a first draft you have gotten the feel of the flow of the paper. In the revision, you are going to get consistency, continuity, precision, and power.

Read your paper cold. Forget you wrote it. Look for problems, and expect to find them. A discussion of some common problems follows.

Avoid gaps. Pretend you have no idea what this paper is about. Do not think about what you meant to put into the paper but did not. Your job is to spot gaps and fill them in with what was in your mind, but did not get into the paper.

One of the commonest gaps in student writing is the general, summary statement that has no supporting data. Supporting data includes examples, reasons, arguments, details, and so on. Writers often assume you will believe them if they make statements like these and do nothing to show you why they believe them to be true:

> Pollution is easy to control.
> Crime is a bigger problem than ever before.
> The death penalty should be abolished.
> Women are equal to men in every way.

None of these statements, no matter how much you may believe it, is by itself convincing to all readers. Without back-up evidence—facts, opinions of experts, explanations, illustrations, and so on—any reader has a right to doubt you. You have left a wide gap.

As you edit your paper, look for expressions of opinion. For each one ask yourself if there is enough evidence to convince a reader that this opinion is valid. Look for exaggerated statements, overstatements that are impossible to support. Writers who exaggerate are not taken seriously, regardless of how many supporting statements they add. On the other hand, if a writer qualifies his statements, showing why each would not be true in every case, he or she is more likely to be believed.

After you have spotted the gaps, fill them in. Be sure each generalization is supported with convincing back-up data. Add what the reader needs to know to make sense of your paper.

Avoid incoherent paragraphs. Each paragraph should present a single idea and should hang together as a whole.

Whenever you present an idea, it needs to be developed. Look for a paragraph that consists of a single sentence. Chances are that it needs to be developed. Each idea in your paper needs at least a few sentences to explain and illustrate it. The idea itself should be stated in what is called a *topic sentence.* The other sentences develop that idea. A good report has no paragraphs that consist of a single sentence. Each paragraph, including this one, has a topic sentence and a few developing sentences. Look for gaps in your paragraphs.

Sometimes you have a single sentence paragraph because you separate a sentence from the paragraph it belongs to. The solution to this problem is easy. Put the sentence with its rightful paragraph.

Go through your paper and decide what each of your paragraphs is about. If there is no topic sentence, one that summarizes the message of the paragraph, add one. Take out any material that does not belong.

A paragraph is a group of sentences that are related. A composition is a group of paragraphs that are related. Just as you do not want gaps or irrelevant information in your composition, you do not want gaps or irrelevancies in your paragraphs.

Avoid excess water. Read the paper again to see where you can cut out needless parts. You want a strong, concise paper. Look for unnecessary words. Often *who*, *which*, or *that* can be scrapped. Try putting two short sentences together, getting rid of a few words as you go. Do you repeat? Cut that out. Repeated words are tedious. If you cannot omit them, change them for variety.

Avoid switching. Good writers are easy to follow because they do not switch tracks. They avoid changing topics, tenses, point of view, or number.

Do not switch topics. If your outline reflects the main ideas in your report, then any material that does not fit neatly under one of the headings does not belong there. It is easy to get side-tracked in writing. Our brains lead us into intriguing byways that often have little or nothing to do with the point of what we are writing. Cut these out, but save them. They might belong somewhere in the report or might make a good beginning for another paper at another time.

Do not switch tenses. If you start out writing in the past tense, stay with it. If you choose the present tense, as in this unit, use the past only when you have a very good reason for doing so.

Do not switch point of view. Your teacher may require that you write a report or term paper in the third person point of view. This means you avoid using "I" for yourself or "you" for the reader. The third person point of view is more formal. Instead of saying "I" you say, "this writer." Use "he" or "she" instead of "you." Unless your teacher assigns use of the third person, decide which person you are going to use and stick to it.

Do not switch number. The subject of any sentence is either singular or plural. Make sure you do not mix tenses in words later in a sentence that refer to the subject of the sentence. Here is a sentence that switches number:

The girl who left yesterday took *their* bathing suits with *them*.

There was just *one* girl. And she took *her* bathing suit with *her*.

Avoid usage and punctuation errors. Go through your paper a final time to see if you can pick up any errors in usage, grammar, or spelling. Most are hard to catch, but easy to fix. A friend who does not make the same errors you do may be able to help you spot them. Be sure each complete sentence has a period, not a comma, at the end. Correct all your errors on your first draft before you write up your final paper.

Preparing your final copy

Learn to type. Not only does your finished report look better and present the teacher with an easier reading task, but it also is easier and quicker for you to produce— after you have mastered the skill, that is. The time spent on a typing course will save you many welcome hours later. Most students can, in a single typing course, learn to type faster than they can write longhand, and, of course, the result is much more professional looking. After you have mastered the basics of typing, each paper you type provides further practice.

Until you learn to type, be sure you take time to write up your final paper in your best handwriting. Keep a dictionary handy and check every word you do not know how to spell. Good spellers can sense which words they are not sure about and look them up when they need to. And the final writing stage is "when you need to." It will help if you put a note "sp?" in the margin of your first draft whenever you are not sure how to spell a word.

3. Can you write a term paper?

A term paper is typically longer than a report and uses more sources of information. It is never a summary of a single source, as a book report might be. A term paper is a composite of information, a bit broader in scope than a report. The previous section considered three topics, each too broad for a report: "Events Leading to the Revolutionary War," "Organic Gardening," and "Animals Used for Clothing." Any one of these topics might work well for a fairly long term paper, one that would be over eight pages in length.

A term paper is different

Do not be deceived, however. Even in a term paper, the problem you are most likely to have is choosing a topic that is too broad. If you find there are whole books written on a topic you have chosen, then it is probably too broad. You need a topic limited enough to have both unity and a sense of completeness. You cannot possibly do justice to too broad a topic. You have neither time nor space to present the subject fully.

Writing a term paper can be a chance to move into an area about which you have always wanted to know more. Use this excuse to explore. Do not settle for a topic that does not intrigue you. Ask your teacher if you can exchange an assigned topic for another you would like better.

Most teachers allow you more freedom in the choice of a term paper topic than in a report topic since a report is often assigned to assure that you understand a particular subject. Find out now if you can choose your own term paper topic.

Writing a term paper is a very effective way to develop skills in finding out what kinds of information are available and in using that information to answer questions. Teachers assign term papers because they want you to develop skills that will serve whenever you need to know about a subject.

What are some of these skills? First, there is the skill of using a library efficiently and effectively. Your first sorties into a library can be frustrating or confusing. Now, while you are in school, is the time to get over any problems, so the rest of your life you will be able to get information when you need it. There is no way for anyone to predict what he or she will need to know in any future situation. The best possible preparation is to learn how to get information.

While writing a term paper you learn how to select the information you need for a specific purpose and how to take notes you can use. You learn to digest material you read, taking it in and making it part of you. And you learn how to organize what you have gathered—from other places as well as from printed materials—and pull it together into a unified and orderly whole and present it in a clear and effective way. Finally, you learn how to give appropriate credit to the writers of your sources of information by indicating when material is quoted and by appropriately footnoting both quotations and your own summaries of someone else's ideas. In the process you learn how to prepare a set of footnotes and a bibliography.

All of these skills will serve you in high school and college. In addition, you have experience in pulling together the kind of long report that is called for in many professions. It is good to know how to write a term paper.

Scheduling the job

Because it takes a long time to gather the necessary information, organize it, and write the paper, most teachers allow from two weeks to a full term to complete a term paper. This fact alone creates one of the greatest problems students face —the overwhelming temptation to put the assignment off. If it is not due until Thanksgiving, why start now? This attitude will get you into big trouble. The reason the teacher assigns the term paper so far ahead of time is that it will take you that long, working on it for at least a short while every day.

One way to gauge your time is to count backwards from the day the term paper is due. Allow yourself at least a full hour per page for typing or writing out the final draft after the initial writing of the paper is completed. You want to allow time to make some necessary changes even at that late date. You may need even longer than an hour per page to get the footnotes and bibliography in final form. So allow yourself about 12 full hours for the final typing of a 10-page term paper with its page of footnotes and page of bibliography. Do not count those 12 hours as the night before, but rather as three hours a day for four days. That means that your first draft has to be ready four days before the final paper is due. Mark that on your calendar. You will need at least 10 full hours to write out the first draft. Count back four more days and circle the calendar again. Now, unless as you have counted backwards you have gone past the day the assignment was given, you can use from now until the day marked for beginning the first draft to gather information and take notes. If you stay with this schedule, there is no need to panic. You have allowed yourself enough time to do well.

Beginning a term paper

First, choose a topic. It may be an informative one, or a controversial one. If it is informative, such as "Events Leading to the Revolutionary War," then assemble all of the accounts, probably in chronological order. You will likely not take a position on this subject, but simply present the facts.

If you choose a controversial topic, like abortion, then your job is to present fairly both sides of the argument and then come up with a conclusion of your own. You do not have to take sides, however. You may decide that the issue is a complex one and that there are strong, valid arguments on both sides. Your conclusion might be that you are not ready to take a side. As with report writing, the important thing is to be honest. Do not pretend to take a side if you have no position.

Once you have decided on a topic, brainstorm with yourself or with a friend. Sit down and think of all the questions that could be asked about your subject. Make a list of these. The answers to some of these questions will make up your term paper. For example, if you have chosen the subject "Unidentified Flying Objects", (UFO's), your first questions might be: Do UFO's really exist? Can we believe the people who have reported seeing beings from outer space? Which reports can we believe? How do experts account for UFO's? Were UFO's around before the twentieth century? Where are they most likely to be reported? Are there pictures that experts agree are reliable? Has anyone seen a UFO around here? Who is keeping track of UFO's? How would I know a UFO if I saw one?

Reading for a term paper

Start reading. You will soon discover there have probably been entire books written on your subject. So you will need to limit your topic. If you get most interested in UFO sightings around your area of the country, decide to limit your term paper to that. Then your best material will probably come from newspaper accounts.

At the same time, you will be following your interest by reading just for your own background. You will want to get some definitions straight. For example, is a UFO the same as a flying saucer?

A good place to start reading is in an up-to-date encyclopedia. If you have time, read a whole book or more on the subject, knowing that most of the reading will not pertain to your more narrowly limited term paper topic. This will not be a problem at first, however. The more informed you are on the whole topic of UFO's, the better. As in report writing, do not take notes at this stage. If you find material that is on your narrow topic, get a 4″ by 6″ card or piece of paper and put the author and page number in the upper left hand corner. Then note what the passage is about. But stop there. Use that card as a placemarker to come back to later. Go on reading. You can later use that card to make notes on. If you start taking notes too soon, you may write material you will later decide to throw away because you have had to narrow your topic even further. Take time now to read widely.

Eventually your preliminary reading period has to stop. Your teacher may suggest when it is time to start collecting data on note cards. At this point write yourself a "scratch" outline. This is a list of topics you want to include in your paper. Go back to your list of questions and decide which of these now pertain to your more narrowly limited topic. Jot down some headings for answers to these questions. Add other information you think should be part of your paper. Number your main headings with Roman numerals, as you would when writing a report.

For a term paper on UFO sightings in your part of the country, you would need different information than you would for a paper on various theories to account for UFO's. Check to see if every item on your scratch outline belongs in your paper. Decide which would be the best order for the items and rearrange them. This scratch outline is a reminder to yourself as you take notes. Expect to make changes in it as you read.

Gathering information

Because one of the goals of term paper writing is learning to use a library, many teachers expect you to get most of your information from printed materials. But you may well discover in your library useful films, filmstrips, pictures, recordings, or tapes. Check the TV listings each week, especially those on public TV. You may be lucky and find a program relevant to your term paper topic. If you do, have your pen ready so you can take notes as you watch. Be sure to get down information such as who is speaking and who produced the program. If you miss some important facts, you can usually get them by calling your local TV station.

Sometimes you learn by performing experiments. Often the results of experiments are written up as term papers for science classes.

Another way to gather information is to ask other people. If you want to know what it is like to pursue a particular career, the best way to find out is to talk with someone doing it. There is no better way to learn what it was like to live on your street or in your neighborhood years before you were born than to go out and talk with people who have lived there for a while.

When you go out to talk to a person in order to collect information, you are conducting an interview. Students usually find preparing a set of questions ahead of time helps. You may decide to include information gathered from a number of people, each of whom was asked the same question or questions. If so, you are taking a survey to collect information. You can also send out a questionnaire, a set of questions on paper. It is sent out to a number of persons, who record their answers and return the questionnaire to you. This type of survey is commonly used for term papers.

Try one of these more sophisticated information-gathering techniques—the interview or the survey—if it is appropriate for your subject. Whether you interview people or not, your conversations with other persons about the subject of your paper will help your thinking. Talk with as many persons as you can about your term paper. What they know may help you.

Information can also come from written or printed records. You have written records in your family—pieces of paper that document marriages, births, property ownership, or savings accounts. In addition, you have in your home non-written records—photographs. You may even have tape recordings or movie films that preserve past events.

Records of property are stored by city or county governments. Documents recording past events are kept by historical societies. Legislative records are in government repositories. None of these collections, however, is as complete as the collection of recorded information in a library. No matter how many non-library sources you use for your term paper, you will probably gather information in the library as well.

The three most useful library resources for term paper information are a good, up-to-date encyclopedia, the subject cards in the card catalog for the library, and *The Readers' Guide to Periodical Literature.* If all three of these sources have plenty of information on the subject you have chosen, you will have no trouble finding material.

If you are currently at the information-gathering stage of a term paper, stop right here and go to unit 7 of this book. There you will find out how to most effectively use the library to gather information.

Bibliography cards

Now is the time to begin working on your bibliography. You may protest, "But I don't even know what I am going to say in my paper." True enough. But you do know what sources you are using. And it will be more difficult later to go back and list all of these. Start now by putting all the information you need for each source on a separate 3" by 5" card or piece of paper. Bibliography cards for a term paper are just like those for a report.

If you are reading an encyclopedia article on flying saucers, your bibliography card should look like this:

```
Hynek, J. Allen. "Unidentified Flying Objects."
    The World Book Encyclopedia (1977), Vol. 20,
    p. 17.
```

For general encyclopedias you do not need to put down the name of the publisher and place of publication. If the encyclopedia article has no author, start with the title.

A bibliography card for a book that is not a reference work should look like this:

```
Klass, Philip J. UFO's Explained. New York:
    Random House, 1974.
```

You list the full name of the author, last name first, the exact title of the book, the place of publication, the publisher, and the date of publication.

A bibliography card for a magazine article should look like this:

```
Oberg, J. E. "Astronauts and UFO's—the Whole
    Story!" Space World, vol. 158, February, 1977,
    pp. 4–28.
```

List the name of the author of the article, if it is given. Then include the exact title of the article, the name of the magazine, the volume number if there is one, the date of publication, and the inclusive page numbers of the article. Do not make a bibliography card for a dictionary, *The Readers' Guide to Periodical Literature,* or any other index you used to find articles.

A bibliography card for a newspaper article should look like this:

```
Shipler, David K. "Issue of UFO's Irks
    Authorities in the Soviet Union." The New York
    Times, December 26, 1976, sec. 1, p. 20.
```

Here, as you can see, you list the name of the author if it is given, the title of the article, the name of the newspaper, the date, the section of the newspaper in which the article appeared (if a section number is given), and the page number.

If your information comes from a television show, list it this way:

```
"60 Minutes." CBS. April 28, 1978. J. Allen Hynek
    interviewed by Mike Wallace.
```

If you want to record the results of an interview, make out a bibliography card like this:

```
Interview with Sandra Mitchell. Evanston,
    Illinois. November 20, 1978.
```

If you punctuate your bibliography cards exactly as on these samples, all you will have to do when typing or writing up the final bibliography is to alphabetize these cards. Arrange your cards by either the last name of the author or by the first word of the title if no author is given. Copy the cards, punctuation and all.

Notetaking

For a term paper, you need to be more systematic and careful than when taking notes for a report. A term paper is longer, and you have a lot more information to keep track of. Because the scope is broader, organizing the material is more difficult. A good set of notes will help you later.

Get yourself a set of 4″ by 6″ note cards or a scratch pad. Most students find 3″ by 5″ cards too small for notetaking. At the top left of each card put the name of the author, or if there is no author listed, the title of the article. Also include the page number of your source. Then read your source carefully all the way through. Go back and copy those parts of the article or chapter that seem to summarize a lot of information. Be very selective. Do not copy unimportant details or parts you think you can remember. Write only summary sentences or factual material such as statistics that will be relevant to your paper. Unless your teacher recommends otherwise, copy word for word, using quotation marks. Do not rewrite in your own words at this stage.

If you leave out part of a quotation, write three spaced dots (. . .), called an ellipsis, to show where words or sentences were left out. If words are left out in the middle of a sentence, indicate that as in the following example.

"There was considerable controversy over the first witness . . . though most people believed he was sane."

If the end of a sentence or the beginning of the next sentence is left out, use four dots (a period and three spaced dots).

"The markings on the land were negligible. . . . Flattened grasses were all the police could detect."

If a complete sentence is left out, you again use three spaced dots after the period (four dots).

"Sheriff Macaulay was not convinced. . . . Two days later he came back to look at the site."

If you quote only a small part of a sentence, you do not need to use an ellipsis. Quotation marks will do.

The general attitude in the town was one of "shocked and frightened disbelief."

Put separate ideas onto separate cards. Do not try to save cards or paper. Your cards will be easier to rearrange and to organize later if you have no more than a sentence or at most a few sentences on each. If you put ideas on different subjects onto the same card, you may have to cut the card apart later. Never have information from more than one source on the same card. Write on only one side of a card.

If part of your information is the result of interviews, put the notes onto cards, writing the name of the person you interviewed at the top left of each. For each separate interview you will need a separate bibliography card.

As you take notes keep your scratch outline in front of you. Decide where the material on each note card belongs on the outline. Put the same Roman numeral in the upper right hand corner of each card as the number in front of the corresponding topic on your outline. If the note you are taking does not fit into any of the topics on your scratch out-line, either revise or expand the outline to include it or throw away the card. If you cannot find any information for a certain topic on your outline, you have two choices. Either omit that heading and narrow the scope of your paper, or look further for material. If you find you have information on a card that fits under more than one topic on your outline, put part of it onto another card, and scratch that part out on your first card.

After your reading is finished and your note cards com-pleted, it is time to do your final outline. Doing it now makes writing the first draft easier. Most teachers require you to hand in an outline with the term paper. The scratch outline you did was for you. The one you do now is for your reader.

The final outline

Find a big table or desk, prop your scratch outline up in front of you, and lay out all your note cards in piles accord-ing to the Roman numerals you have in the upper right hand corners. Then start your outline. At the top put the title of your term paper. Under this title, write the word "Outline." Then write your thesis sentence. This is a state-ment of the central idea of your paper. The outline itself would follow.

Here is an example of an outline. It is in the form yours should be when you attach it to the front of your term paper.

BUSING TO ACHIEVE SCHOOL INTEGRATION
Outline

Thesis sentence: The busing of school children to achieve integration is more likely to succeed in a community with similar socioeconomic levels where adequate preparation has been made and where school budgets are healthy.

I.   Reasons for school integration
     A.   The limitations of the "separate but equal" law
     B.   The 1954 Supreme Court ruling
II. Cities with busing problems
     A.   Detroit, Michigan
     B.   Boston, Massachusetts
     C.   Other communities
III. Cities with successful busing
     A.   Berkeley, California
     B.   Evanston, Illinois
     C.   Other communities

IV. Characteristics of successful school busing programs
   A. Similar socioeconomic level
   B. Adequate preparation
     1. Of the teachers
     2. Of the community
   C. Adequate budgets for quality programs
   D. More and better instructional materials

The hard work in writing an outline is to decide which parts fit under which other parts. Look at the Roman numerals on your scratch outline. For most short term papers, three to five main divisions are enough. If you have more Roman numerals than five, look them over carefully to see if any two or more are about the same subject. If they are, put them together. Or you may need to make up a new heading because what you have are actually the subheadings.

Although you are likely to need only Roman numerals and capital letters, here is the correct form for further breakdown of an outline:

I.
  A.
    1.
      a.
        (1)

Remember, whenever you have one subheading, you need at least one more.

All the headings at any level, such as all those numbered with a Roman numeral, must be parallel in content and form. This means they must be parallel in type of material and part of speech. Here are two headings that are parallel:

I. Causes of water pollution
II. Ways to avoid pollution

Here are two that are not:

  A. Industrial wastes
  B. To clean up oil spills

To be parallel, subheading B. should read:

  B. Oil spills

Subhead "A." and the second wording of subhead "B." would be logical subheadings under heading "I".

I. Causes of water pollution
  A. Industrial wastes
  B. Oil spills

Now you are ready to write out the first draft of your term paper. You do it as you would a report. Keep your outline in front of you and write out what should be said about each topic in turn. Keep your reader in mind as you write. Look over the note cards you made for each heading. Decide which note cards, if any, have information you want to quote in the paper. Read over the other note cards and then write what they say in your own words.

You need to write at least a paragraph to develop each subheading of your outline. In most cases you will need several paragraphs. If you are using a quotation, be sure it fits in smoothly with the flow of your own words. Make it easy for your reader to get your message.

If you quote 100 words or less, use quotation marks. If you quote more than 100 words, set off the quotation by indenting it on both sides and single spacing it, like this:

> Not all teachers insist on footnotes, so be sure they are required before you include them. Footnotes serve a variety of purposes. In addition to documenting sources, a footnote may also (1) explain a point more fully, (2) make an editorial comment, (3) add an interesting sidelight, (4) be a cross reference to another part of the report, or (5) offer a difference of opinion. For an oral report you will want footnotes on any of your speaker's cards that have material needing documentation. You won't read these, but you may be called upon to give the source of a fact or quotation you worked into your speech.[1]

---

[1]"How to Do Research," The World Book Encyclopedia, Vol. 22, p. 27.

You do not need quotation marks when you set off a long quotation by indenting.

Whenever you quote five or more consecutive words from one of your sources, you need to use quotation marks and a footnote. You also need a footnote when the information or idea is not your own even if it is in your own words. Footnotes tell the reader exactly where to find the material you quoted or summarized. If you fail to use quotation marks or footnotes where needed, you are guilty of plagiarism. This is literary theft. You plagiarize if you pretend that someone else's writing is your own. A reader assumes that anything in your paper that is not quoted or footnoted is written by you.

As you write your first draft, enter your footnotes at the

Documentation

bottom of the page on which the quoted or summarized material appears. See the example of this in the long, indented quotation above.

The finished paper

Follow the suggestions on revising given earlier in this unit. Make changes on your first draft. If you have not done it, compose a first paragraph that tells the reader just what the whole paper is about. Because a term paper is long, it is especially important to present the thesis statement, the same one that is on your outline, as early in the paper as possible.

In addition to beginning with your summary or thesis statement, you should end your term paper with a conclusion. This is usually a full paragraph that again summarizes the main ideas of the paper. It should cover the whole subject so well that someone could read just the conclusion and have a good idea of the content of the whole paper.

When you type up the final paper, double space it except for long quotations, footnotes and bibliography. Ask your teacher if your footnotes are to go at the bottom of the pages of your term paper or on a separate page at the back of the paper. Put the number of the footnote a half a space higher than the rest of the line. Leave no space before a footnote number in the text of your paper or after the number in the footnote itself.

Leave a margin of 1½ inches on the left and approximately 1 inch on the other three sides, except for the outline and first page which start 2 inches from the top.

If you write your term paper longhand, single space it throughout, double spacing between paragraphs. Set off long quotations by double spacing before and after them and indenting just as you would if you were typing.

Attach a title page to the front of your paper. Number pages starting with the first page of the term paper itself. Center all numbers at the top of each page except for the first page where the number should be centered at the bottom of the page.

Put the paper in a binder with a blank page first, then the title page, the outline, the paper itself, the footnotes if they are not at the bottom of the pages, the bibliography, and a blank page.

Then proofread for typing or careless errors, and your term paper is complete.

Activities

The unit-end activities have been designed to help you to practice some of the things you have learned in this unit and to test some of your writing skills. Please do not write in this book, but place your answers on a separate sheet of paper. Answers to the activities can be found in the **Answer Key** that begins on page 290.

Test your outlining skill

Suppose you are writing a term paper on water pollution and have started with the following list of the most important items. How would you rearrange them into an outline with the main headings and subheadings?

The Pollution of Lake Michigan
Thesis sentence: Because Lake Michigan is extensively polluted, only strong laws will provide an effective solution.

The causes of pollution
Sewage treatment regulations
Solutions to the problem
Pesticides used for farming
Increased cost of water purification
Undesirable levels of algae
Evidence of pollution
Industrial wastes
Maximum water temperature regulation
Thermal pollution from nuclear energy plants
Pesticide controls
Contaminated fish
Inadequately treated sewage
Laws limiting industrial emissions

Using verbs properly

One of the most common writing problems is the improper use of verbs, especially the various tenses of irregular verbs. In the following examples, fill in the past tense and past participle of the verb for which the present tense is given.

Example:

1. She *begins* now.
   a. She <u>b</u> <u>e</u> <u>g</u> <u>a</u> <u>n</u> yesterday.
   b. She has <u>b</u> <u>e</u> <u>g</u> <u>u</u> <u>n</u>.

1. The wind *blows* now.
   a. The wind _____ yesterday.
   b. The wind has _____ .
2. The balloon *bursts* now.
   a. The balloon _____ yesterday.
   b. The balloon has _____ .
3. It *breaks* now.
   a. It _____ yesterday.
   b. It has _____.
4. He *brings* it now.
   a. He _____ it yesterday.
   b. He has _____ it.
5. He *comes* now.
   a. He _____ yesterday.
   b. He has _____ .
6. He *dives* today.
   a. He _____ or _____ yesterday.
   b. He has _____ .
7. He *drags* his sled.
   a. He _____ his sled yesterday.
   b. He has _____ his sled.
8. He *drinks* it today.
   a. He _____ it yesterday.
   b. He has _____ it.
9. He *drowns* today.
   a. He _____ yesterday.
   b. He has _____ .
10. He *flies* today.
    a. He _____ yesterday.
    b. He has _____ .
11. He *gives* it today.
    a. He _____ it yesterday.
    b. He has _____ it.
12. He *is* here today.
    a. He ____ here yesterday.

112

b. He has _____ here.
13. He *leads* today.
   a. He _____ yesterday.
   b. He has _____.
14. He *rides* it today.
   a. He _____ it yesterday.
   b. He has _____ it.
15. She *runs* today.
   a. She _____ yesterday.
   b. She has _____ .
16. It *shrinks* today.
   a. It _____ or _____ yesterday.
   b. It has _____ or _____ .
17. She *steals* it today.
   a. She _____ it yesterday.
   b. She has _____ it.
18. She *swings* today.
   a. She _____ yesterday.
   b. She has _____ .
19. She *throws* it today.
   a. She _____ it yesterday.
   b. She has _____ it.
20. She *writes* it today.
   a. She _____ it yesterday.
   b. She has _____ it.

Using commas properly

Another common writing problem is the improper use of commas. Test your knowledge of the use of commas by punctuating the sentences given below.

Example:
  1. Come back Susan and take this letter with you.

Answer:
  1. Come back, Susan, and take this letter with you.

  1. I have made my scratch outline done my reading and taken notes.
  2. The President of the United States who has greater responsibility for this country's welfare than any other person is also Commander-in-Chief of the U.S. Armed Forces.
  3. It is time to go inside the house Tom.

4. On July 4 1976 Americans celebrated 200 years of independence.
5. I would like to watch TV but I have to write my report.
6. "Don't go without me Mary" Jane called.
7. At the salad bar were cottage cheese marinated herring tossed salad and olives.
8. I went right to sleep last night and so the thunder did not disturb me.
9. Whenever I have a long complicated term paper due I try to work on it for at least a little while every day.
10. "John" she called "I have something to show you."

Test your knowledge of good usage

Good writing also requires a knowledge of English usage. This activity will help you judge whether you need to spend more time learning about using English correctly. Complete each sentence with the correct word from the two choices given in parentheses.

Examples:
1. My dog has _____ (dragged, drug) that big bone all the way home.

Answer:
1. dragged

1. I _____ (did, done) the dishes last night.
2. He _____ (doesn't, don't) live here.
3. Everyone finished early _____ (accept, except) me.
4. I have _____ (laid, lain) on that bed every night.
5. Take my _____ (advice, advise); stay home.
6. I _____ (ain't, am not) going to call him _____ (anyhow, nohow).
7. _____ (It's, Its) a great day for kite flying.
8. Spencer and _____ (I, me) went fishing.
9. I will _____ (learn, teach) you how to play golf.
10. I would _____ (have, of) watched TV if I had been you.

A checklist of usage

Take a 3″ by 5″ card and cover up the past tense and past participle of these irregular verbs. See if you know them. Make a list of any you do not know and learn them.

Present tense	Past tense	Past participle
She *begins* now.	She *began* yesterday.	She has *begun*.
The wind *blows* now.	The wind *blew* yesterday.	The wind has *blown*.
It *breaks* now.	It *broke* yesterday.	It has *broken*.
He *brings* it now.	He *brought* it yesterday.	He has *brought* it.
He *comes* now.	He *came* yesterday.	He has *come*.
She *digs* now.	She *dug* yesterday.	She has *dug* the hole.
He *dives* today.	He *dived* or *dove* yesterday.	He has *dived*.
She *does* the job today.	She *did* the job yesterday.	She has *done* the job.
He *drags* his sled.	He *dragged* his sled yesterday.	He has *dragged* his sled.
She *draws* today.	She *drew* yesterday.	She has *drawn*.
He *drinks* it today.	He *drank* it yesterday.	He has *drunk* it.
She *drives* today.	She *drove* yesterday.	She has *driven*.
He *drowns* today.	He *drowned* yesterday.	He has *drowned*.
She *falls* today.	She *fell* yesterday.	She has *fallen*.
He *flies* today.	He *flew* yesterday.	He has *flown*.
She *freezes* today.	She *froze* yesterday.	She has *frozen*.
He *gives* it today.	He *gave* it yesterday.	He has *given* it.
She *grows* today.	She *grew* yesterday.	She has *grown*.
He *is* here today.	He *was* here yesterday.	He has *been* here.
She *knows* it now.	She *knew* it yesterday.	She has *known* it.
He *leads* today.	He *led* yesterday.	He has *led*.
She *lends* it today.	She *lent* it yesterday.	She has *lent* it.
He *rides* it today.	He *rode* it yesterday.	He has *ridden* it.
It *rings* today.	It *rang* yesterday.	It has *rung*.
She *runs* today.	She *ran* yesterday.	She has *run*.
He *sees* it today.	He *saw* it yesterday.	He has *seen* it.
It *shrinks* today.	It *shrank* or *shrunk* yesterday.	It has *shrunk* or *shrunken*.
She *sings* today.	She *sang* yesterday.	She has *sung*.
It *sinks* today.	It *sank* yesterday.	It has *sunk*.
He *speaks* today.	He *spoke* yesterday.	He has *spoken*.
She *steals* it today.	She *stole* it yesterday.	She has *stolen* it.
He *swims* today.	He *swam* yesterday.	He has *swum*.
She *swings* today.	She *swung* yesterday.	She has *swung*.
He *takes* it today.	He *took* it yesterday.	He has *taken* it.
She *throws* it today.	She *threw* it yesterday.	She has *thrown* it.
He *wears* it today.	He *wore* it yesterday.	He has *worn* it.
She *writes* it today.	She *wrote* it yesterday.	She has *written* it.

A guide to speaking skills

5

Can you speak easily to a large audience? Or do you feel "butterflies" in your stomach whenever you must speak to a crowd? The ability to speak, and speak well, before an audience is an important skill to have if you wish to be successful.

This unit discusses the different kinds of formats that speeches might follow. And it describes techniques that will help you prepare and deliver an effective speech.

The contributors of this unit are Dr. Richard J. Jensen, Assistant Professor of Speech Communication, University of New Mexico, Albuquerque, New Mexico; and Dr. Timothy G. Plax, Associate Professor of Speech Communication, University of New Mexico, Albuquerque, New Mexico.

1. Why should you practice speaking skills?

The key to spoken communication

Many of your daily activities depend on your ability to speak. For example, your teacher may assign you the task of talking to the class. You may be asked by your club to speak at a conference. You may be asked to give a speech to a church group. Or you may have to go through an interview when applying for a part-time job.

These in- and out-of-class situations all have something in common. They all require effective spoken communication. Obviously, the success of many of your everyday life experiences depends on your ability to make known to others your needs, wants, and ideas. And this sometimes must be done before large groups.

To develop speaking skills, stop for a few moments and think about spoken communication. Ask yourself the following questions: What is public speaking? How does a person prepare a speech? What kinds of speeches are there? What is the best manner of speaking in public? How can I be comfortable while speaking naturally?

This section and other sections in this unit have been designed to answer these questions for you. The answers to these questions will help you improve your communication skills. With this information you will be able to master the skills you need to become a more effective communicator.

What public speaking is

To understand public speaking, you must recognize its elements. And you must understand how these elements are related to each other. You can do this by asking and answering the following questions: What are the important elements of public speaking? What goes on while a speech is being delivered? What problems can occur while you are speaking? How can you solve or avoid these problems?

118

Public speaking defined. Public speaking is an attempt by a speaker (transmitter) to send a message to a listener (receiver). The message that is received should be as close as possible to what the speaker had in mind.

This is a very difficult task. It is nearly impossible for a listener to get the exact meaning intended by a speaker. Meanings are in people, not in words. However, a speaker should try to aid a listener as much as possible. A speaker who realizes the difficulty of achieving his or her speaking goal will probably work harder to get the message across. And as in everything, hard work pays dividends.

Successful public communication occurs, then, when what was in the mind of the speaker is successfully received by the listener. Public speaking is effective when the speaker gets his or her thought through to the listener.

For example, you may find yourself trying to describe rock music to your parents. You should realize that your parents will probably never totally understand rock music. But you should help them understand as much as possible. You might do this by comparing rock music to the kind of music that was popular when they were your age. You would thus be building on their experiences to explain your own.

Elements of speaking. Every example of public spoken communication includes certain elements.

1. The speaker.
2. A speech, or message.
3. A channel, or how the message is sent.
4. An audience, or group of listeners.
5. The effect of the speech.
6. The feedback, or responses to the speaker from the listeners.

For example, your teacher may give you a speech assignment which involves describing one of your hobbies to your classmates. After consideration, you decide on boating.

In this situation, you are the *speaker*. The *speech* is composed of the information you have gathered on boating. The *channel* is your voice and other materials, such as visual aids, you use to convey your speech materials. The *audience* is your classmates, and your speech would obviously have some *effect* on your audience. How the class responds to your presentation—laughter, applause, sleeping, and so forth—is the *feedback*. The interaction of all of these elements determines the success or failure of your attempt at public communication.

Steps in public speaking. Public speaking involves several steps. It begins when you, the speaker, decide what it is you are going to speak about. Next, you put your ideas into words. In order to do this you gather information and organize it into speech. After you have developed your speech, you deliver it to your audience. The audience receives the speech. And lastly, the audience reacts to the speech. It is possible that individual audience members will affect one another's reaction to the speech. How someone responds to your speech will influence his or her neighbor's reaction and vice versa.

No matter what the reason for the speech, or what kind of audience the speech is being delivered to, this sequence will happen. Your success in a public speaking situation will depend upon your ability to understand and control this sequence of events.

Some common misunderstandings

Many people do not understand what is involved in public communication. These misunderstandings lead people to perform poorly in public speaking situations. The following will make you aware of some of the more common misconceptions. Hopefully, knowing about them will enable you to avoid the problems caused by them.

Being a successful speaker is easy. Some people feel all you have to do is stand up and talk. Others believe there is such a thing as a "born public speaker." The fact is that giving a successful speech requires a great deal of care and preparation. Effective communicators are *not* born. They must work hard to become skillful speakers.

Public speaking is frightening. Some people see public speaking as a frightening experience. These people avoid situations in which they might have to speak. This fear of public speaking can normally be overcome by forcing yourself into public speaking situations. In other words, the more times you speak the easier it will become for you.

Public speaking is different from everyday communication activities. Each of you is involved in numerous daily activities which require you to communicate. Although a public speaking situation requires more careful preparation than your casual conversations with a friend, both require similar kinds of communication skills.

A speech must always be dramatic. A hundred years ago people gave very dramatic speech presentations. However, this is no longer the case. Speeches today are delivered in a style that tries to communicate information effectively and naturally. This *may* involve some dramatization. But dramatization is no longer an essential part of good public speaking.

Breakdowns in public speaking are common. When they occur, it is normally the result of a problem in the speaker, the speech, the channel, the listener, or any combination of these elements.

Breakdowns in public speaking

An example of a speaker-caused breakdown might involve a poor choice of words. If you were speaking to a group of adults you would want to use different language than if you were speaking to a group of small children. A speech-related breakdown could involve the lack of a clear purpose or central idea. Specifically, if you failed to spend adequate preparation time, no clear purpose would emerge from your ideas.

You must realize that a speech is given to an audience. Think about that audience carefully while you are preparing your speech.

A typical channel breakdown occurs when distracting noises are present during a speech. You have probably been in situations where loud noises like a motorcycle, an air conditioner, or a plane overhead made it difficult for you to hear a speech. Unless a speaker raises his or her voice to compensate for noise, much of the message will be lost.

Your failure to listen to someone's speech or someone's failure to listen to yours is a great cause of misunderstanding. This lack of attention is an example of a listener breakdown.

Generally, most breakdowns can be avoided through careful speech preparation. Knowing how to prepare a speech is essential.

2. How do you prepare a speech?

Planning and practice are needed

Probably the most important cause of a poor speaking performance is lack of preparation. As in any other activity you might try to do, giving a speech requires careful planning and practice. Confidence in your ability to actually deliver the speech will come from your knowledge that you have prepared well.

Whatever the occasion, whether it is a teacher giving a lecture to a class, a minister delivering a sermon, or you describing your vacation to your classmates, the method of preparation and practice is the same.

There are basically six steps involved in the preparation and practice of a speech. These are:

1. Audience analysis.
2. Choosing a topic.
3. Determining the purpose.
4. Gathering materials.
5. Developing an outline.
6. Rehearsing the speech.

What follows is a discussion of these steps.

Audience analysis. As a public speaker you should do all that you possibly can to improve your chances for success *before* you give your speech. The first step you must take is to carefully analyze your audience. Once you know who your audience is going to be, you can try to adapt what you are going to say to their interests.

If your speech is a class project, try to find out about the likes and dislikes of the class members. If the speech is to be given to a civic group or other community organization, find out all you can about the group's membership, its goals, and what topics would interest its members.

Audiences can be different in several ways. They may differ in membership. Some audiences will be all male or all female. Other audiences will contain both males and females. Audiences will vary in size. They may be large or small. Audiences will differ in age. They may be young, old, or young and old. Audiences will differ in how much they know about the topic of your speech. An audience can be generally well-informed, uninformed, or misinformed about your topic.

Audiences also have attitudes. They may get along well, they may not like each other, or they may not even care for you. Audiences will have varying political views. They may generally have a conservative or liberal attitude toward the topic of your speech.

Finally, audiences differ in composition. An audience may be composed of individuals with a lot in common or nothing in common. And some audiences may consist of a group of subgroups with things in common and subgroups with nothing in common.

In any speaking situation, then, your knowledge of the audience is extremely important. You will have a great advantage if you *know* your audience in advance. In fact, a successful speech presentation will depend to a great degree on careful analysis of your audience.

Choosing a topic. Once you know as much as you possibly can about your audience, your next step is to choose a topic for your speech. Many people find this difficult.

The first thing to do in selecting a speech topic is to examine your own interests and experiences. Many people have the feeling that they have nothing of interest to talk about. This is totally incorrect. Just about every experience you have ever had would provide an interesting speech topic.

Ask yourself the simple question, "What am I interested in that this audience would be willing to listen to?" If you still cannot find a speech topic begin to ask other people for ideas. Then sit down and make a list of all the topics you have gathered.

Once you have made the list, take each topic individually and examine it. Judge each topic based on your own background knowledge, the interest you think the topic would hold for the audience, and whether or not the topic would be suited for the occasion on which the speech is to be given.

If the topic requires you to do extra research be sure that

you know where to find the outside information. If you carefully analyze your audience and yourself you will be able to focus on your topic much easier. Remember to examine your own interests first. Avoid overlooking possible topics because you think you have nothing interesting to say to the audience.

Determining the purpose. The next step is to determine the purpose of your presentation. Your audience is going to want to know whether you plan to *inform*, to *persuade*, or to *entertain* them. You should know before you prepare the speech what you want the audience to leave the occasion with. Do you want the audience to gain some knowledge about your topic? Or do you want them to have an emotional reaction to it? Whatever your purpose, it will be accomplished only if it is made clear to your audience.

Your major purpose in an informative speech is to present information to the audience. For example, you might tell how to operate a CB radio, how to do the latest dance, how to tune up a car, or even something as simple as how to chew gum properly.

Persuasive speeches are designed to convince the audience to change in some way. A persuasive speech tries to get the listener to modify his or her behavior or thinking. This type of speech can include such things as telling people why they should see a particular movie, why they should change their style of dress, why they should drop a bad habit, or perhaps why they should change their opinion on an issue.

Entertaining speeches normally give an audience pleasure. These speeches are often humorous. But they can also be serious. Generally, your purpose is not to persuade or inform, just entertain. You might give an entertaining speech during assemblies or after a banquet. Speaking competitions often include an event called "entertaining speeches."

You should realize that a speech can contain two or more types of public communication at the same time. For example, a persuasive speech normally contains a good deal of information. Also, you can entertain an audience to help persuade them. And you can inform people while entertaining them. However, you should analyze the speaking situation and your purpose in giving the speech before deciding on which type of public communication to use.

For example, you may be asked by a local civic group to speak on the role of student government at your school. You carefully analyze your audience and decide to speak on how student government trains future leaders. As you prepare the text of your speech, you must make sure that you include a specific statement early in the speech which conveys your purpose to your audience.

In this speaking situation you would expect your audience to respond favorably to your speech because members of civic clubs generally see themselves as leaders of the community. You have adapted your speech to what you know about the beliefs of your audience. And you have planned to make that adaptation clear by stating a very specific purpose. Chances are the audience will respond positively to your speech.

Keep in mind that it is not enough for you to have a general purpose. The purpose must be as specific as possible. The more specific the purpose, the more likely your audience will be able to easily identify it. This will make it more likely that you will get the audience response you originally hoped for. Make sure the purpose of your speech is so clear that members of your audience could summarize it in a sentence or two if asked.

Gathering materials. Once you have analyzed your audience, selected a topic, and stated a purpose, you must next determine how much and what types of information you must have to prepare what you want to say. There are basically three approaches to collecting background materials for a speech.

1. You can directly *observe* the subject matter. For example, if your talk is going to be about tennis, you might either watch a tennis match or a tennis coach teaching a player how to improve his or her game.
2. You can *talk* to persons who are knowledgeable about your topic. If your subject is football, your school's football coach would be a good person to interview.
3. You can do *research* in the library about your topic. Libraries contain many different kinds of sources that you can draw on for information. For example, if your subject is tennis, you could find magazines and articles about tennis in the periodical section of the library.

Developing an outline. An organized speech must have a beginning, a middle, and an end. These divisions are also referred to as *introduction, body,* and *conclusion.* Your audience should be able to easily spot these divisons during your talk since each division plays a particular role in a successful speech.

Your introduction should tell your audience what you are going to say. It should attract the audience's attention. And it should promote good relations between you and your audience.

You might get the audience's attention through a well-chosen quote or short story which will cause them to want to listen. Although it may sometimes be a one sentence statement of your main point, the length of an introduction should vary with the particular audience and occasion.

Most importantly, plan your beginning carefully. Make sure it is relevant to your speaking situation. You may even want to write out your introduction to be sure it achieves your purpose. Remember, you may lose your audience if the first minute or two of your presentation is boring. Your introduction is your chance to get the audience on your side.

The body of your outline is in fact the main part of your speech. It contains all the main points and subpoints which explain and support the topic of your speech. There are several things you should keep in mind when preparing this part of your speech outline:

1. You must decide on the number of main points and subpoints to include. This is generally determined by the amount of time you have to speak. Do not have too many main points or subpoints. Short talks normally have one to five main points. Limit your subpoints to things you believe your audience would be especially interested in.

2. You must decide on the arrangement of main points and subpoints. This normally depends on the topic, the audience, and the speaking situation. Points can be arranged in a number of ways. First, by *time sequence:* you could present a chronologically arranged history of football. Second, by *space sequence:* you could talk about football in terms of where it was invented and where early games were played. Third, by *order of priority:* a speech on getting things done during the day could be built around a list of chores that must be completed, arranged in order of importance. Fourth, from *familiar to unfamiliar:* to explain baseball you could begin with those things about the game most familiar to your audience in order to get their attention, then gradually move to the more unfamiliar aspects of the game. Fifth, from the *simple to the complex:* in preparing a speech about dancing, you could start with a discussion of some basic steps and move to more complex dance arrangements.

3. You must decide on the number and type of transitions you will use. Transitions are sentences that link the points of a speech together. If used correctly, transitions will help you to move naturally from point to point in a speech.

Your conclusion should end your speech effectively. Its purpose should depend upon the nature of the speech, the nature of the occasion, your goals, and the attitude of the audience. The conclusion should summarize the major points of the speech, and may also be used to leave the audience with one last important thought concerning the speech's topic.

As important as developing a good speech outline is knowing how to use such an outline correctly. The speech outline should be the *guide* to a speech, not an actual speech. The outline should be a list of the ideas you are going to use in your speech and a plan of how you will present these ideas.

A word of caution

When practicing your speech, you should have the outline in front of you. However, the more you practice, the less you should depend on your outline. As you practice, begin to put the ideas contained in the outline into your own words. Above all, do not become too tied to your outline.

3. How can you deliver your speech?

When preparing to speak you must decide how to deliver your speech. There are several different ways to do this. Each way has both advantages and disadvantages.

Speaking from a manuscript. You can write out your speech and read it aloud to your audience. This way of delivering a speech has several advantages. It allows you to describe your ideas very carefully. There is no chance of forgetting your speech. You can refer back to the speech at a later date to see exactly what you said. You can distribute exact copies of the speech, and your audience can get an accurate record of what you said.

However, this type of speaking does have several major difficulties. Most people do not read well, so these kinds of presentations usually are less natural. Also, you are less free to make spontaneous changes in your presentation. You are tied to your manuscript and have to make the best of it.

Memorizing your speech. If you decide to memorize your speech, you also start by writing it out word for word. But you deliver it from memory. Many people feel confident with this approach. But it has several problems.

You may forget your chain of thought or leave out parts of your speech. It is highly embarrassing to stand in front of an audience with nothing to say because you have forgotten what comes next. And you may focus so much energy on remembering the exact words of a memorized speech that the presentation will seem unnatural or even phony.

The impromptu speech. You can also decide to use very few words or no notes and speak in a spontaneous manner. The advantage to this type of speaking is that you will not be tied to a manuscript or outline and can simply say whatever comes to your mind. It allows for a lively, spontaneous style of delivery. And an impromptu speech will permit you to adjust your content to the mood of the audience.

The biggest weakness to this style of speaking is that a lack of preparation may cause your speech to lack organization. Few persons can give a carefully structured, well-organized speech off the top of their head. Too often impromptu speeches ramble on and the audience has a hard time identifying the purpose.

Extemporaneous speaking. The most commonly used type of delivery is the extemporaneous speech. In this kind of delivery you carefully select ideas and organize them into an outline. Then you rehearse from the outline several times, and only use the outline to refer to when needed while speaking. The advantages to this type of delivery are:

1. The delivery is spontaneous. Your speech will be a little bit different every time you present it, thus avoiding some of the problems of presentation associated with memorized or written speeches.
2. The speech is as carefully prepared as one that is written. A well-prepared extemporaneous speech takes a great deal of research and planning.
3. The outline serves as a guide. If you lose your train of thought, the outline may be referred to. This solves one of the major problems of memorized speeches.

As you can see, the extemporaneous style has most of the advantages of the other styles but with fewer disadvantages. The main problem with this method is that you may get so tied to the outline that you will begin to ignore the audience. If the outline is used correctly, you will seldom refer to it.

When choosing one of the above styles, consider which fits the occasion and the purpose. All have advantages and disadvantages. It is up to you to find the style that works best for you.

Once you have completed all of your preparations, you must begin to consider the actual presentation of your speech. Many people do not put as much thought and effort into delivering the speech as they do in choosing a topic or preparing the speech. This is a mistake. All of your preparations will have been for nothing if your delivery is poor.

You should work very hard at making your oral presentation as effective as possible. You must think about what your

Techniques of delivery

voice sounds like to an audience. You must decide how you can use your voice to increase the audience's understanding of what you are saying. And you must think about what effect your physical appearance may have on an audience.

What your voice sounds like. Your audience will judge you partly on how you sound. If your voice is dry and boring, it will turn off your audience. On the other hand, if you seem excited by your topic and your voice is full of energy, it may help increase the audience's interest in the topic. There is no way you can avoid being judged on your presentation by the audience.

Avoid creating distractions for the audience with your voice. Listeners may be bothered if you mispronounce words or do not say them clearly.

You should be careful as you prepare a speech to make sure you can correctly pronounce every word. If you do make a mistake in pronouncing a word, it will reduce your effectiveness. The audience may begin to question your knowledge of the subject of your speech. If you do not know how to pronounce a word, look it up in the dictionary or ask a knowledgeable person.

You should also be very careful about your articulation of words and phrases. Audiences can be distracted when they have a hard time understanding a speaker or the speaker uses a lot of vocal insertions such as "ah," "er," "like," or "you know." If you overuse these kinds of insertions, your audience may begin to focus on how many times you use them and lose track of the rest of your message.

A speech should be delivered in a way which will help your presentation, not get in the way of your message. Think about your delivery and work to improve your pronunciation and articulation.

Using your voice. Your voice is a remarkable instrument that will do a great number of things. Most people do not realize how many things can be done with the voice in terms of *pitch*, *volume*, *speaking rate*, and *quality*, or the overall sound of your voice.

Pitch refers to depth or highness of the tone of your voice. Changes in pitch may be used to add emphasis to ideas. Normally your pitch will vary as you speak. If your voice lacks variation in pitch, the delivery will become monotonous. You should make an effort to raise and lower your pitch as you speak. This will help you to get variety into your delivery.

Volume refers to the loudness or softness of your voice. Again, you can call attention to a particular idea in your speech by changing your volume as you say it. At times you may want to raise your voice to emphasize particular words or phrases. The opposite is also true. If you are speaking quite loudly, you can call attention to your ideas by speaking more softly. The important thing is to remember to vary the volume of your voice during your speech. Changes in volume while you are speaking will help you to keep the attention of your audience.

Rate is the speed at which people talk. Some people speak very rapidly while others speak more slowly. You should realize that you can use changes in speed to give emphasis to ideas. If an idea is not important, you might speak faster to get past it. If an idea is more important, you can make it stand out by speaking slowly. This change in your rate of speed will tell the audience it should pay more attention.

You might also think of the length of pauses you place between words when trying to put emphasis on ideas. If you want to call attention to a certain part of your speech, you may pause a bit longer just before or after you say it. If used properly, the pause can be a valuable speaking tool. The change in delivery will "tip" your audience to the important parts of your speech.

The quality of your voice is the characteristic tone of your voice. Quality is what makes your voice different from other voices. A voice may have a pleasant, neutral, or unpleasant quality about it. You should work at making your voice as pleasant as possible to your audience. This will help to make the audience feel more positive to you and your speech.

Here are some ideas you might consider in using your voice to communicate meaning:

1. Learn to emphasize important words. Make it clear to the audience through changes in pitch, volume, rate, and quality that there are certain words and ideas which you want them to pay special attention to. By doing this, you will increase your chances of successfully getting your ideas across to the audience.

2. Be sure to make clear the distinctions between ideas. You must make it clear, by pauses and other changes, when you are moving from one idea to another. You can increase clarity by helping your audience understand where you are in a presentation and which ideas you feel are most important.

3. Make words sound like you mean them. You must convey your interest in the topic to the audience. Make

your delivery lively and interesting. If you act bored, your audience will sense your feelings and react to them.

4. Speak in a conversational manner. Your delivery is an extension of you as a person. Try to speak in a natural, conversational style—much as you would in face-to-face conversation. If you are natural and spontaneous, you will put your audience at ease. And this will increase your chances of communicating your ideas to the audience.

Your physical appearance. Your audience will judge you as a speaker not only on the quality of your voice, but also on your physical appearance. Make sure that your appearance adds to your presentation, not distracts from it. Be aware of eye contact, posture, movements, and gestures.

Effective speakers use eye contact to emphasize ideas. Listeners tend to trust individuals who look them in the eye when speaking to them. When delivering a public speech, try to initiate eye contact with as many audience members as possible. This will show the audience that you are interested in communicating with them. It will also give you a means of evaluating the audience's reaction.

Your posture may send messages to your audience that you do not intend to send. If you slump over the podium or sit in a slouched position, the audience may take this as a sign that you are bored by your topic. Try to show through your posture that you are full of energy and are excited about the presentation you are going to make.

Movement while speaking can distract the audience. If you walk back and forth in front of your audience or make quick movements, the audience may start watching them and forget about what you are saying. Limit yourself to those movements that are essential for the presentation.

You should also be concerned about gestures. You can distract from your speech by using too many arm gestures. Some speakers will try to include unnatural gestures. They force themselves to use many hand and arm motions.

The best thing to do is to use only gestures that feel natural and are comfortable. If you feel uncomfortable using many hand and arm gestures, do not use them. As you give more and more public speeches, you will find it easier to use gestures naturally.

Where you are giving a speech will influence your use of gestures. Gestures that are appropriate for an audience of ten may not be as effective when used before an audience of several hundred. Experience will help you decide what kinds of gestures to use and when to use them.

Finally, think about your personal appearance. Avoid wearing clothes or jewelry that might distract from your speech. Be neat and clean. Whether you like it or not, some people in the audience will react to your speech based on their reaction to your appearance. You should consider both your audience and the occasion. Your dress and appearance should be appropriate to each.

Using visual aids

Many speakers are able to liven up what would otherwise be an average or dull presentation by the use of visual aids. You may decide that you can make your speech more effective by including the use of one or more visual aids.

There are several types of visual aids. However, all fall into one or the other of several groups. These groups are diagrams and graphs, maps and globes, pictures, models, and objects.

Effective use of visual aids depends on following a few simple rules.

1. The visual aid should be large enough for the entire audience to see.
2. The visual aid should be as simple as possible.
3. The visual aid should be an important part of the content of the speech.

Whatever visual aid you decide to use, be sure to practice using it prior to the speech. And during the presentation of the speech, keep the visual aid out of sight until you actually need it.

4. What else should you know?

Conversational communication

A common mistake many people make is in thinking that public speaking is different from everyday conversation. Speakers seem to think that when they stand before an audience the rules of communication change. Obviously, there are some slight differences. But the communication is essentially the same. One person is attempting to communicate with another person or persons.

One trait of a good speaker is that he or she recognizes the similarities in both public and conversational communication and uses a conversational style of voice in both. Never try to "sound" like what you *think* a public speaker does. When delivering a speech you can generally speak at about the same volume (loudness), rate (speed), and pitch as you normally do. And in most cases, there will probably be sound equipment available that will make your task easier.

Remember that you should speak to an audience just as you would if you were speaking in your home or across a table at your favorite hangout. You should send out your message and look for the audience's response. Try to imagine that you are not speaking to an audience but *with* a group of friends. Above all, try to be yourself—be natural.

Suggestions for improving your speaking

In addition to all the tips and suggestions that have been given you to this point, there are several other things you can do to help improve yourself as a speaker. Your speaking can be improved by following some rather simple rules:

1. Once you have your speech prepared, practice it aloud. You might even find a friend to listen to your speech and ask him or her to make some constructive comments about the speech. Say your speech aloud, not silently to yourself. Do this several times until you feel

comfortable. If you are not comfortable with parts of a speech, change them.

2. If possible, practice the speech in the room in which it is to be given. Musicians always check out the sounds in a room before they play a concert. When giving a speech, your voice is your instrument. Your presentation is the concert.

3. You may also want to consider using a sound tape recorder or a video tape recorder as a method to help you improve your speaking skills. Record the rehearsal of your speech. This will give you the opportunity to criticize your own presentation.

When considering these suggestions, it is also important to note that *although there are many similarities, there are also many differences between public speaking and social conversation:*

1. In public speaking, you usually speak to more persons than you would in social conversation.

2. In public speaking, the audience does not usually interrupt or speak back during the presentation. They communicate in other ways how intently they are listening to you. An experienced speaker learns to read the signs given off by his or her audience to see if they are listening.

3. In public speaking, you are often physically separated from your audience by a desk, podium, or an open space. You must learn to project yourself across this space and try to overcome this separation.

4. The public speaking situation is often much more formal or serious than the social conversation. Your audience expects an effective message from you and you must deliver it.

Together with these differences, you must understand the similarities between public speaking and social conversation. When you speak publicly, you are talking to a larger group of people than when you are making social conversation. But even so your intent is the same in both situations. You are trying to either inform, persuade, or entertain. Keeping this in mind should help you to be more at ease. And being at ease should help to make you a more effective communicator.

And finally

Speaking in public is largely as easy or as difficult as you care to make it. If you have carefully organized, researched, and practiced your presentation, there is no reason to believe you will falter or fail in your delivery. If you have studied the interests, likes, and dislikes of your audience, there is no reason to believe your speech will be poorly received.

Remember that the ability to speak efficiently and effectively before an audience is a skill that is well worth developing. No matter what career you plan to enter after you complete school, well-developed speaking skills can make a difference in how well you succeed.

And even if you never have to speak before an audience, the self-confidence well-developed speaking skills can create will be of use to you in many different situations. Many useful ideas have failed to become influential because of someone's inability to state these ideas clearly and concisely. Many problems have been caused by misunderstandings of things that were said. Many talented people have proved unable to succeed at chosen careers because they lacked the self-confidence and forcefulness to deal with others effectively.

No matter what the event, no matter what the time, no matter what the place, your chance of successfully handling a situation will depend largely on your ability to communicate your ideas forcefully and effectively to others. And such ability is closely related to the level of development of your speaking skills.

Remember, be confident, control your breathing, think about how your voice sounds, consider your physical appearance, and, perhaps most importantly, *think before you talk*. Project a confident image and you will find your ability to influence others growing.

Activities

The unit-end activities have been designed to help you to practice and gain the ability to use the various communication skills discussed in this unit. Please do not write in this book, but place your answers on a separate sheet of paper. Where appropriate, answers to the activities can be found in the **Answer Key** that begins on page 290.

Getting ready

There are many steps involved in the preparation of an effective speech. It is easy to forget a step or two along the way. And yet this would be the kind of mistake that could ruin a presentation. If you are about to begin the preparation of a speech, use the following questions to make sure you "cover all the bases."

	Yes	No
1. Have I carefully studied and analyzed the audience?	___	___
2. Have I chosen a topic for my speech that not only interests me, but is also adaptable to the likes and dislikes of my audience?	___	___
3. Have I set the purpose of my speech?	___	___
4. Have I carefully gathered all of the information and materials I will need to document my speech?	___	___
5. Have I developed a well-organized and logical outline for my speech?	___	___
6. Have I rehearsed my presentation to the point that I am sure I can deliver the speech confidently and without hesitation?	___	___

Give a speech

The best way to calm any apprehension you might have about speaking before an audience is to practice. The more often you speak before an audience, the easier it will become.

However, even if you are taking a speech class, you will probably not get many opportunities to speak before an audience. A simple way to get such practice is to speak before groups of your classmates or friends. Try to find several classmates or friends who are also interested in improving speaking skills. Hold practice "speaking sessions" with them, and critique one another's presentations.

You need not take the time to prepare extensive speeches. Each person should be given two minutes to prepare a one-minute speech on a selected topic. Topics should be kept simple. You might consider topics such as the following:

1. My favorite television program
2. A hobby I enjoy
3. My most memorable moment
4. A person I enjoy
5. Why I like school
6. Why I dislike school

Listeners could critique each presentation, using guidelines such as the following as the basis for criticism:

	Good	Fair	Poor
1. Organization of the presentation	___	___	___
2. Clarity of purpose	___	___	___
3. Effectiveness of the conclusion	___	___	___
4. Variation in vocal pitch	___	___	___
5. Volume	___	___	___
6. Speaking rate	___	___	___
7. Clarity of enunciation	___	___	___
8. Eye contact with audience	___	___	___
9. Physical presence	___	___	___
10. Overall reaction to the presentation	___	___	___
11. Comments: _____			

After a speech has been given and critiqued in writing, all of the participants should discuss their critique with the speaker.

The ability to accept constructive criticism and to use this criticism to strengthen weaknesses is essential to the development of an effective speaker. You must have a strong sense of self confidence that you then project to your listening audience. Most audiences can sense a speaker's self confidence and this, in turn, can mold the audience response to the speaker's presentation. A good way to develop this necessary self confidence is to learn to react rationally to criticism. And the best way to learn to accept criticism is to get it and use it.

If you are interested in extending your skills as a speaker, you might wish to consult any or all of the following sources. Each has been prepared by an expert or experts in the field of communication skills. And each is used in classes dealing with formal training in the skills of communication.

Allen, R.R., Parrish, Sharol, and Mortenson, David. *Communication: Interacting Through Speech.* Columbus, O.: Charles E. Merrill Publishing Co., 1974.

Ewing, Raymond. *Participating.* Boston: Houghton Mifflin Co., 1975.

Galvin, Kathleen M., and Book, Cassandra L. *Person to Person: An Introduction to Speech Communication.* rev. ed. Skokie, Ill.: National Textbook Co., 1978.

Reid, Loren. *Speaking Well.* 3rd ed. New York: McGraw-Hill Book Co., 1977.

Wilkinson, Charles. *Speaking of Communication.* Glenview, Ill.: Scott, Foresman & Co., 1975.

A guide to vocabulary skills

6

You need words to communicate your feelings and ideas to others. And you need words to understand what others are trying to say to you. Do you have a well-developed vocabulary? Are your word skills at a high enough level so that you are able to communicate effectively?

This unit explains some of the bases and uses of words. And it gives you a program designed to help you build your word-using skills.

The contributors of this unit are Dr. Joseph O'Rourke, Research Associate in the College of Education, The Ohio State University, Columbus, Ohio; and Dr. Edgar Dale, Emeritus Professor of Education, The Ohio State University, Columbus, Ohio.

1. How can words help you?

You live in a world of words

You need words. Words help you to communicate, to share your ideas and feelings with others. So expanding your vocabulary is a very practical thing for you to do.

The more words you know the more effectively you can speak, listen, read, write, and think. Words are the tools you think with. And every idea you wish to communicate to others must be expressed in a language of some kind— words, painting, music, gestures, or signs. But mainly you communicate by using words. Therefore, the more words you know, the more ideas you can understand and share.

Your vocabulary is your life

The words you know show the experiences you have had. If you know the words *layout, pike, tuck,* and *half gainer,* you probably like the sport of diving. If you do not know these words, you probably have no interest in diving.

Knowing words such as *serve, lob, deuce, fault, backhand,* and *match point* shows an interest in tennis. *Linebacker, tight end, single wing,* and *blitz* indicate an interest in football. *Simmer, parboil, broil, baste,* and *scallop* relate to cooking.

Your success in school is related to the size of your vocabulary. Students with the poorest vocabularies often get the poorest grades. Students with the best vocabularies often get the best grades.

You cannot understand a subject unless you know the key words in that subject. For example, the more key words you know in biology, the more you will be able to learn about that subject. If you do not know words such as *legislative, executive, judicial, amendment, preamble, representative,* and *impeachment,* you will not be able to understand much about the Constitution of the United States.

Words are also important outside of school. If you do not

142

know the right words, you cannot effectively express your thoughts in social situations or on the job. Words make it possible for you to communicate ideas.

You need to increase the size of your vocabulary and become more skillful with words. But this does not always mean learning big, hard words. It means learning to use the exact words you need to explain your ideas to others. For example, the words *leave* and *abandon* have somewhat similar meanings. But there is a difference between *leaving* someone and *abandoning* someone. Is there a difference between an *uninterested* person and a *disinterested* person? You need the right word for the right occasion.

Choosing the right word is important. But keep in mind that words are not things. Words are symbols, something that stands for something else.

The word *chair* does not look like a *chair*. But to communicate effectively about the thing *chair*, you need to know the word, the symbol or the name for the thing *chair*.

Try to ask for a *chair* without using the word-symbol for *chair*. You will find yourself saying something like the following: "Please bring me a thing with four legs and a back that you sit on." Such a statement is both long and confusing. A listener could just as well interpret your request to be for a horse or camel as for a chair. So learning the names, the symbols, the words for things is a shortcut to more effective communication. And the more word-symbols you know how to use, the more exact the meaning of your communication will be.

But you still might say, "What good is it to learn words I may never use?" The answer to this question is simple. In school subjects, and in materials you will read in and out of school, you will meet many unfamiliar words. Whether you are in junior high school or a senior in college, you will still come across unfamiliar words. The larger your vocabulary is, the fewer the unfamiliar words you will be likely to encounter. And the fewer unfamiliar words you have to work with, the more efficient will be your reading and studying.

If you have some method of attacking new words, you will have a better chance of learning and remembering them. The material that follows will permit you to develop a method for attacking new words.

If you look closely at the parts of the word *tonsillectomy*, you will discover that this word is not much harder than the words *tonsil* and *tonsillitis*—words you already know. The word part *ectomy* means "cut out," and you can easily guess what kind of operation a *tonsillectomy* is.

But the important point is that once you have learned that the *ectomy* in *tonsillectomy* means "cut out," your learning does not stop there. You will see *ectomy* in hundreds of words, especially in science. And you will know that whenever you see *ectomy*, the word of which it is a part will have something to do with "cutting out." What, do you think, is an *appendectomy?*

Should you learn big words? Only if you want to, maybe for fun. If you are superstitious you should know this word: *triskaidekaphobia*. Break it down into its parts: *tris* (3), *kai* (and), *deka* (10), *phobia* (fear). The word means fear of the number 13.

However, many of the words you need to know are short and easy to learn. But even simple words have different meanings. For example, notice the different meanings of the word *for*:

> He went home *for* good.
> He went home *for* his ball glove.
> She went home, *for* she was tired.

You can increase your vocabulary and your language skills by noticing the slight differences in the meanings of simple words, such as the word *bank*:

> money in the *bank*
> the *bank* of a stream
> *bank* your money
> *bank* the fire
> a snow *bank*.

A gambler may "break the *bank*." A pool shark can hit a "*bank* shot." You can "*bank* on it." You should be aware of the slight difference of meaning between words such as *praise* and *flatter, subtle* and *crafty, bold* and *reckless, thrifty* and *stingy*, and so on.

Using synonyms and antonyms

Synonyms are words that mean almost the same thing. Learning synonyms is a good way to build your vocabulary. It helps to organize words into groups. For example, under the idea of "little," you can mentally file such synonyms as *tiny, wee, minute, miniature, dwarf, elf,* and *pygmy*.

It is sometimes interesting to notice how many different

synonyms there are for a word. How many synonyms can you think of for the word *prison*? Some are fancy words, some are down to earth: *house of correction, penal institution, penitentiary, jail, workhouse, dungeon, lockup, hoosegow, calaboose, jug, pokey,* and *clink*.

You can sharpen your vocabulary skills by learning the synonyms for common words. But you should also learn words that are dissimilar, words that have opposite meanings. Such words are called antonyms. When you study antonyms, you begin to understand the relationships between words. If there is an *up*, there must be a *down*. If there is *light*, there must be *dark*. One idea does not exist without the other.

Therefore, when you learn a new word, it is a good idea to also learn its antonyms. It will not take long, and one word is easier to remember when you associate it with another. Some examples of words and their antonyms are:

male—female   *explode—implode*
masculine—feminine   *alpha—omega*
billygoat—nannygoat   *perigee—apogee*
buck—doe   *prologue—epilogue*

Notice that in studying word opposites you are making relationships between words and ideas. You are comparing and contrasting ideas. Thus, studying antonyms helps you see connections between opposite words such as

healthy—ailing   *sanitary—unsanitary*
sane—insane   *nutrition—malnutrition*
robust—frail   *immigrate—emigrate*

Fun with metaphors

Learning words should not be a chore for you. You should experiment with words and play with words. Many of our most commonly used expressions come from trying out words in different situations. Words are elastic and people can stretch the meanings of words. This process is called making metaphors. For example, a person may be described as "having a heart of stone." Obviously, the person's heart is not really stone. But it is compared to stone. The person's heart is given the characteristics of stone—hard, cold, and lifeless.

Look for metaphors in the newspapers. Listen for them on the radio and television. Notice how often your parents, teachers, and friends use metaphors. You probably use metaphors more often than you realize.

Many metaphors refer to parts of the body. How often

have you heard the metaphors used in the following expressions? "Keep a stiff upper *lip*." "Don't stick your *neck* out." "Don't split *hairs*." "She got an *earful*." "You said a *mouthful*." Other examples of the use of metaphors include the expressions "high *brow*," "won by a *nose*," "see *eye* to *eye*," "a *belly* laugh," "use your *head*" and "don't lose your *head*."

Electricians use metaphors when they talk about the flow of electric *current* (like a stream of water). Geologists refer to the earth's *crust* (like a loaf of bread), and plumbers use *elbow* joints (like the part of a person's body).

Some metaphors, often those derived from the names of fruits and vegetables, become slang. People often call a poorly made product a *lemon*. People also refer to folding money as *lettuce*. Baseball fans know that Hank Aaron hit the *apple*, or baseball, hard. Players may become involved in a *rhubarb*, or argument. And umpires may get the *raspberry*, a sound made by the tongue and lips.

Rearranging letters to form new words

Another way to learn new words by playing with words is by noticing their constructions. For example, games such as crossword puzzles require you to look closely at how a word is spelled and how the letter of one word blends into another word. Some people like to work anagrams, the changing of a word into another word by moving the letters. Two examples of anagrams would be *are—ear*, and *thorn—north*.

Some people play with words by making palindromes. Palindromes are words or phrases that read the same backward or forward. For example, read these words and phrases forward then backward: *radar, kayak, rotor, level, gold log, stops spots*. Can you think of other palindromes? Try people's names, such as *Bob* and *Anna*.

Remember, your vocabulary is your life. It has a serious side and a playful side. You need both. Words help people express important thoughts, such as those found in the Declaration of Independence and the Gettysburg Address. And words also help people enjoy the language of puns, jokes, and witty remarks. Increase and refine your vocabulary and you increase and refine your ability to communicate with and to understand the people around you.

2. How can a dictionary help you?

The dictionary is an important tool for improving your vocabulary. Most people do not really know what kind of information is available in the dictionary. They know the dictionary only as a list of words. But as you read this section, you will discover that the dictionary is more than a book in which you may find a word's meaning, pronunciation, and spelling.

An important word resource

A person has an experience and gives the experience a name. That name is a word. Thus the dictionary is also a collection of the named experiences people have had. It is a storehouse of quick, easy-to-find information.

For example, where did the *gardenia* get its name? The dictionary tells you that the gardenia is named after the Scottish naturalist Alexander *Garden*. It also tells you that a *volt*, a measure of electrical energy, is named after the Italian physicist Alessandro *Volta*. And the dictionary tells you that a *watt*, a unit of electric power, gets its name from the Scottish engineer James *Watt*.

When you do research on a topic, you need a resource, something that will provide you with information. The dictionary is a word resource. It tells you many things about a word, such as the word's meaning, spelling, and pronunciation. And the dictionary also tells you where the word came from, its origin and its history.

The dictionary can help you choose the right word for the right occasion. It can help you to better understand the shade of difference in the meaning of similar words. And the dictionary can help you to expand the size of your vocabulary. The dictionary is the most important word resource tool you have.

Using compound words

The dictionary tells you how words are formed. Sometimes two complete words are joined together to form a compound word such as *bullhead, firehouse,* and *meanwhile*. However, parts of words are also joined together to form compound words. Many words are made from meaningful parts. A meaningful part added to the beginning of a word is called a prefix. A meaningful part added to the end of a word is called a suffix. The word to which a prefix or suffix has been added is called a root.

The dictionary shows you how a word changes its meaning when a prefix or suffix is added to the root: meter—*dia*meter; grade—*de*grade; grammar—grammar*ian*; diction—diction*ary*. The dictionary shows you how parts of words combine to form new words: *bio* (life) + *graph* (write) + *er* (one who) = *biographer*, one who writes about someone's life.

Most persons do not get enough practice in compounding. They do not learn how to use prefixes, roots, and suffixes to understand the meaning of compound words. You can get this practice by looking closely at words in the dictionary. The word *postscript* is a compound of two meaningful parts, *post* (after) and *script* (write). The word *predict* is a compound of the meaningful parts *pre* (before) and *dict* (say). These prefixes in turn may be compounded with other roots to form words carrying the idea of *before* and *after*. For example:

Before: preview, preface, preliminary, prepositions, prescription, precede, preamble, prelude, preclude, precursor.

After: postwar, postpone, posterior, posterity, posthumous, post meridian, post-mortem, postnasal, postlude.

Note also that the two opposite ideas of *pre* (before) and *post* (after) combine to form the word *preposterous*, something contrary to reason or common sense.

If you want your vocabulary to grow, you have to concentrate on the process of compounding. You have to recognize the importance of meaningful word parts that combine with one another to form new words. Keep in mind that the number of words you will learn is directly related to your ability to recognize and use compounds—not only whole words but the meaningful parts of words. The dictionary will help you to do this.

The following are some useful things you should know about using dictionary entries.

Word entries. Entry words are the main words or head words in the dictionary. You should know that:

1. Main entry words are in large, boldface type.
2. Main entry words are listed in strict alphabetical order.
3. Different spellings of the same word may be listed together, for example **usable**, also **useable**. They may also be listed as separate entry words, for example, **amoeba** or **ameba**.
4. Main entries may be single words, compound words, phrases, abbreviations, prefixes, suffixes, or root words.
5. Homographs, words that are spelled alike but have different meanings, are listed separately with superscript numbers. For example: **count**[1] (add up); **count**[2] (a nobleman).

Guide words. Each set of facing pages containing word entries has a guide word on each outside top corner. The guide word on the left-hand page tells you what the first entry on the set of facing pages is. The guide word on the right-hand page tells you what the last entry on the set of facing pages is. For example, if you are looking for the word **bribe**, you will find it on the facing pages between the two guide words **breeze** and **brick**.

Guide words are timesavers. If you practice using guide words, you will become skillful at it and be able to find words quickly and easily.

Parts of speech. Did you know the dictionary tells you what part of speech any word is? It tells you whether the word is a noun, adjective, verb, and so forth. And the dictionary shows you how the word may be used in a phrase or sentence. The parts of speech are listed alphabetically— adjective first, then noun, then verb. The dictionary also lists the plural form of nouns. So the dictionary is also a useful grammar resource.

Etymology. The dictionary will inform you of the etymology, the original meaning or derivation, of a word or its parts. For example, notice the original meaning of the parts in the word *helicopter: heli* (spiral) + *pter* (wing). A helicopter is kept aloft by "spiraling wings," that is, by horizontal propellers. Notice the etymology or derivation of the word *insect: in* (into) + *sect* (cut). If you look closely at an insect, such as an ant, you will see that it appears to be "cut into" sections or parts.

Synonyms and antonyms. The dictionary lists the synonyms, and may list antonyms for many words. As mentioned earlier, practice in the use of synonyms and antonyms can improve your vocabulary.

The dictionary as a source for synonyms is especially important. If you look up a word in the dictionary and do not understand the definition, you can look at the synonyms for that word and find one you know well. The synonym will give you a clue to the meaning of the word you looked up.

Word usage. The dictionary gives you hints about word usage, the grammatically proper use of certain words. Usage notes in the dictionary will help you to be grammatically correct in your use of words. For example, the dictionary can help you decide whether to use the spelling *all right* or *alright*. It tells you that *all right* is the preferred spelling in formal usage and that *alright* is not generally acceptable.

Of course, a word may be acceptable in one situation and not in another. For example, the word *ain't* is not acceptable in formal usage. But you sometimes hear the word *ain't* used in informal conversations. The dictionary lists this word as substandard.

The dictionary explains the use of colloquialisms, words used in everyday, informal speech. And it also includes slang, flashy, popular words used in a special way.

Colloquialisms and slang are part of the living, changing language. Colloquialisms and slang are included because the dictionary is also a resource for understanding how contemporary language is used.

Definitions. Many words have more than one meaning. Such words can be used in many different senses. So the dictionary can help you to learn additional meanings for words you already know.

For example, the word *about* may mean "dealing with" (*about* money), "nearly" (*about* empty), or "nearby" (somewhere *about* the garden). A recently ill person can now be "up and *about*." Your friend may be "*about* to leave." A soldier may do an "*about* face."

So extending your vocabulary is not only a question of learning new words. It is also a matter of extending the number of meanings you can attach to a word you already know. The dictionary can help you do this.

3. How can you build your vocabulary?

Be on the alert

If you wish to think and communicate more effectively, you must increase your vocabulary and improve your word-using skills. The best way to develop a rich vocabulary is to have rich experiences—travel; going to movies, plays, and concerts; seeing things; meeting people; listening to good conversation; and selecting good television and radio broadcasts. But most people do not have the opportunity to experience all these things directly. That is why it is also important to read widely.

Perhaps you cannot experience directly all the things you would wish to experience. But you can read about these things. You can build a good vocabulary by reading a wide variety of books, magazines, and newspapers. The more you read, the more your vocabulary will grow. And, in turn, a growing vocabulary will make you a better reader. One helps the other.

Although reading is one of the best ways to learn words, you have to learn to read actively, not passively. Read with the idea that you are going to use the information you pick up and the new words you meet. Be on the alert. Be ready and willing to attack unfamiliar words.

In addition to reading actively and learning new words, you have to be willing to do something about your vocabulary. The more you do about your vocabulary, the more it will grow. You must decide that you will make a conscious effort to learn the new words you meet in your reading. You must pick up the habit of really looking at words. You must become word conscious.

Begin to look carefully at the words that appear in the various subjects you study in school. For example, in a health

Being word conscious

class you might learn such words as *vitamin, protein, carbo-hydrate, dietetic, rickets,* and *cholesterol.* These important words are classified under a special subject. Classifying words is an easy way to remember them. It is a systematic method for learning words.

You already know thousands of words and you will learn thousands more. But the many words you now know, you know at different levels of understanding. Each time you learn a new word, that word passes through the following four levels of understanding:

1. I have never seen the word. For example, *zizz,* a short sleep; *ai,* a three-toed sloth.
2. I have heard of the word, but I do not know it well. For example, *abyss,* a deep, empty space; *cam,* part of a machine.
3. I would recognize the word when used in context. For example, there was a dangerous *crevasse* in the glacier; frequent battles had almost *annihilated* the Indian tribe.
4. I know the word. For example, *government, continent,* and *geography.*

As you can see from the preceding examples, there are some words you just do not know. You have never heard of them. But there are many other words that are farther along on your learning scale and you at least recognize them. Some words you have heard of and know in general how these words are used. But you understand these words only vaguely. Finally, there are some words you know fairly well, and still others you know very well.

In any systematic method of building vocabulary, you must move the partly known or dimly known words into sharp focus. Using the words you almost know will sharply increase your active vocabulary, the vocabulary you use frequently. An athlete gets better because he or she practices. The more you practice using words, the better you will become at it.

Learning and using word parts

The quickest way to increase your vocabulary and improve your understanding of words is by learning key prefixes, suffixes, and roots. Once you know these, you can begin practicing the procedure called analyzing words, or taking words apart. Learning to analyze words helps to give your memory a boost. If you do not know the meaning of a word, you might know the meaning of part of the word. This can give you some clue to the meaning of the entire word.

For example, it is a simple matter to analyze a word such as *bicycle*. The prefix *bi* means "two," and the word *cycle* means "wheel." Have you noticed the use of the prefix *bi* in other words? How many wives or husbands does a *bigamist* have? Notice the *bi* in the word *bigamist*—*bi* (two) + *gam* (marriage). When you *bisect* a line you cut it into how many parts? Notice the *bi* in *bisect*—*bi* (two) + *sect* (cut). Once you understand the significance of the prefix *bi*, you have a leg up on such words as *biennial, bicentennial, bilateral, binomial, bivalve,* and *bicuspid.*

By learning important prefixes, suffixes, and roots you can unlock the meaning of many unfamiliar words. For example, the root *cred* means "believe" or "trust." Notice the root *cred* in the word *credit*. When a person buys "on credit" the seller trusts him or believes the buyer will pay later. Did you recognize the ideas "trust" or "believe" in the word *credit* before? Analyzing word parts makes you word conscious.

Knowing key roots helps you recognize and remember many words. The root method gives you a mental filing system that helps you understand the relationship among many words.

The prefixes, suffixes, and roots listed in the tables that follow are among those that are most frequently used in the English language. Knowing the meaning of these word parts can help you to understand and to remember the meaning of many words. Study these tables. See if you can think of an additional example for each word part.

Word parts you should know

Table of commonly used prefixes

Prefix	Meaning	Example
a	not	atheism
ab	from	absent
ad	to	adhere
ante	before	anteroom
anti	against	antislavery
apo	away from	apogee
bene	well, good	beneficial
bi	two	bicycle
cent	hundred	century
circum	around	circumnavigate
co	with, together	cooperate
col	together, with	collaborator

153

Prefix	Meaning	Example
com	together, with	compose
contra	against	contradict
de	down	descend
dec	ten	decade
deci	tenth	decimal
di	two	dipthong
dia	through, between	diameter
dis	not	dishonest
du	two	duet
dys	bad	dystrophy
e	out	eject
epi	upon	epidemic
eu	well, good	eulogy
ex	out	exit
hept, sept	seven	heptagon, September
hex, sex	six	hexagon, sextet
hyper	over	hypersensitive
hypo	under	hypodermic
il	not	illegal
im	not	immovable
in	not	inactive
inter	between	international
ir	not	irregular
kilo	1,000	kilocycle
macro	large	macroscopic
mega	large	megaphone
meta	change	metaphor
micro	small	microphone
milli	1/1,000	millimeter
mis	wrong	misspell
mono	one	monorail
multi	many	multitude
novem	nine	November
ob	against	objection
oct	eight	octopus
penta	five	pentagon
per	through	perforate
peri	around	perigee
poly	many	polygon
post	after	postscript
pre	before	precede
pro	forward	progress
proto	first	prototype
pseudo	false	pseudonym

Prefix	Meaning	Example
quad	four	quadruplet
quin	five	quintuplet
re	back	refund
re	again	readmit
retro	back	retrorocket
semi	half	semicircle
sub	under	submarine
super	over	supersede
sym	together	symmetry
syn	together	synonym
tetra	four	tetrameter
trans	cross	transcontinental
tri	three	triangle
ultra	beyond	ultraviolet
un	not	unsafe
uni	one	unicycle

Table of commonly used suffixes

Suffix	Meaning	Example
able, ible	can be done	readable, credible
ancy	state of	infancy
al	relating to	natural
and, end	to be done	multiplicand, dividend
ant, ent	person who	immigrant, resident
cule	small	animalcule
dom	state of	freedom
ectomy	surgical removal	tonsillectomy
ence	state, quality, condition of	dependence
er	comparative degree	faster
er, or	person who	farmer, actor
ess	feminine ending	actress
et, ette	little, small	islet, kitchenette
ful	full of	skillful
ful	enough to fill	cupful
fy	make into	deify
hood	state of	manhood
ian	related to	Parisian
ical	of the nature of	comical
icle	little	particle

Suffix	Meaning	Example
ine	like	canine
ine	feminine suffix	Josephine
ish	to form adjectives	Turkish
ism	state of	hypnotism
ist	person who	biologist
less	without	witless
let	small	ringlet
ling	small	duckling
logy	science of	zoology
ly	in the manner of	fatherly
ment	state of	amazement
ness	state of	sickness
oid	like, resembling	spheroid
or	person who	auditor
orium	place for	natatorium
ory	place where	laboratory
osis	abnormal condition	neurosis
ship	state of	friendship
ule	little, small	molecule, tubule
ward, wards	direction	homeward, backwards
wise	way	clockwise

Table of commonly used roots

Root	Meaning	Example
agr	field, land	agriculture
alt	high	altitude
annu	year	anniversary
aqua	water	aquarium
aster, astro	star	asterisk, astronomy
aud	hear	audible
auto	self	autobiography
baro	weight	barometer
bio	life	biography
cide	kill	suicide
crat	rule	democratic
cred	believe	incredible
cycl	circle, wheel	cyclist
demos	people	democracy
dent	tooth	dentist
dic, dict	say	predict
do	give	donate

Root	Meaning	Example
dorm	sleep	dormitory
duc	lead	conduct
enni	year	bicentennial
equ	equal	equality
fac	make, do	manufacture
fer	carry, bear	transfer
flect	bend	deflect
fract	break	fracture
frat	brother	fraternity
fug	flee	fugitive
gen	race, birth	generation
geo	earth	geology
gon	angle	trigonometry
graph	write	autograph
greg	herd	congregation
homo	same	homonym
ign	fire	ignite
insul	island	insular
ject	throw	eject
leg	law	legal
loc	place	location
log	speech	dialogue
magni	great	magnify
man	hand	manual
mater, matri	mother	maternity
math	learning	mathematics
maxima	greatest	maximum
meter	measure	centimeter
metro	mother	metropolis
migr	move	migrate
min	small	minute
mnem	memory	amnesia
monstr	show	demonstrate
mort	death	immortal
mot	move	motion
nom	law, arrangement	astronomy
nov	new	novelty
onym	name	synonym
ov	egg	ovary
path	feeling	sympathy
patri	father	patriotism
ped	foot	pedestrian
pend	hang	pendulum
phag	eat	esophagus

157

Root	Meaning	Example
phil	love	philatelist
phon	sound	phonics
port	carry	import
pter	wing	helicopter
rupt	to break	rupture
saur	lizard	dinosaur
sci	know	science
scope	to watch	telescope
scrib, script	write	inscribe, manuscript
sect	cut	dissect
somn	sleep	insomnia
son	sound	unison
soph	wise	philosopher
soror	sister	sorority
spect	look	spectator
spir	breathe	respiration
tang, tact	touch	tangible, tactile
tele	distant	televise
ten	hold	tenacious
tom	cut	anatomy
tract	pull	tractor
urb	city	suburb
ven	come	convention
ver	true	verdict
verb	word	verbal
vers	turn	reverse
vid	see	evidence
vir	man	virility
vis	see	visual
viv	live	survive
voc	call	vocal
volv	roll, turn	revolve

4. What is your word skill level?

The following lists contain important words. You will come across these words in various areas of study, such as history, health science, and social studies. Knowing these words will help you to understand school subjects better and to communicate with others more effectively.

The words lists are arranged from **Level 1** through **Level 8**. While these skill levels are not the same as grade levels, they are roughly equivalent to grade levels from 5th through 12th grade. For example, words tested and listed at skill **Level 1** are words that you would be likely to encounter at 5th grade, skill **Level 2** at 6th grade, and so on.

Choose the level suitable for you and see how well you know the words. First, test your knowledge of words by completing the **Word Quiz**. Please do not write in this book, but place your answers on a separate sheet of paper. Check your score. The correct answers follow each **Word Quiz.**

Next, go through the list of **Words to Know** for the level you have chosen. Note the words you do not know. Based upon the results of the **Word Quiz** and the degree of your familiarity with the list of **Words to Know**, you may wish to either proceed to higher levels, or drop back to lower levels for review.

Ask your parents, a friend, or your teacher about the meaning of any unfamiliar words. You might also look up the meaning or pronunciation of certain words in the dictionary. You will notice that some words have several meanings. Learning the various meanings of a word is an important part of developing your vocabulary skills.

You should review the list of **Words to Know** from time to time to check your progress. You should progress from one level to another as your word skill increases.

Word Quiz—Level 1

Complete each sentence by choosing the correct word from the choices that have been provided. Correct answers are at the end of the **Word Quiz.**

1. A DON'T WALK sign means you are __ to cross the street.
   a. allowed   b. reminded
   c. forbidden

2. He offered a __ about how to prepare for a bike hike.
   a. suggestion   b. donation
   c. question

3. The astronauts __ from their capsule to the orbiting spaceship.
   a. rescued   b. transferred
   c. separated

4. A person who commits a crime must pay the __ .
   a. cost   b. amount   c. penalty

5. A person who does not know what to do should get __ .
   a. ready   b. confused   c. advice

6. The shortening of a word is called an __ .
   a. abbreviation   b. accent
   c. adjustment

7. The Pilgrims left England and formed a __ in America.
   a. territory   b. nation   c. colony

8. The __ is the line where the sky and earth appear to meet.
   a. atmosphere   b. equator
   c. horizon

9. The subject matter of a book arranged alphabetically is called the __ .
   a. preface   b. contents   c. index

10. __ means dealing fairly with everyone.
    a. Freedom   b. Liberty   c. Justice

11. In the word *submarine, sub* is a __ .
    a. suffix   b. root   c. prefix

12. The area near the North Pole is called the __ Zone.
    a. Tropic   b. Arctic   c. Torrid

13. An __ machine works by itself.
    a. oiled   b. automatic   c. operated

14. You use a __ to find direction.
    a. barometer   b. altimeter
    c. compass

15. The letters D, K, and T are called __ .
    a. abbreviations   b. consonants
    c. vowels

16. The __ is an imaginary line around the earth, equally distant from the North and South Poles.
    a. latitude   b. equator   c. longitude

17. It is hard to walk on ice because there is little __ between your feet and the ice.
    a. contact   b. gravity   c. friction

18. Heat is one form of __ .
    a. fuel   b. gas   c. energy

19. A __ is a person from another country.
    a. native   b. foreigner   c. citizen

20. To rule or control a country is to __ it.
    a. free   b. establish   c. govern

21. A __ to drive a car gives you permission to drive it.
    a. ticket   b. sticker   c. license

22. __ is doing something often so you can do it well.
   a. Work   b. Recreation   c. Practice

23. __ holds us onto the earth's surface.
   a. Friction   b. Gravity   c. Weight

24. A __ is a meaningful syllable at the end of a word.
   a. prefix   b. root   c. suffix

25. To put off doing something until later is to __ it.
   a. forget   b. reject   c. postpone

Answers: 1.c., 2.a., 3.b., 4.c., 5.c., 6.a., 7.c., 8.c., 9.c., 10.c., 11.c., 12.b., 13.b., 14.c., 15.b., 16.b., 17.c., 18.c., 19.b., 20.c., 21.c., 22.c., 23.b., 24.c., 25.c.

Words to Know —Level 1

abbreviation
accident
accomplish
account
acre
addition
adjective
adjustment
advertise
afford
album
aluminum
anniversary
anxious
atlas
attention
auction
autograph
barbecue
border
budget
business
capital
capsule
cargo
carol
cartoon
century
cereal
channel
citizen

clarinet
clue
commercial
communication
community
computer
concert
continent
conversation
copper
country
coupon
danger
defend
design
desire
dial
dictionary
dinosaur
discussion
disease
drug
duty
education
election
emergency
employee
encyclopedia
envelope

exchange
experience
fable
fertile
fin
fraction
freedom
fuel
funeral
gallon
genius
germ
government
governor
grammar
gymnasium
hobby
independence
industry
infection
instrument
insurance
interest
intermission
invention
judge
knowledge
language
lawyer
liberty

loan
mayor
misspell
modern
nation
normal
ocean
paragraph
paralyze
percent
perspire
pilgrim
pioneer
planet
poison
popular
pronoun
property
puppet
race
recipe
recreation
reflection
religion
responsible
review
romance
royal
sanitation
season
sex
signature
similar

skeleton
spine
state
stomach
submarine
syllable
symbol
tax
temperature
thermometer
tornado
town
traffic
transfer
transportation
treasure
triangle
tuba
vehicle
ventilation
verb
verse
vitamin
vocabulary
volcano
volunteer
witness

Word Quiz—Level 2

Complete each sentence by choosing the correct word from the choices that have been provided. Correct answers are at the end of the **Word Quiz.**

1. The Latin word for sand is *arena*. In a Roman stadium the gladiators fought in the ___, a sandy floor.
   a. contests   b. open air   c. arena

2. The unprinted edge of a page in a book is called the ___
   a. leaf   b. margin   c. border

3. A ___ makes an explosive vapor by mixing air with gasoline.
   a. distributor   b. carburetor
   c. throttle

4. People gathered together in one place for a special purpose is a *meeting*, or ___.
   a. a society   b. a company
   c. an assembly

5. The English physician, William Harvey, discovered the ___, or movement of blood in the human body.
   a. pressure   b. circulation   c. force

6. When the colonists first came from England they found ___ life harsh and severe.
   a. outdoor   b. American   c. colonial

7. Good athletes ___, or pay close attention to what they are doing.
   a. practice   b. concentrate   c. enjoy

8. Another word for *subtract* is ___.
   a. conduct   b. product   c. deduct

9. A follower who accepts the beliefs and teachings of a leader is a ___.
   a. promoter   b. disciple   c. partner

10. A ___ is a long story with several characters and a plot.
    a. drama   b. history   c. novel

11. Dance pupils often appear in a musical program called a ___.
    a. chorus   b. recital   c. comedy

12. A *pharmacy* is another name for a ___.
    a. drug   b. druggist   c. drugstore

13. The Statue of Liberty ___, or stands for, human freedom and justice.
    a. means   b. assures   c. represents

14. A *role* in a play is ___.
    a. a scene   b. a part   c. an act

15. The *treasurer* takes care of the ___.
    a. treasure   b. vault   c. funds

16. Your ability to learn is called ___.
    a. concentration   b. intelligence
    c. heredity

17. The ___ branch of the government deals with making laws.
    a. executive   b. legislative   c. judicial

18. When birds *migrate* they ___.
    a. feed the young   b. travel   c. nest

19. A short, paper-covered booklet on a particular subject is called a ___.
    a. pamphlet   b. volume
    c. magazine

20. A doctor's written direction on the preparation and use of medicine is called a ___.
    a. subscription   b. inscription
    c. prescription

21. A suggested plan for doing something is a ___.
    a. desire   b. proposal   c. preference

22. A __ collects and stores water for present and future use.
    a. reservation b. conservatory
    c. reservoir

23. Changing the kinds of crops that grow in a field from year to year is called __ of crops.
    a. fertilization b. cultivation
    c. rotation

24. A liquid used to prevent a disease is called a __.
    a. prevention b. serum c. cure

25. A *debt* is something you owe. A *debtor* is the person who __ money.
    a. owes b. lends c. keeps

Answers: 1.c., 2.b., 3.b., 4.c., 5.b., 6.c., 7.b., 8.c., 9.b., 10.c., 11.b., 12.c., 13.c., 14.b., 15.c., 16.b., 17.b., 18.b., 19.a., 20.c., 21.b., 22.c., 23.c., 24.b., 25.a.

Words to Know—Level 2

abolish, absorb, abuse, accent, achievement, acrobatic, activate, actual, adjourn, admission, affect, agent, alcohol, algebra, although, alto, annual, antenna, appendix, astronomy, atom, automatic, barely, biographer, blackmail, bonus, bouquet, bronze, caffeine, cancel, cancer, capable, captive, caution, chapter, character, chemical, chime, circular, civilian, civilization, clinic, coast, collapse, collision, column, committee, complexion, composition, concern, concrete, conduct, conference, conservation, constitution, construction, contribution, convention, cooperate, council, current, cymbal, decimal, degree, democracy, dissolve, drama, due, element, equator, evaporate, event, expand, fabric, fiction, flexible, formula, fragile, galaxy, glacier, glossary, grief, harmony, hibernation, illegal, inflammable, investigate, investment, labor, laboratory, landscape, lawful, manufacture, missile, navigation, notion, noun, nylon, oasis, oath, opera, operation, opinion, orbit, ore, peasant, peninsula, petroleum, population, portable, president, principal, produce, product, profit, progress, protect, punctuate, quality, radar, ransom, rectangle, reform, refrigeration, region, registration, rehearse, resources, script, security, sensitive, session, sincere, slogan, souvenir, structure, subject, supreme, theme, tissue, ton, tragedy, transparent, treaty, tropical, union, vaccine, vitamin, volume, wealth

163

Word Quiz—Level 3

Complete each sentence by choosing the correct word from the choices that have been provided. Correct answers are at the end of the **Word Quiz.**

1. The philosopher, Plato, taught pupils in the Academy, a private grove near Athens. Today an *academy* is a __ .
   a. private park   b. private school
   c. private library

2. Detectives find out things. In the word *detective* did you notice the word *detect*? It means __ .
   a. hide   b. discover   c. search

3. If a person accused of a crime was somewhere else when it happened, he or she has __ .
   a. a reason   b. a witness
   c. an alibi

4. Charles Lindbergh did not fail in his __ to fly across the Atlantic.
   a. suggestion   b. attempt
   c. proposal

5. The chief designer of a building is the __ .
   a. engineer   b. superintendent
   c. architect

6. A partner is __ .
   a. sociable   b. an associate
   c. an association

7. Benjamin Franklin's *Autobiography* is the story of his own __ .
   a. books   b. friends   c. life

8. A good mind is one of the __ of study.
   a. essentials   b. characteristics
   c. benefits

9. A __ influences someone to act dishonestly.
   a. gift   b. bribe   c. reward

10. Another name for a chest of drawers is a __ .
    a. buffet   b. bureau   c. cabinet

11. If someone *compliments* your work, he __ it.
    a. finishes   b. criticizes   c. praises

12. A *concussion* is __ .
    a. a serious argument   b. a brain injury   c. an aftereffect

13. A doctor who examines unnatural deaths is called __ .
    a. an intern   b. an inspector
    c. a coroner

14. An engine's piston chamber is called a __ .
    a. block   b. cylinder   c. compressor

15. The bottom number in a fraction is called the __ .
    a. denominator   b. whole number
    c. numerator

16. A person who helps you decide what to do is __ .
    a. a friend   b. an adviser   c. a guide

17. When you buy something at a *discount*, the price is __ .
    a. fair   b. reasonable   c. lower

18. The supreme ruler of an empire is __ .
    a. a king   b. a chieftain
    c. an emperor

19. A highway patrol officer makes you obey the speed limit. He __ the law.
    a. obeys   b. enforces   c. favors

20. An *expedition* is __ .
    a. a long cruise   b. an exploring journey   c. a short trip

21. A car runs well when the engine __, or works as it should.
    a. starts   b. responds   c. functions

22. People about the same age are in the same __ .
    a. group   b. generation   c. class

23. Bears __ , or sleep through the winter.
    a. alternate   b. accommodate
    c. hibernate

24. With a microscope you can see __ objects.
    a. distant   b. large   c. tiny

25. Two flat, wormlike animals with many pairs of legs are __ and __.
    a. centipedes   b. velocipedes
    c. millipedes

Answers: 1.b.,   2.b.,   3.c.,   4.b.,   5.c., 6.b.,   7.c.,   8.c.,   9.b.,   10.b.,   11.c., 12.b.,   13.c.,   14.b.,   15.a.,   16.b.,   17.c., 18.c.,   19.b.,   20.b.,   21.c.,   22.b.,   23.c., 24.c.,   25.a.,c.

Words to Know—Level 3

abdomen	ceremony	discipline	income	orchestra	senator
accelerate	certificate	document	increase	parallel	sincerely
adverb	choir	duet	inhale	parliament	society
affection	circumfer-	eclipse	injection	pasteurize	soloist
allegiance	ence	eliminate	insulation	patriotism	soprano
altitude	classify	environ-	interior	pedestrian	statesman
amateur	command-	ment	invert	perspira-	summary
amend-	ment	epidemic	irrigation	tion	surgery
ment	competi-	equality	latitude	persuade	sympathy
analyze	tion	establish	legend	plastic	symphony
anatomy	compound	excellence	legislature	political	system
artery	confidence	exhale	longitude	pollution	temporary
atmosphere	congress	exploration	loyalty	positive	tenor
authentic	conjunc-	exterior	malnutri-	preposition	testimony
authority	tion	Fahrenheit	tion	process	treason
automation	contagious	federal	manuscript	production	unit
bacteria	corpuscle	feud	meter	pronunci-	unite
ballot	criticism	finance	metric	ation	vaccination
biography	cubic	fossil	monoto-	protein	variety
boundary	culture	genuine	nous	proverb	verdict
bulletin	debt	graph	moral	receipt	veto
calculate	decrease	handicap	mortgage	representa-	victory
calorie	delegate	hazard	national	tive	violation
campaign	demolish	heir	negative	resident	visual
candidate	diameter	homicide	numeral	rhythm	voluntary
cavity	diary	humid	occupation	rural	
cello	digestion	ignition	omit	satellite	

Word Quiz—Level 4

Complete each sentence by choosing the correct word from the choices that have been provided. Correct answers are at the end of the **Word Quiz.**

1. A *dispatch* is an official ___ .
   a. message   b. command   c. speech

2. A ___ is a pipe that carries hot air from a furnace to a room.
   a. pump   b. blower   c. duct

3. A person who feels great bliss or joy is ___ .
   a. romantic   b. in ecstasy
   c. in a trance

4. ___ persons do their jobs with skill.
   a. Efficient   b. Conscientious
   c. Sincere

5. To sew in designs on cloth is to ___ the cloth.
   a. knit   b. embroider   c. crochet

6. Customary rules of behavior in polite society are called ___ .
   a. manners   b. ordinances
   c. etiquette

7. If you try hard, you are ___ yourself.
   a. forcing   b. exerting   c. overtaxing

8. Judges in court dispense or ___ justice.
   a. inspire   b. recommend
   c. administer

9. *Anthropology* means ___ .
   a. love of mankind   b. study of man
   c. having human form

10. The *blockade* of a port by ships ___ the port.
    a. clears   b. controls   c. opens

11. When she decided not to take the plane, she ___ her reservation.
    a. requested   b. made   c. canceled

12. The opposite of *simple* is ___ .
    a. solemn   b. sincere   c. complex

13. A *decade* is ___ .
    a. an athletic event   b. a geometric figure   c. a ten-year period

14. ___ is getting rid of a problem.
    a. Discussion   b. Elimination
    c. Agreement

15. Money paid out is called ___ .
    a. credits   b. receipts
    c. expenditures

16. If you gain something by deceit, the judge may find you guilty of ___ .
    a. dishonesty   b. fraud   c. trickery

17. In a theater the *gallery* is the ___ balcony.
    a. lowest   b. middle   c. highest

18. A *hypocrite* ___ .
    a. is very critical   b. imagines he's ill
    c. is a false person

19. A sudden desire to do something is an ___ .
    a. impulse   b. impact   c. instigation

20. Some scientists believe space is endless. It has ___ boundaries.
    a. defined   b. infinite   c. definite

21. A red swelling on the body is ___ .
    a. an inflammatory   b. an inflammable   c. an inflammation

22. If a dead relative leaves you his house, you ___ it.
    a. occupy   b. annex   c. inherit

---

23. *Ex* (out) + *clude* (shut) = *exclude*, meaning __ .
    a. shut in   b. shut out   c. shut up

24. *Psychology* is the study of the __ .
    a. mind   b. body   c. spirit

25. Depending on the pronunciation, the word *invalid* has two meanings. What are they? __ __
    a. of no value   b. priceless
    c. a sick person

Answers: 1.a., 2.c., 3.b., 4.a., 5.b., 6.c., 7.b., 8.c., 9.b., 10.b., 11.c., 12.c., 13.c., 14.b., 15.c., 16.b., 17.c., 18.c., 19.a., 20.b., 21.c., 22.c., 23.b., 24.a., 25.a.,c.

Words to Know—Level 4

abolition, absence, abstract, accessory, accumulation, acknowledge, acquaintance, activate, acute, adaptable, adjoins, administration, admittance, advantageous, alimony, alteration, alternate, altimeter, ample, apparently, apprenticeship, approximate, arid, autopsy

ballad, baritone, barometer, bazaar, biology, bowels, calculator, camouflage, casual, cavern, Celsius, centennial, chaperon, characteristic, charitable, circuit, circulation, circumnavigate, circumstances, clause, coma, consumer, contraction, contrast, convenient, cornea, crisis, culture

currency, custody, debatable, declaration, decompression, dedicate, deduction, deed, defendant, degrade, dehydrate, delusion, detail, detract, diabetes, dialogue, diplomatic, disability, disable, disarm, disband, disclaim, disinherit, dislodge, dismantle, disown, disrupt, distinctly, distinguish, economic

embezzle, enzyme, epilepsy, exceed, excess, germicide, graft, gram, heredity, inheritance, inquiry, isthmus, italics, kilometer, leukemia, manslaughter, manual, membrane, memento, minimum, monopoly, mural, neutral, neutron, nucleus, occupant, octave, omelet, option, ovary

overture, parasite, patience, perpendicular, petrify, policy, poverty, predicate, prepaid, primitive, privilege, probability, probation, propaganda, protoplasm, radiation, reinforce, reproduce, republic, respiration, sarcastic, sedative, segregation, semicolon, sequence, slander, species, stanza, statistics, strategy

suspense, technician, textile, theory, tributary, trustee, vacuum, vomit

Word Quiz—Level 5

Complete each sentence by choosing the correct word from the choices that have been provided. Correct answers are at the end of the **Word Quiz.**

1. Benjamin Franklin wrote "Poor Richard's ___," which gave information on dates, astrology, and the weather.
   a. Diary   b. Journal   c. Almanac

2. If a country's supply of wheat is ___, it has *more* than enough.
   a. adequate   b. abundant
   c. sufficient

3. Pus forming at a certain point of an infection is called ___.
   a. a tumor   b. an abscess   c. a welt

4. An *apostrophe* is a punctuation mark as in ___.
   a. "Can you?"   b. "I cannot!"
   c. "I can't."

5. Something that is *audible* can be ___.
   a. eaten   b. heard   c. seen

6. A *bankrupt* person has been legally declared unable to ___.
   a. borrow money   b. use credit
   c. pay debts

7. The short blessing at the end of a ceremony is called the ___.
   a. sermon   b. conclusion
   c. benediction

8. The study of plants is called ___.
   a. biology   b. botany   c. geology

9. A floating object to warn sailors about rocks and other obstacles is a ___
   a. bob   b. bobbin   c. buoy

10. Tough elastic tissue, like the outer part of your ear, is called ___.
    a. marrow   b. cartilage   c. bone

11. *Chlorine* is a gas used ___.
    a. by plants   b. to purify water
    c. to produce unconsciousness

12. The word *miscalculate* means ___.
    a. to mix up   b. to count wrong
    c. to scheme

13. A ___ is one who consults a lawyer.
    a. witness   b. perjurer   c. client

14. The ancients described the Colossus of Rhodes, a huge bronze statue, as gigantic or ___.
    a. sturdy   b. famous   c. colossal

15. A ___ travels regularly to work by bus, train, or auto.
    a. businessman   b. traveler
    c. commuter

16. A flattering remark is ___.
    a. complimentary   b. insincere
    c. inspirational

17. The pitcher threw three strikes, one after the other. He threw three ___ strikes.
    a. accurate   b. successful
    c. consecutive

18. The two disputing candidates were involved in a lively ___.
    a. conversation   b. assembly
    c. controversy

19. A *cordial* meeting is ___.
    a. cautious   b. unsociable
    c. friendly

20. An authoritative statement of religious belief is a —.
a. prayer   b. creed   c. ritual

21. Something you usually do is —.
a. constant   b. methodical
c. customary

22. The — is hard skin around the base of your fingernail.
a. callus   b. cuticle   c. quick

23. If you *decelerate* your car, you —.
a. maintain speed   b. speed it up
c. slow it down

24. A *declarative* sentence —.
a. asks a question   b. makes a statement   c. gives a command

25. A *gladius* was a short Roman sword. A flowering plant with swordlike leaves is called a —.
a. gladiator   b. gladiolus

Answers: 1.c., 2.b., 3.b., 4.c., 5.b., 6.c., 7.c., 8.b., 9.c., 10.b., 11.b., 12.b., 13.c., 14.c., 15.c., 16.a., 17.c., 18.c., 19.c., 20.b., 21.c., 22.b., 23.c., 24.b., 25.b.

Words to Know—Level 5

abrupt
accurate
advantage
alliance
ambassador
amphibian
analysis
ancestry
anemic
armament
ascend
baritone
benefactor
beneficiary
bigamy
boycott
capacity
category
censor
census
climax
combustion
commencement
commentator

commit
comparable
complexity
compromise
condemn
condense
confirm
conservative
conspicuous
constellation
contemporary
contradict
controversial
crescent
critical
data
deceit
decompose
deficient
deflate
density

deport
derive
descendant
desolate
diagnosis
diagonal
dietetic
dimension
diminish
diplomat
discrimination
dissect
distinct
dividend
drought
ecology
edible
editorial
elaborate
electoral
embroider
emphasis
enable
endorse
endurance
equivalent
erosion

exclude
external
extinct
extinguish
extract
felony
fiord
fragment
gauge
grievance
habitat
heritage
hybrid
hygiene
illiteracy
immune
imply
incision
inferior
infinitive
inflate
inhabitant
insomnia
instinct
interjection
internal
international

intersect
invasion
isolate
literacy
mammal
mineral
modify
monarchy
municipal
myth
novelty
nutrition
obituary
optical
origin
parenthesis
photosynthesis
preamble
preface
premier
principle
proclamation
prosecute
prosperity
ration

rebellion
regulate
remnant
resistance
revolution
segment
solar
sphere
supplement
surplus
tariff
technique
tolerance
transmit
tuition
tumor
typical
ultraviolet
unanimous
urban
utility
versus
vertical
virus
warrant

Word Quiz—Level 6

Complete each sentence by choosing the correct word from the choices that have been provided. Correct answers are at the end of the **Word Quiz.**

1. A poem without the author's name is an __ poem.
   a. unauthorized   b. unknown
   c. anonymous

2. The word *habitable* means __ .
   a. instinct   b. regular   c. livable

3. Famous Venetian boats propelled by one oar are called __ .
   a. canoes   b. gondolas   c. dories

4. Running a car engine slowly when it's not in gear is called __ .
   a. choking   b. revving   c. idling

5. To *gorge* yourself is to eat __ .
   a. quickly   b. lightly   c. greedily

6. Macbeth said to Banquo's ghost, "Never shake thy gory locks at me." *Gory* means __ .
   a. long   b. uncombed   c. bloody

7. The speaker's answers were not planned. They were __ .
   a. unintentional   b. haphazard
   c. indirect

8. An *abacus* is a __ frame.
   a. weaving   b. counting   c. quilting

9. A building that is *adjacent* to another building is __ it.
   a. next to   b. taller than
   c. lower than

10. Your *alma mater* is your __ .
    a. best friend   b. school or college
    c. trusted partner

11. A person skilled in manual arts is called a *craftsman* or an __ .
    a. artifact   b. artist   c. artisan

12. A *bipartisan* political program is supported by __ .
    a. one party   b. biased persons
    c. two parties

13. Ancient Rome was supplied with water by means of __ .
    a. aquariums   b. aquacades
    c. aqueducts

14. Sugar and starch are two kinds of __ .
    a. fats   b. carbohydrates   c. calories

15. When the colonists left England they had certain rights granted them by __ .
    a. settlement   b. charter
    c. exploration

16. The writing of letters back and forth between two persons is called __ .
    a. courtesy   b. information
    c. correspondence

17. A strong campaigner against crime is a __ .
    a. crusader   b. radical   c. informer

18. Temporarily inactive plants are __ in the winter.
    a. frostbitten   b. dormant
    c. durable

19. A person who does not get enough vitamins is said to be suffering from vitamin __ .
    a. depreciation   b. deprivation
    c. deficiency

20. A *dubious* statement is __ .
    a. doubtful   b. deceitful
    c. untruthful

21. If you furnish someone with increased knowledge, you __ him.
a. inspire   b. enlighten
c. encourage

22. An __ , such as Virgil's *Aeneid*, is a
long, narrative, heroic poem.
a. epic   b. elegy   c. ode

23. Threatened by floods, the inhabitants
__ the town.
a. evaded   b. evacuated   c. invaded

24. *Culture* means taking care of or grow-

ing. *Floriculture* means growing __ .
a. wheat   b. fruit   c. flowers

25. In mythology Flora was the goddess
of flowers and the sister of Faunus,
the god of animals. The phrase "flora
and fauna" means __ .
a. sisters and brothers
b. plants and animals

Answers: 1.c., 2.c., 3.b., 4.c., 5.c.,
6.c., 7.b., 8.b., 9.a., 10.b., 11.c.,
12.c., 13.c., 14.b., 15.b., 16.c., 17.a.,
18.b., 19.c., 20.a., 21.b., 22.a., 23.b.,
24.c., 25.b.

Words to Know—Level 6

accessible	commend	despite	infiltrate	petition	solemnity
accomplice	compre-	detest	instigate	phenome-	solitude
adapt	hend	detraction	jeopardy	nal	southerly
adequate	condensa-	digit	lapse	philoso-	spontane-
administer	tion	distinction	liter	pher	ous
adoles-	condenser	doctrine	malprac-	pi	stabiliza-
cence	confide	domestic	tice	plaintiff	tion
affidavit	confront	dominant	media	pledge	stalactite
aggravate	constitute	dynamic	medieval	porous	stalagmite
aggressor	convey	edition	micro-	portray	status
alias	conviction	elapse	meter	presump-	submit
alumni	coordinate	elements	migratory	tion	subsonic
analgesic	copyright	embargo	mock	prism	subtitle
antibiotic	correspon-	embryo	mutual	profanity	superficial
apparatus	dent	equation	northerly	prosecutor	syringe
apprehend	counsel	esophagus	noteworthy	radical	tenor
aptitude	creed	exasperate	nuclear	recurrent	tension
aquatic	crisis	feudalism	obituary	relic	terminal
arrogant	crusade	fluent	outcast	renais-	texture
bigoted	cultivation	foremost	overseer	sance	theorize
capability	deceitful	forum	pact	repeal	threshold
centimeter	decimeter	fraternal	papyrus	replenish	titanic
character-	defective	fungus	pathetic	resolution	tyranny
ize	dehuman-	generaliza-	patronize	sane	velocity
chivalry	ize	tion	pedometer	seminary	vendor
chronic	delirious	genetics	perforate	sensation	
coincide	deprivation	horizontal	perturbed	shuttle	
collaborate	designate	impel	pessimist	skeptic	

Word Quiz—Level 7

Complete each sentence by choosing the correct word from the choices that have been provided. Correct answers are at the end of the **Word Quiz.**

1. A preservative added to food to keep it fresh is called an __ .
   a. absorbent   b. addition   c. additive

2. Opposite of the term *Arctic Zone* is the term __ Zone.
   a. Temperate   b. Antarctic   c. Torrid

3. *Atheism* means not believing in __ .
   a. theology   b. religions   c. God

4. __ diseases can be easily transmitted from person to person in a community.
   a. Hereditary   b. Communicable
   c. Acquired

5. A sideboard or cupboard in a dining room is a __ .
   a. service   b. bureau   c. buffet

6. The __ supports a lever when the lever is used to lift something.
   a. pressure   b. fulcrum
   c. resistance

7. When two lanes of a highway come together into one they __ .
   a. immerge   b. emerge   c. merge

8. If you have an eager and earnest desire to accomplish something, you have __ .
   a. zest   b. zing   c. zeal

9. Listening to conversations by using a secret telephone connection is called __ .
   a. debugging   b. eavesdropping
   c. wiretapping

10. *Verbatim* means __ .
    a. word for word   b. syllable for syllable   c. letter for letter

11. A courageous person has __ .
    a. value   b. valor   c. validity

12. A forbidden action is __ .
    a. vengeful   b. unjustified   c. taboo

13. Something you can touch is __ .
    a. pliable   b. digital   c. tangible

14. To *tantalize* someone is to __ him.
    a. tease   b. torture   c. mock

15. The opening words of a letter are called the __ .
    a. salutation   b. heading
    c. inside address

16. A person who is not frank is __ .
    a. deceptive   b. secretive
    c. conniving

17. A temporary structure to support people working is called __ .
    a. framing   b. shoring   c. scaffolding

18. *Self-denial* means __ .
    a. denying guilt   b. destroying oneself   c. personal sacrifice

19. __ means *very great joy.*
    a. Cordiality   b. Rapture   c. Delight

20. Delaware was the first state to *ratify* the Constitution. *Ratification* means a __ .
    a. formal proposal   b. formal amendment   c. formal approval

21. A person engaged in the real estate business is a __ .
    a. reagent   b. realist   c. realtor

172

22. A *recession* means ___ .
    a. much credit buying   b. business is poor   c. high interest charges

23. Taking over mortgaged property is called ___ .
    a. direct purchase   b. payment on demand   c. foreclosure

24. ___ acts are performed regularly.
    a. Recurring   b. Alternating
    c. Habitual

25. Which one makes big sales to stores? ___
    a. A wholesaler.   b. A retailer.

Answers: 1.c., 2.b., 3.c., 4.b., 5.c., 6.b., 7.c., 8.c., 9.c., 10.a., 11.b., 12.c., 13.c., 14.a., 15.a., 16.b., 17.c., 18.c., 19.b., 20.c., 21.c., 22.b., 23.c., 24.c., 25.a.

Words to Know—Level 7

abdicate
abduct
acknowledgement
access
acquit
alien
alignment
alliteration
alloy
ameba
anesthetic
antagonist
anticipate
antidote
antonym
aristocracy
assess
auxiliary
biceps
cardiac
carnivorous
casualty
cataract
celestial
censorship
chaos
chasm
chiropractor

chronic
chronological
classical
clergy
commemorate
comply
comprise
concoct
condolence
confirmation
congestion
conjugate
consistent
constructive
contaminate
contemplate
contour
coordination
corrupt
credible
deface
default
denim

denomination
depreciate
dexterity
diligent
diplomacy
disclose
disprove
edit
eligible
elude
encore
enterprise
equilateral
ethics
evolution
excavate
excise
exempt
exotic
fallacy
fatality
filament
futile
gastric
gender
genetic
harass
hemisphere
homonym

hypotenuse
illegitimate
illiterate
immaculate
impeach
imperialism
implication
inclusive
induce
influenza
initiate
insight
integrity
intensive
interrogative
intervention
intricate
inventory
larceny
levy
libel
magistrate
misdemeanor
neuter
obsolete
odometer
ordinance
percussion

perennial
perjury
perspective
precede
precinct
prelude
premonition
propellant
proton
puberty
quorum
ratify
realism
rearmament
recede
recipient
recline
reconcile
rectify
recur
refrain
relinquish
reminiscent
remorse
remote
revive
revoke
rhapsody

secede
skeptic
sonnet
spectrum
synonym
tactful
tapestry
technology
tedious
telepathy
trend
ultimatum

Word Quiz—Level 8

Complete each sentence by choosing the correct word from the choices that have been provided. Correct answers are at the end of the **Word Quiz.**

1. __ speeds up your heartbeat.
   a. Anesthesia   b. Analgesic
   c. Adrenalin

2. __ describes a deep, dark seemingly bottomless hole in the earth.
   a. Fissure   b. Abyss   c. Opaque

3. __ nerves deal with the sense of hearing.
   a. Cerebral   b. Optic   c. Auditory

4. To give praise unwillingly is to __ it.
   a. begrudge   b. withhold   c. retain

5. The surgical removal of tissue from a living body is called __ .
   a. autopsy   b. pathology   c. biopsy

6. In ancient times a __ was used to hurl stones.
   a. battering ram   b. crossbow
   c. catapult

7. The __ is the frame, wheels, machinery, and running gear of an automobile.
   a. body   b. chassis   c. assembly

8. To __ is to figure or calculate.
   a. compute   b. compensate
   c. comprise

9. A __ statement is scornful.
   a. conflicting   b. contradicting
   c. contemptuous

10. __ may be described as rage or violent anger.
    a. Madness   b. Wrath   c. Rivalry

11. When a person says one thing and does another it destroys his __ .
    a. credulity   b. credentials
    c. credibility

12. Fine glassware is called __ .
    a. china   b. crystal   c. porcelain

13. The __ carries out the provisions of a will.
    a. bequeather   b. recipient
    c. executor

14. A __ often involves continual talking to delay the passing of a law.
    a. caucus   b. filibuster   c. quorum

15. The chemical compound __ is applied to the teeth to decrease decay.
    a. chlorine   b. fluoride
    c. phosphate

16. The __ are the "cutting" teeth.
    a. molars   b. bicuspids   c. incisors

17. The Washington Monument, a tall, single, four-sided stone, is an example of __ .
    a. an epitaph   b. a mausoleum
    c. an obelisk

18. A __ is a five-angled, five-sided figure.
    a. hexagon   b. pentagon   c. heptagon

19. The word __ means a long, adventurous journey.
    a. sojourn   b. wayfarer   c. odyssey

20. The last letter of the Greek alphabet is __
    a. alpha   b. delta   c. omega

21. An __ disaster is one that is likely to happen soon.
    a. disputable   b. indubitable
    c. impending

22. An __ speech is done without preparation.
    a. impulsive   b. impromptu
    c. impetuous

23. A __ disease directly affects the lungs.
    a. vascular   b. neurological
    c. pulmonary

24. The word __ refers to the withdrawal of the Southern states from the Union.
    a. recession   b. secession
    c. concession

25. The words __ and __ both mean *eggs*.
    a. yegg   b. ova   c. roe

Answers: 1.c., 2.b., 3.c., 4.a., 5.c., 6.c., 7.b., 8.a., 9.c., 10.b., 11.c., 12.b., 13.c., 14.b., 15.b., 16.c., 17.c., 18.b., 19.c., 20.c., 21.c., 22.b., 23.c., 24.b., 25.b.,c.

Words to Know—Level 8

abridge, accentuate, acoustics, adhere, advocate, affiliate, alleviate, ally, alternative, ambiguous, annuity, antagonize, anthology, antiquity, appropriation, arbitration, astigmatism, audit, benevolent, bequeath, betrothal, bias, bigot, calculus, canine, chromosome, citation

clemency, coalition, coherent, collateral, colloquial, commodity, compassion, compensate, competence, component, composure, compulsory, computation, concede, conceive, concept, concise, concurrent, condone, conform, conquest, conscientious, consecrate, consensus, consolidate

constraint, constriction, consumption, contempt, contraband, convalescence, convene, converge, convulsive, correlation, corrode, cumulative, curtail, cynical, decade, decomposition, deficit, deteriorate, deviate, dilemma, discreet, disperse, egotism, eject, electorate

emancipation, encompass, epitaph, erroneous, excerpt, explicit, extortion, extremist, foreclose, hemorrhage, herbicide, hieroglyphic, horticulture, humus, hypochondriac, impediment, imperative, impromptu, indict, indoctrinate, induct, indulge, injunction

inoculation, insidious, intimation, intravenous, liter, mandate, martial, melancholy, metaphor, microwave, misconception, mobilize, moderation, monologue, morality, naturalization, nautical, notoriety, nutrient, ornate, ornithology, paraphrase, partisanship, pistil, premeditate

profound, promissory, protocol, prudent, sediment, simile, simultaneous, stagnation, stamen, statute, strategic, subordinate, subpoena, subsistence, suffrage, terminate, theorem, valid, vehemence, vengeful, versatile, vibrant, witticism, writ, zealous

Activities

The unit-end activities have been designed to help you to practice and gain the ability to use the various classroom and study skills described in this unit. Please do not write in this book, but place your answers on a separate sheet of paper. Answers to the activities can be found in the **Answer Key** that begins on page 290.

Using the dictionary
Use a dictionary to answer the following questions.

1. What is the abbreviation of the word *pound*? How many *ounces* in a pound? How many *grams*?

2. What is the plural of *Jones*?

3. What does the symbol **i.e.** mean?

4. Why is the symbol **e.g.** used for the abbreviation of the term *for example*?

5. What is an acronym? What does the acronym *ZIP*, as in "ZIP Code" mean?

6. What is *californium*? Where does it get its name?

7. What is the plural of the word *alumnus*?

8. What is the symbol for *pi*? For *earth*? For *paragraph*?

9. How do you pronounce *comparable, inexplicable,* and *schism*?

10. What parts of speech can the word *rust* be?

11. What is the difference in meaning between the words *uninterested* and *disinterested*, *respectively* and *respectfully*, *flaunt* and *flout*?

Making words
Use the dictionary to make additional words from the letters of the key words given below.

Example: **Answer:**
17. fire   17. fir, ire, fie, rife, ref

1. nail	5. turn	9. chesty	13. listen
2. rail	6. lead	10. cheat	14. fortune
3. bear	7. mean	11. course	15. vowel
4. rate	8. tear	12. pearl	16. father

Adding letters to endings of words
Using the clues in column B., make a new word by adding the correct letter or letters to each word in column A.

Example:
19. ten <u>n</u> <u>i</u> <u>s</u>   a popular game

A.
1. rode —
2. plum —
3. pin — —
4. lock — —
5. sand — —
6. boot —
7. ball — —
8. brow — —
9. comb — —
10. cub —
11. fan —
12. for — —
13. kin —
14. miser —
15. oat —
16. past — —
17. past — —
18. pie —

B.
cowboy contest
round and full
to squeeze
jewelry
open shoe
place for selling
kind of dance
glance through
battle
solid square
long tooth
to sign falsely
a twist
unhappiness
a pledge
soft, pale color
minister
landing place

177

Finding hidden words

Using the clues in column B., find the "hidden words" in column A.

Example:

15. <u>diner</u>   confused noise

A.	B.
1. yore	rock containing metal
2. lapel	once around the track
3. lavender	seller
4. malaria	solo
5. obliterate	can read
6. usable	fur
7. uttermost	speak
8. wallop	cut off
9. wholly	red berry tree
10. flute	stringed instrument
11. palms	charity
12. invent	opening
13. glance	to cut open
14. graze	destroy completely

Adding the correct prefix

Add the correct prefix to each root word in column A. to match the word's definition in column B.

Example:

15. <u>i n</u> active   not active

A.	B.
1. ___ expensive	not expensive
2. ___ employed	not employed
3. ___ movable	cannot be moved
4. ___ proper	not proper
5. ___ practical	not practical
6. ___ legal	not legal
7. ___ legible	not legible
8. ___ religious	not religious
9. ___ rational	not rational
10. ___ typical	not like the type
11. ___exact	not strictly correct
12. ___ divisible	cannot be divided
13. _____ slavery	against slavery
14. _____ toxin	fights poison

Complete these sentences

Add the correct prefix to complete each of the following sentences.

Example:

7. A <u>s</u> <u>u</u> <u>b</u> atomic particle is smaller than an atom.

1. A _ _ _ marine goes under the ocean.
2. _ _ _ terranean means under the ground.
3. _ _ _ normal temperature is below normal.
4. _ _ _ sonic planes fly at less than the speed of sound.
5. Extra-fine sugar is _ _ _ _ _ fine.
6. _ _ _ _ _ natural powers are beyond the natural.

Adding the correct suffix

Change the following adjectives to nouns by adding the correct suffix.

Example:

8. tender <u>n</u> <u>e</u> <u>s</u> <u>s</u>

1. selfish _ _ _ _
2. reckless _ _ _ _
3. damp _ _ _ _
4. brave _ _

5. savage _ _
6. content _ _ _ _
7. prepared _ _ _ _

A guide to research skills

Have you ever had to write a research paper? Do you know where to look for the data you need to do research? For most students, the hardest part of writing a research paper is gathering the data. And the biggest trick to gathering the information is knowing where to look for it.

This unit lists some of the more common sources you can go to for various kinds of information. And it describes the organization and uses of the library, your most important reference tool.

The contributor of this unit is Jeanette E. Mitchell, Instructor in Library Sciences, University of Hawaii, Honolulu, Hawaii.

1. How do you use a library?

Libraries exist to provide access to accumulated knowledge in any form, whether on clay tablets or on microfilm. These materials are arranged so as to simplify the task of finding information. In order to use a library independently and efficiently, you have to understand how the materials are organized.

Most school and public libraries arrange and classify books according to the *Dewey Decimal Classification System*. Most college, university, and research libraries arrange and classify books according to the *Library of Congress Classification System*. Both systems are easy to use. You will find either one very helpful when you try to locate a book on the shelf.

Dewey Decimal System. Small and medium-sized libraries generally use the Dewey Decimal Classification System. In this system, devised by Melvil Dewey in 1876, all nonfiction books are divided into 10 main subject areas. According to Dewey, all knowledge could be divided into nine large categories, or classes, with an additional class for works that would not fit into any of the other classes. This additional class includes general works, or those covering several broad subjects.

Each main class is divided into 10 smaller classes, and each of these is further subdivided into 10 more classes. For very narrow and specific classifications, there is a decimal point followed by one or more additional numbers. Numbers designate the various classes:

000-099 Generalities (encyclopedias, bibliographies, periodicals, journalism)
100-199 Philosophy and Related Disciplines (psychology)

200-299 Religion
300-399 The Social Sciences (economics, sociology, civics,
      law, education, vocations, customs)
400-499 Language (language, dictionaries, grammar)
500-599 Pure Sciences (mathematics, astronomy, physics,
      chemistry, geology, paleontology, biology, zoology,
      botany)
600-699 Technology (medicine, engineering, agriculture,
      home economics, business, radio, television,
      aviation)
700-799 The Arts (architecture, sculpture, painting, music,
      photography, recreation)
800-899 Literature (novels, poetry, plays, criticism)
900-999 General Geography and History

The following example of a Dewey Decimal number shows
how a number is "built," or developed:

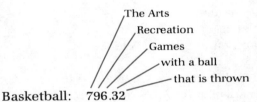

                           The Arts
                             Recreation
                               Games
                                 with a ball
                                  that is thrown
Basketball: 796.32

The Dewey Decimal number appears on the spine of each
book. In this way, all books about the same subject have the
same number, and so are shelved together. The number also
appears on the catalog cards for each book, so that the user
will know which section of the shelves to search.

The author's initial, or a symbol designating the author's
name (Cutter number), appears below the Dewey Decimal
number on each book and on the catalog card. Together,
these two symbols make up the *call number* for the book.
The call number stands for a particular book on a certain
subject, written by a given author. The call number should
be noted exactly so that you will be able to find the book.

Library of Congress System. When it became evident in
the early 1900's that the collection in the Library of Congress
would become very large, a new system, called the Library of
Congress Classification System, was developed. This system
provides for more precise classification in most fields, and
more room for expansion, than does the Dewey Decimal
System. Many large libraries now use the Library of Congress, or L.C., System, as it is usually called.

The Library of Congress System uses letters of the alphabet to designate 21 main classes, or areas of knowledge:

        A General Works
        B Philosophy, Psychology, and Religion
C, D, E, F History
        G Geography, Anthropology, and
          Recreation
        H Social Sciences
        J Political Science
        K Law
        L Education
        M Music
        N Fine Arts
        P Language and Literature
        Q Science
        R Medicine
        S Agriculture
        T Technology
        U Military Science
        V Naval Science
        Z Bibliography and Library Science

A second letter is added to designate a subdivision of each class. To indicate a specific topic, one or more numerals are added after the letters. To complete the call number for a particular book, a very short, modified Cutter number is added for the author's name. For example, *Desert Wildlife*, by Edmund Carroll Jaeger, carries the following L.C. call number:

          Science
           Zoology
           Deserts
             Author number, or modified Cutter number
QL116.J25

The card catalog

Most libraries have an index, or catalog, of their collection, often including such nonbook items as records, filmstrips, and so on. This index is usually on cards that are filed in alphabetical order in trays or drawers. This *card catalog* can be changed as new books are added or old or worn-out books removed from the collection. Just as the index to a book indicates the subjects covered, and on what pages, the card catalog lists the books and other materials in the library and indicates the location of each.

Kinds of catalog cards. For each book or item in a collection, one or more cards is placed in the catalog. Usually there is an author card, a title card, and one or more subject cards. All these cards look very much alike, but one card, usually the author card, is called the *main entry.* All the other cards for a particular book are based on the main entry. These other cards are termed added entries. Shown below are examples of a main entry card and added entry cards found in a card catalog.

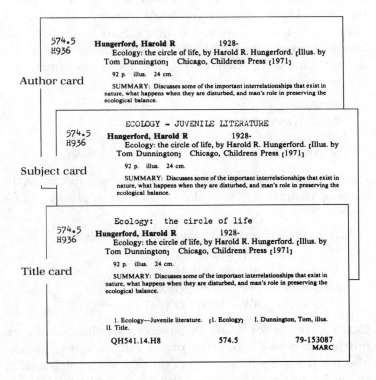

Added entries for a book follow the pattern of the main entry, except that each has an added line at the top giving the title, or the subject, or some other heading that might be used by someone looking for the book.

How catalog cards are filed. Each catalog card is filed in alphabetical order, according to the words on the top line. The main entry is filed under the author's name. The added entry for the title is filed under the title. The subject cards necessary for the book are filed according to the first word or words on the top line. Each drawer of the catalog has entries for authors, subjects, and titles, all interfiled in alphabetical order. This type of catalog is called a *dictionary catalog*.

These few rules, used by most libraries in filing cards, will help you to locate information in the card catalog:

1. Cards are arranged in alphabetical order, letter by letter to the end of the word, then word by word to the end of the heading. Marks of punctuation are disregarded.
2. When a title begins with "a," "an," or "the," the card is filed beginning with the next word in the heading.
3. Abbreviations are filed as if they were spelled in full: Dr. as doctor, St. as saint, Mr. as mister, and so forth. This includes abbreviated geographical names: N.Y. as New York, Gt. Brit. as Great Britain, and U.S. as United States.
4. Names beginning with Mc, Mac, or M' are all filed as though they were spelled Mac, and as though the name is one word:

McAdam, Henry   Machinery
MACADAMIA NUTS   McLean, Alan
Macbeth   MacLean, John
McHenry   Macmillan, Thomas

5. Under U.S.—HISTORY, and similar sections in the card catalog, historical subheadings are filed in chronological order:

U.S.—HISTORY—REVOLUTIONARY WAR
U.S.—HISTORY—WAR OF 1812
U.S.—HISTORY—CIVIL WAR
U.S.—HISTORY—1920—1929
U.S.—HISTORY—WORLD WAR, 1939-1945

6. Catalog entries for books *by* a person are filed before the entries for books *about* that person. (Remember, entries about a person will be subject entries, with the heading in capital letters. The title of the book will be found below the author's name)

Cross-references. Sometimes when you are looking for a book or other material on a particular subject, you may not find any cards under the word you are using. Instead, you may find instructions to look under another word:

CARS see AUTOMOBILES

This "see" reference is one type of cross-reference.

You may sometimes find a number of entries under the

subject you are looking for, together with directions to look under an additional subject or subjects. This type of cross-reference is called a "see also" reference, and directs you to other subject headings under which you will find additional materials that might contain information on your subject.

Computer printouts. When the library's catalog is a computer printout, it will resemble a card catalog in many ways. However, you will save yourself a lot of time if you read the instructions for using the printout before you try to use this kind of catalog. If you do not understand any part of the instructions, ask for help.

Finding a book on the shelf

When you have located a catalog entry for a book or other material you want, copy down the call number, the author, and the title. Caution: Do not confuse the subject heading with the title of the book. Remember, if the heading is in capital letters, it is the *subject* of the book. You will find the title on the line below the author's name. Once the call number, author, and title are copied on a slip of paper, you are ready to find the section of shelving that includes the call number of the book you want. There will usually be a floor plan of the library and signs on the shelves to help you. Ask for help if you need it.

As you search for the book you have learned about in the catalog, it is a good idea to watch for other books that might be helpful to you. This is called "browsing," and is a good habit to develop. Even the best description on a catalog card may not indicate a book's usefulness to you.

Browsing has its drawbacks, however. If someone else has checked out a book, you might never know about it unless you use the card catalog. If you know that the library has a book, and it is not on the shelf, the librarian will search for the book among recently returned books not yet reshelved. If the book is checked out to another user, a "reserve" may be attached to the card so that you can be notified when the book is returned.

Using other libraries

At any time in your research you may have need for materials that your library does not have. The library may borrow these materials for you on inter-library loan, or you may be able to get permission to use a nearby special library. If you do, it is important to understand and obey the rules. Otherwise, permission to use the library may be withdrawn.

2. What is in the Reference Department?

Using the Reference Department

The Reference Department contains a number of special books you will find helpful. These books are not designed to be read from cover to cover, but to be consulted for items of information.

If you need only a quick answer to one or two questions, or the location of one article, it would not be very efficient to learn all about the Reference Department of your library. The librarian will find what you need very quickly.

However, if you are beginning fairly extensive research that will involve the use of materials in the Reference Department, it will save you time to learn how to be an independent user. This will enable you to work at your own pace, without waiting for help at every step. And you will not need to be dependent upon another person's interpretation of your assignment or question.

Choosing a reference book

Think of reference books as tools. Go to the tool that is designed for the job you have to do. Just as there are bread knives for slicing bread and steak knives for cutting steak, there are special reference books for particular kinds of information. Although you might find the correct spelling of a noun in the index of an encyclopedia, you would find it more quickly in a dictionary. Some facts about an elephant could be found in a dictionary, but an encyclopedia article is more likely to be a complete source of information. But it probably would not be efficient to use a general encyclopedia to find out who won the World Series in 1976. Information such as this is much more likely to be found in an almanac.

Each type of reference book is designed to give you quick access to certain kinds of information:

Information Needed	Reference Book
words	dictionary
"something about"	encyclopedia
geographical information	atlas (for maps)
	gazetteer (for facts)
records and statistical information	almanac
"how to"	handbook
people	biographical dictionary
names and addresses	directory
books and materials	bibliography

Some reference books cover many fields of knowledge; others are very specialized and cover one field in depth. Browsing along the shelves of the Reference Department and examining the specialized reference tools available can save you time when you have an assignment. Use the catalog to find what works are available in the subject field of interest to you. Then, examine each book for any special features.

The following bibliography is a sampling of some of the reference books you may find useful in completing assignments. But it is only a sample list. You will find many other helpful books as you learn to use the reference section of your library. If any of these books seem as though they might be helpful and your school library does not have them, try the public library.

Selected reference books

000-099 Generalities

028 Reading and Reading Aids

Books for the Teen Age. New York Public Library.
An annually revised, annotated list of mostly adult books on subjects of special interest and appeal to teen-agers.

Smorgasbord of Books: Titles Junior High Readers Relish, Betty M. Owen. Scholastic Book Services, 1974.
An annotated reading list by the long-time editor of the Teen-Age Book Club.

Your Reading: A Booklist for Junior High School Students. 5th ed. National Council of Teachers of English, 1975.
A list with imaginative groupings, such as "On solving a mystery" and "On growing up female." Also includes a good selection of nonfiction titles and reference materials.

031 American Encyclopedias

Collier's Encyclopedia. 24 vols. Macmillan Educational Corporation.
A well-illustrated, general encyclopedia with broad articles.

Compton's Encyclopedia and Fact-Index. 26 vols. F. E. Compton Company.
Especially useful for students who need "an easy reference set." The divided index, placed at the end of each volume, includes definitions and very short articles.

The Encyclopedia Americana. 30 vols. Americana Corporation.
A general encyclopedia, strong on science and technology, written for the nonspecialized user.

The New Columbia Encyclopedia. Columbia\University Press, 1975.

A one-volume encyclopedia designed for quick reference; strong on place names and biographies.

The New Encyclopaedia Britannica in 30 Volumes. Encyclopaedia Britannica, Inc.
Called Britannica 3 because of its three-part organization, this encyclopedia is divided into a one-volume *Propaedia: Outline of Knowledge,* a 10-volume, short-article *Micropaedia: Ready Reference and Index,* and a 19-volume long-article *Macropaedia: Knowledge in Depth.*

The World Book Encyclopedia. 22 vols. World Book–Childcraft International, Inc.
A general, family encyclopedia with clearly written text and outstanding illustrations; has both specific articles and survey articles.

The World Book Year Book. World Book–Childcraft International, Inc.
Published annually as a supplement to *The World Book Encylopedia,* each volume contains a review of significant events of the preceding year.

100-199 Philosophy and Related Disciplines

103 Philosophy—Encyclopedias

The Encyclopedia of Philosophy, Paul Edwards, ed. 4 vols. Macmillan, 1967.
Contains 1,450 signed articles dealing with philosophy past and present, East and West.

200-299 Religion

291 Mythology

Bulfinch's Mythology: The Age of Fable; The Age of Chivalry; Legends of Charlemagne, Thomas Bulfinch. 2nd rev. ed. Harper & Row, 1970.
One of the standard collections of myths and legends.

300-399 The Social Sciences

301 Sociology

The Negro Almanac, Harry A. Ploski and Warren Marr. 4th ed. Bellwether, 1981.
This book is the most comprehensive single source on Black Americans.

310 Statistics

The Statesman's Year-Book: Statistical and Historical Annual of the States of the World. St. Martin's.
Reliable, current descriptive information and statistical data on the governments of the world.

317.3 General Statistics of the U.S.

Information Please Almanac: Atlas and Yearbook. Simon & Schuster.
Up-to-date information on world events, sports, the arts, industry, manufacturing, religion, science, economics, and other topics of general interest.

Historical Statistics of the United States: Colonial Times to 1970. U.S. Bureau of the Census, 1975.
This bicentennial edition, the third in a series, contains a wide variety of U.S. statistical information.

The World Almanac and Book of Facts: The Authority Since 1868. Newspaper Enterprise Association.
Crammed with statistics, records, and events of the preceding year.

341.23 United Nations

Yearbook of the United Nations. Department of Public Information, United Nations.
Part One covers activities of the organization. Part Two covers activities of the intergovernmental organizations.

355.09 Military History

The Encyclopedia of Military History: From 3500 B.C. to the Present, R. Ernest and Trevor N. Dupuy, eds. Rev. ed. Harper & Row, 1977.
Chapters are chronologically arranged, with a subarrangement by country.

400-499 Language

422 English Etymology (Word History)

The Oxford Dictionary of English Etymology, Charles T. Onions, ed. Oxford University Press, 1966.
The most complete, most reliable etymological dictionary of the English language:

423 English Language Dictionaries

American Heritage Dictionary of the English Language, William Morris, ed. American Heritage and Houghton Mifflin, 1975.
The most common definition is given first in this dictionary which covers biographies of

noteworthy persons, geographic data, literary and legendary characters, acronyms, abbreviations, and foreign words and phrases used in the English language.

A Dictionary of Modern English Usage, Henry W. Fowler. 2nd rev. ed. Sir Ernest Gowers, ed. Oxford University Press, 1965.
Includes essays on the use and misuse of words and expressions, and comparisons between British and American usage and pronunciation.

Funk & Wagnalls Comprehensive Standard International Dictionary. Funk & Wagnalls, 1973.
Describes language as it is used, rather than how it should be used.

The Shorter Oxford English Dictionary on Historical Principles. 2 vols. 3rd ed. Oxford University Press, 1973.
The oldest meaning of a word is given first.

Webster's Third New International Dictionary of the English Language: Unabridged. G. & C. Merriam, 1961.
Defines words as they are used rather than how they should be used.

The World Book Dictionary, Clarence L. and Robert K. Barnhart, eds. 2 vols. World Book–Childcraft International, Inc.
Completely new in 1976 and revised annually; more than 3,000 illustrations.

424 Synonyms and Antonyms

Roget's International Thesaurus. 4th ed. Harper & Row, 1977.
Read the directions carefully; words are grouped by ideas; contrasts positive and negative aspects of ideas.

Webster's New Dictionary of Synonyms: Dictionary of Discriminated Synonyms with Antonyms and Analogous and Contrasted Words. 5th ed. G. & C. Merriam, 1978.
Revised and updated classic work whose title and subtitle describe it well.

426 Rhyming Dictionaries

New Rhyming Dictionary and Poets' Handbook, Burgess Johnson, ed. Rev. ed. Harper & Row, 1957.
The introduction gives directions for use and has forms of versification in English.

427 Slang

A Dictionary of Contemporary American Usage, Bergen and Cornelia Evans. Random House, 1965.

A very readable and witty book, explaining grammar and rhetoric, word usage, literary concepts, clichés, phrases, idioms, and figures of speech.

A Dictionary of Slang and Unconventional English, Eric Partridge. 7th ed. Macmillan, 1970.
A classic reference source for a wide variety of slang.

500-599 Pure Sciences

503 Science—Encyclopedias and Dictionaries

McGraw-Hill Dictionary of Scientific & Technical Terms. 2nd ed. McGraw-Hill, 1978.
Contains definitions of 100,000 terms.

McGraw-Hill Encyclopedia of Science and Technology. 15 vols. 4th ed. McGraw-Hill, 1977.
An authoritative set with broad survey articles covering physical, life, and earth sciences as well as engineering and technology.

505 Yearbooks

Science Year: The World Book Science Annual. World Book–Childcraft International, Inc.
Essays, special reports, short articles, and lists of awards and prizes; covers science and technology.

McGraw-Hill Yearbook of Science and Technology. McGraw-Hill.
Aims to cover all the natural sciences and their major applications.

591 Zoology

The International Wildlife Encyclopedia, Maurice and Robert Burton, eds. 20 vols. Marshall Cavendish, 1969-70.
Covers 1,229 animals or animal groups.

600-699 Technology

629.403 Astronautics—Encyclopedias

The New Space Encyclopaedia: A Guide to Astronomy and Space Exploration. Rev. ed. Dutton, 1973.
Explains more than 800 terms and concepts in astronomy and space science.

630 Agriculture

Outdoors U.S.A. U.S. Department of Agriculture. Government Printing Office, 1967.
Covers vacationing, recreation, and conservation.

700-799 The Arts

780.3 Music—Encyclopedias and Dictionaries
Encyclopedia of Pop, Rock, & Soul, Irwin
 Stambler, ed. St. Martin's, 1974.
 Spans the years 1950 to 1972; has 500 entries
 covering individuals, groups, record produc-
 ers, impressarios, rock festivals, musicals, and
 recent forms of music.
Harper's Dictionary of Music, Christine Ammer.
 Harper & Row, 1972.
 Has 2,800 entries covering composition of
 music, its performance, famous composers,
 abbreviations, forms of music, and instruments.

784.4 Folk Songs
*The Folk Songs of North America in the English
 Language*, Alan Lomax, ed. Doubleday, 1960.
 Includes the words, music, and origins of
 more than 300 American folk songs.

796.03 Sports—Encyclopedias
*The Baseball Encyclopedia: The Complete and Of-
 ficial Record of Major League Baseball*. 4th ed.
 Macmillan Publishing Company, 1979.
 A complete baseball record book, including
 yearly performances of batters and pitchers,
 managers' records, and much more.
*Rules of the Game: The Complete Illustrated
 Encyclopedia of All the Sports of the World*.
 Diagram Group. Bantam, 1976.
 Explains the rules for more than 230 sports.

800-899 Literature

808.81 Poetry
Granger's Index to Poetry, William James Smith,
 ed. 6th ed. Columbia University Press, 1970.
 Indexes 374 anthologies of poetry by title, first
 line, author, and subject.
Short Story Index, Dorothy E. Cook and Isabel S.
 Munro. H. W. Wilson, 1953.
 Indexes by author, title, and subject some
 60,000 stories in more than 4,000 collections.
 Supplements cover the years 1950 to 1978.

808.88 Quotations
*Familiar Quotations: A Collection of Passages,
 Phrases, and Proverbs Traced to Their Sources
 in Ancient and Modern Literature*, John
 Bartlett. 15th ed. Rev. and enlarged. Little,
 Brown, 1980.
 Quotations arranged chronologically by author.

*The Home Book of Quotations, Classical and
 Modern*, Burton Stevenson. Rev. ed. Dodd,
 Mead, 1967.
 Quotations are grouped under a large variety
 of subjects.

810.3 American Literature—Handbooks
American Authors and Books. W. J. Burke and
 W. D. Howe, eds. 3rd rev. ed. Crown, 1972.
 This dictionary of American literature includes
 authors' names, with dates of birth and death,
 and titles and dates of published works.

820.3 English Literature—Handbooks
*A Dictionary of Literature in the English Lan-
 guage, from Chaucer to 1940*, Robin Meyers, ed.
 2 vols. Pergamon, 1970-71.
 This classic work covers "3,500 authors who
 have used English as their medium of expres-
 sion throughout the world over a period of
 600 years."

900-999 General Geography and History

902 History—Chronologies
*An Encyclopedia of World History: Ancient,
 Medieval, and Modern*, William L. Langer, ed.
 5th ed. Houghton Mifflin, 1972.
 A chronologically arranged history of the
 world, covering major events from Paleolithic
 times to 1970.

903 History—Dictionaries
Dictionary of World History, G. M. D. Howat.
 Thomas Nelson & Sons, 1973.
 Short entries cover people, events, cultural
 trends, and "isms" through 1970.

910 General Geography
Webster's New Geographical Dictionary. G. & C.
 Merriam Company, 1977.
 This pronouncing dictionary covers not only
 current geographical names, with alternate
 spellings, but also historical place names from
 Biblical times onward. Gives gazetteer informa-
 tion: location, area, population.

911 Historical Atlases
Atlas of the American Revolution, Don
 Higginbotham and Kenneth Nebenzahl.
 Rand McNally, 1974.
 Contains 54 historical maps originally en-

graved and published during the American Revolutionary War.

Atlas of the Second World War, Peter Young, ed. Putnam, 1974.

The 215 maps, 250 illustrations, and explanatory text cover the land, air, and sea operations of all major participants in World War II.

912 Atlases

Hammond Ambassador World Atlas. Hammond, 1979.

Excellent maps, world statistical tables, and a combination gazetteer-index.

National Geographic Atlas of the World. 4th ed. National Geographic Society, 1975.

Maps and text by geographic regions.

Rand McNally Cosmopolitan World Atlas. Enlarged "Planet Earth Edition." Rand McNally, 1978.

An excellent general atlas, with physical, political, and metropolitan area maps, as well as informative articles.

920.03 Biography—Dictionaries

The McGraw-Hill Encyclopedia of World Biography. 12 vols. McGraw-Hill, 1973.

Long, up-to-date articles about "men and women whose lives are important to the understanding of social and cultural history."

Notable American Women, 1607-1950: A Biographical Dictionary, Edward and Janet James, eds. 3 vols. Harvard University Press, 1971.

Readable and informative biographies of 1,359 notable women who died before 1950.

Pictorial Encyclopedia of People Who Made America: Notable Men and Women of Many Races and Viewpoints, from Earliest Times to the Present, Who Helped Influence and Form the America We Live in Today. 20 vols. United States History Society.

The subtitle gives the scope of this very easy-to-read set. Emphasizes the strong influence of background upon accomplishment. Strong on various minorities.

Webster's American Biographies. G. & C. Merriam, 1974.

This tool covers people who made significant contributions to American life and history.

Who Was Who in America. 6 vols. Marquis, 1942-1976.

Covers Americans who died between 1897 and 1976.

Who's Who. St. Martin's Press.

An annual publication. The coverage is principally British, but prominent people of other nationalities are included.

Who's Who in America. 2 vols. Marquis.

Published every two years, this work covers living American men and women and outstanding people in other countries.

973 American History

The Annals of America. 23 vols. Encyclopaedia Britannica, 1968-76.

Set contains 2,202 original source readings in American History.

Special problems

As you begin to use reference books, you may be startled to learn that the facts in one book may not agree with the facts in another. Such a basic fact as the area of a country may not be the same in two encyclopedias. When you encounter this problem, consult a third source. This may solve the problem. When information varies, be sure to identify your source. You may say, "According to *Encyclopedia X,* the elephant may grow to be 10 feet tall."

Another problem in using reference books may arise from the publication date. Obviously, no book can include information about events that took place after the book was published. When using reference books, be sure to look at the copyright date. If, for example, the copyright date is 1977, you are not likely to find any information later than 1976. And, as in the case of an encyclopedia, the specific information you want may not be that recent. So, you may have to supplement, or update, the information using yearbooks or almanacs. Caution: When using yearbooks and almanacs, remember that they usually contain information from the year *preceding* the cover date. The 1977 *World Almanac* is helpful for 1976 events and statistics, but the user who expects 1977 events to be covered will be disappointed.

Research techniques

Here are some time-tested techniques for using reference materials to prepare a report:

1. Understand your assignment. Get it *in writing* before you leave the classroom.
2. Decide upon a "do-able" topic within the guidelines of your assignment. If you had unlimited time and the largest library in the world, you could research any topic. Usually you have a very definite due date and a limited collection to use.
3. Prepare a simple outline. Think through the things you want to know about your topic. Set these items down in outline form, as you learned to do in Unit 4 of this book.
4. Take notes efficiently. Note cards or slips of paper work best. Always identify the title of the reference books and the page number where you found the information. Then, you will be able to return to the books if you need more facts, if you need to prove what you have written, or if you have to prepare a bibliography.
5. Give credit when quoting. If you use the exact words, enclose what you have copied in quotation marks. If you decide to use the quotation in your final work, you will know the extent of the quotation and the source. Other notes will be phrases and rewordings, so there will be no need for quotation marks.
6. Work the notes into your outline. Use a symbol on each note slip or card to identify the part of the outline where the information will fit. Sometimes a piece of information appears to be useful in more than one part of the outline. Label it and shuffle it later. This is one reason for using cards or slips on which to take notes.
7. Do you need a bibliography? Your note cards will be very helpful if you need a bibliography to accompany your report. It is important to find out the format for the bibliography in time to prepare yours correctly.

3. What other reference sources can you use?

Other media listed in the card catalog can be very helpful. Films and filmstrips are often an excellent source of information. The study guides that accompany these media not only provide insight into the films, but also include supplementary text that may give new direction to your research.

Sources listed in the card catalog

Recordings, both disk and tape, will be listed in the card catalog, also. Depending upon your subject, you may find valuable additional information in a recorded format. The record sleeve or supplementary guides often contain facts that will enhance your report.

The vertical file is found in one or more filing cabinets used to group and make accessible pamphlets, clippings, pictures, and other materials that are difficult to store on a shelf. These materials are collected by the library because they are timely and often contain information that does not appear in books.

The vertical file

However, because the materials in the vertical file are ephemeral, or not considered to be of lasting interest or permanent value, they are not listed item-by-item in the card catalog. Instead, the subject headings under which the pamphlets, clippings, and other items are filed in the vertical file will appear in the card catalog as *see also* cross-references:

UNITED NATIONS
see also
materials filed under that heading in the Vertical File

Items in the vertical file usually can be checked out of the library for a limited time.

Microfiche editions	Many libraries have microfiche editions of books that are too rare or too expensive to own in book form. The microfiche format consists of a number of small cards with rows of tiny windows. Each window is a miniature, transparent reproduction of the page of a book.

The cards can be read on a microfiche reader, a simple enlarging device that projects a page at a time upon a lighted screen. As each page is read, the user moves the card to position the next page. The greatest disadvantage of using a book in microfiche format is that it must be read in the library. This, however, can sometimes be an advantage in that these "books" will not be checked out by someone else when you need them.

Newspapers	Newspapers are very useful to researchers because they record events as they happen, and as they are perceived at that time. Back files of newspapers are often photographed and kept on rolls of microfilm. The film can be read on a microfilm reader. The user can move the film forward or backward rapidly to the page desired.

One newspaper, *The New York Times*, is available in many libraries. This paper gives very complete coverage to the news and is very thoroughly indexed, making it a valuable research tool in many fields. Each issue of the index contains instructions for its use, and the few minutes spent reading these instructions will save valuable time.

Usually, one or more local newspapers are also available in microfilm, or in their original format. *The New York Times Index* can be helpful to you in using the back files of your local newspaper because it will identify the date of the issue in which you can expect to find a particular story of national interest. Often, background material appearing in newspaper accounts never becomes available in book form. For example, editorials and letters to the editor indicate contemporary local reaction to events. This type of information can greatly enhance a report.

Magazines	Magazine articles are often a valuable source of information. But you will not be able to find these articles through the card catalog, for they are not listed there. You will, however, probably find what you want through the *Readers' Guide to Periodical Literature*, or its shorter form, the *Abridged Readers' Guide to Periodical Literature*. These publications index the articles and stories in many magazines. The names of

the magazines indexed are listed on the introductory pages. Check to see which of these magazines are available in your library.

The *Readers' Guide*. The paperbound volumes of the *Readers' Guide* index the most recent issues of magazines. A new *Guide* is published twice a month. At the end of three months, the entries are combined into one alphabetical listing and published as a cumulation, again in paperback. At the end of a year, all the entries for that year are cumulated into an annual clothbound volume. Earlier cumulations, before 1965, cover two or more years. The period covered is clearly marked on each volume.

Some information that appears in magazine articles will never appear in book form. For this reason, articles in old periodicals can be extremely helpful when you are writing a report. To locate information on an event that occurred in 1928, for instance, begin your search in Volume VIII of the *Readers' Guide*, which covers June 1929 to June 1932. After locating any entries in this cumulation, use Volume VII (1925-1928).

Sometimes, the tenth, the hundredth, or some other anniversary of an event will inspire many articles. You may benefit from the authors' research if you check *Readers' Guide* for these anniversary periods.

Using the *Readers' Guide*. The *Readers' Guide* is somewhat like the card catalog, but in book form. There are author entries and a variety of subject entries. Both types of entries contain the information you will need to find an article. Because the titles of magazine articles are often misleading or unimportant, there are no title entries. There are title listings for stories, but these entries only refer you to the author entry, where full information for locating the story is given. Entries in the *Readers' Guide* usually contain the following information:

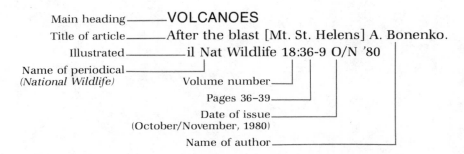

In order to save space, abbreviations are used in the entries. A separate list gives the abbreviations used for these periodicals. You will need to be familiar with these abbreviations. The names of the periodicals, the months of the year (Ja, F, Mr, Ap, My, Je, Jl, Ag, S, O, N, D), and descriptions of special features in the articles are all abbreviated. These abbreviations are explained in the introductory portion of the *Readers' Guide*, and you should read those pages carefully.

Finding a magazine. When you have located the entries for articles you want to read, copy down the meaningful information: author, title, magazine, year or volume number, and page numbers.

The bound volumes of magazines are usually shelved in alphabetical order by title. If you have any difficulty in locating the magazine you want, the librarian will help you. When the library you are using does not have the back files of a particular magazine, a nearby library might have them. Do not waste valuable time browsing among other interesting articles in a magazine. Plan to return to such articles when you do not have an assignment due!

And finally

Your school and community library can be the most important aid you have during your school career and after. The library can give you knowledge. And the library can give you pleasure.

But to be able to use any library, you must understand its organization. If you take the time to learn the basic form of library organization, it will pay you great dividends in understanding and enjoyment.

4. Where else can you get help?

People as a source of information

School and public libraries are not your only sources of information. You will find that people, both locally and nationally, can provide you with a great deal of information for a variety of research reports. Much, however, will depend upon the specific topic you have in mind, as well as upon the kind of report you want to do. You also need to know how to go about getting information from people.

Personal interviews. Personal interviews are one way of getting information that will produce a unique report. A radio program or a newspaper story may give you an idea for a report, as well as the names of people to talk to. Another source of names is the community resource file in the library. This file lists people in the community who are willing to share their knowledge or expertise.

If your topic involves vocational information, personal interviews may enhance your report. Prepare for the interviews by using the vocational information files in the library to learn the scope of the particular vocational area in which you are interested. Then you might interview young people who want to enter that field, people who are in entry-level jobs, middle management people, and, if you can get an interview, a top executive. One question you might ask of those working in the field is, "Does the job match the expectations you had before you began?"

When you request an interview, have a good idea of what you want to learn. Find out as much as you can about the person and the subject ahead of time. This is not to impress anyone with your knowledge, but to avoid asking "dumb questions" and wasting interview time.

During the interview, be sure to listen carefully so that you get your facts straight. You may want to use a tape recorder or take notes, but be sure to ask permission. Some people either "dry up" or become distracted by these procedures. You will get the best interview if you are primarily a good listener and seem to appreciate what you are learning.

Be sure to thank the person for giving you the interview. It is easy to become so excited by the information you are getting that you cannot wait to get home and work it into your report. Be sure to give the person credit in your report, or in the bibliography that accompanies your report.

Interviews by mail. If you are interested in getting information from someone who lives too far away for a personal interview, try contacting the person by letter. An interview by mail, however, is necessarily more limiting than a personal interview.

You cannot ask very many questions in your letter without appearing to ask the person to write your report for you. If you do ask too many questions, you may not get any answer at all. The best procedure is to read everything you can about the person. You might then ask for clarification of some point you do not understand, or for that person's reaction to some event in his or her life.

Make your questions interesting, keep them few in number, and mention the deadline for your assignment. Remember, people are busy. For any number of reasons, the answers to your questions may not arrive in time for your assignment, or may not arrive at all. So, do not depend upon receiving interesting extra information. Prepare your report so that you can turn it in on time even if you do not receive a reply to your letter.

The personal survey. Conducting a personal survey, and then drawing conclusions from it, is another way of producing a unique report. Everybody has opinions, and most people enjoy sharing them. You may choose to get local opinion on questions used in a national opinion poll, or you may choose to use a subject of purely local interest.

Phrase your questions carefully, so that the people you interview can respond easily and unambiguously. You might choose to interview a large number of people, using questions that call for a simple "yes," "no," or "no opinion." Or, you may want to interview a few people in depth, and then quote the exact words of the persons interviewed. If you choose to use in-depth interviews, be sure to ask each person for the correct spelling of his or her name. If anyone does not want to give you his name willingly, do not insist.

Move on to the next interview. If too many of your attempted interviews end up this way, perhaps you should change to the "for," "against," or "don't care" survey where names do not matter. But whichever format you use, summarize the results fairly. Results that were not predictable will tend to make your report more interesting.

Television and radio offer information along with entertainment. You can often get many interesting ideas and information for research reports from these media.

Help from television and radio

Each week there are a number of special programs on television. The sponsors of these "specials" often prepare supplementary materials to inform viewers about the subjects of the programs. These study guides and bibliographies may be requested in advance. They are usually available free, or at very little cost.

Many special programs are recorded on videotape. If so, they may be available through your media center, with the accompanying guides, or may be ordered from the network for classroom showing. Even if there are no supplementary materials, a great deal of information may be gained by watching and taking notes.

Television "talk shows" are another possible source of information. The people interviewed have usually done interesting things or written thought-provoking books. These people can provide insight into new fields of knowledge.

Telecast college credit courses may, of course, be watched by anyone. For each course there are bibliographies and a course syllabus designed to help the students enrolled in the course. These may be excellent background for your research. Watching the programs can be a good way to gather useful information. It is also an excellent opportunity to develop your note-taking technique—a skill so necessary in college.

Radio stations are required to devote a certain amount of time to public-interest broadcasts. These programs may take the form of interviews with people on both sides of a controversial issue. There may be special programs giving historical background before important events, such as elections, space flights, or the commemoration of an historical event. Special radio programs are apt to be planned to meet the needs of the community served by the station. This means that there will be resource people available to help you if you wish to pursue a particular subject that captures your interest.

Government publications are an often overlooked source
of information. They cover a fantastic range of subjects and
the price is right: free or quite inexpensive. Of course, many
of these may be in your library, but you may wish to acquire
your own copies.

Local government. City and county governments publish
statistics and reports about the services they offer, as well as
historical pamphlets, and, quite often, brochures prepared
to attract businesses to the community. Some of these publications can raise more questions than they answer, but this
may give meaningful direction to your research.

State government. States publish a wide variety of information materials. For example, tourist and other travel information will identify for you some of the interesting places in
your state. You can then obtain more information by visiting
or writing a particular place. State geological publications
will identify the mineral resources of the state and interesting rock formations that occur there.

Ecological publications will cover state efforts to preserve
the environment. Birds and animals native to the state are
often described in state publications, and the state forest
preserves will have literature on trees and other plants
found throughout the state.

Anniversary and special centennial books and pamphlets
sometimes reproduce rare historical documents, letters,
diaries, and records to which you would not ordinarily
have access. State agricultural extension agencies publish
very helpful information about all phases of farming
and homemaking. Through county agents, classes are sometimes available on these subjects.

United States government. Federal publications are very
numerous and extremely varied. New publications are listed
in the *Monthly Catalog of United States Government Publications,* published by the Superintendent of Documents,
United States Government Printing Office, Washington, D.C.
20402. Your library will have a number of government documents, and a nearby library may be one of the repository
libraries in which most or all government publications are
collected.

Other publications. There are national organizations for
many types of occupations. These groups may be willing to
send you up-to-date information on the outlook for that oc-

cupation, about training schools or university programs, and the latest figures on the income you can expect in a particular field.

The Reference Department of the library will have directories that contain the addresses of these organizations. You can also find the names and addresses of such organizations in *The World Book Encyclopedia* and other general encyclopedias. You might also check the *Readers' Guide to Periodical Literature* for articles about new and unusual vocational areas.

Many businesses, and most countries, also publish pamphlets which you can send for. Sometimes, you can obtain pictures and posters as well. Some of these materials are labeled "teaching materials," but students are usually welcome to send for them. Most of these materials are either free or involve very little cost. The following handy guides provide lists of free and inexpensive materials that you can order. These guides are often available in school and public libraries:

Free and Inexpensive Learning Materials, George Peabody College for Teachers, Nashville, Tennessee. Distributed by Incentive Publications, Inc., P.O. Box 120189, Nashville, Tennessee 37212.

Vertical File Index, The H.W. Wilson Company, 950 University Avenue, Bronx, New York 10452. Issued quarterly, this publication lists available pamphlets according to subject.

The Consumer Information Catalog, Consumer Information Center, General Services Administration. Lists more than 200 publications on subjects of interest to consumers. Though generally available in libraries, copies of *The Consumer Information Catalog* may be obtained free of charge by writing to the Consumer Information Center, Pueblo, Colorado 81009.

Free! The Newsletter of Free Materials and Services, Dyad Services, P.O. Box 4696, Station C, London, Ontario N5W 5L7. Published five times a year, this newsletter lists free materials available in Canada.

A few moments spent consulting the listings in these guides will be well worth your time and effort.

Activities

The unit-end activities have been designed to help you to practice and gain the ability to use the various research and study skills described in this unit. Please do not write in this book, but place your answers on a separate sheet of paper. Where appropriate, answers to the activities can be found in the **Answer Key** that begins on page 290.

Listing in order

An understanding of the way in which entries would be listed in alphabetical order is essential to the use of the card catalog. Study the entries listed below. Then arrange the entries as you would expect to find them listed in the card catalog.

CARSON McCULLERS
DIVISION
BLOOMINGTON
WRESTLING
SCULPTURE
HERALD
DOG
SEAL
ANATOMY
BOTULISM
MADISON SQUARE GARDEN
MONGOL EMPIRE
SEDATIVE
VIRGINIA
DIME

AIRPLANE
HAWAII
RICHARD McBRIDE
SEA
FERDINAND VON ZEPPELIN
LUDWIG BEMELMANS
MELON
ERNEST HEMINGWAY
DENMARK
SECRETION
URUGUAY
HEMISPHERE
MAINE
ANDREW MELLON
AJAX

Locating sources

While your local or school library probably contains all of the information you will need to complete a class assignment, this information will do you little good if you are unable to locate it. You should familiarize yourself with the Dewey Decimal System of classification and with the categories of information covered under the various classifications. A number of topics have been listed below. Using the information given on pages 182-183 of this unit as your resource, determine under which general number in the Dewey Decimal System of classification information related to each listed topic would be found.

1. Supply and demand in a modern mixed economy.
2. Whitehead's impact upon modern philosophy.
3. Critical studies of Shakespeare's comedies.
4. An English-French/French-English dictionary.
5. How to begin and care for an organic garden.
6. A list of recent books and articles written about World War II.
7. Studies in abnormal psychology.
8. A history of the United States.
9. A study of Hindu religious beliefs.
10. An anthology of English-language poetry.
11. A photographic study of the surface of the moon.
12. Climate and landform regions of the earth.
13. How to play baseball.
14. Basic principles of algebra.
15. The architectural works of Frank Lloyd Wright.
16. Vocational education in American schools.
17. The plays of Eugene O'Neill.
18. The political system of Canada.
19. The process of photosynthesis in plants.
20. Europe during the Middle Ages.
21. City government in the United States.
22. Case studies in consumer economics.
23. The art of French cooking.
24. The basic rules of baseball.
25. Careers in public service.
26. Earning a license to fly a plane.
27. The physical structure of the dog.
28. The Age of Andrew Jackson.
29. Basic principles of accounting.
30. Critical essays on the state of contemporary art in the United States.

Using the *Readers' Guide*

The *Readers' Guide to Periodical Literature* indexes articles
and stories published in periodicals, or magazines. Entries
in the *Readers' Guide* are simple to understand once you
have had some practice working with them. Using the sample entry on page 197 as a guide, give the meaning of each of
the following entries from the *Readers' Guide.*

AVIATION
> Safety devices and measures

Airlines busier—and safer, too. il U.S. News 90:10
   Ja 26 '81

CAMERAS
Revolution in amateur picture-taking. il Bus W p220-2+
   0 27 '80

COLLEGE graduates
> Employment

Where the jobs are for the class of '81. il U.S. News 90:65-6
   Ja 26 '81

COMPUTERS
> Home use

Computers: at the crossroads & beyond. R.L. Perry. il Mech
   Illus 77:62-3+ Ja '81

POWER resources
> Canada

Alcohol fuels are no longer small potatoes. D. Folster. il
   Macleans 93:50 Mr 24 '80

RAILROADS
> Trains

Heading home; trip from San Francisco to Chicago on the
   Zephyr. P.L. Buckley. il Nat R 28:904+ Ag 20 '76

TORNADOES
Understanding tornadoes. il USA Today 108:12-13 D '79

UNITED STATES
> Forest Service

Hunting bears for science [work of L. Rogers] il pors Nat
   Geog World 64:4-9 D '80

Help from newspapers

A commonly overlooked source of information is the newspaper. Many people read the newspaper only for the sports, funnies, and listings of television programs. But there is a tremendous amount of different kinds of information in each issue of a newspaper. Familiarize yourself with the kinds of information available in a newspaper by studying several issues of a local daily. Try to find newspaper articles that could be related to the following topics of general information.

Art	Economics	Literature
Biography	Foreign Affairs	Political Science
Criticism	History	Public Opinion
Drama		

Library checklist

When you hear the word "library" you probably think of "books." Yet, as you have learned in this unit, most libraries contain many kinds of resource materials in addition to books. Use the checklist shown below to make an inventory of the resource materials available in your school or local library.

	Yes	No
Films	⎯⎯	⎯⎯
Filmstrips	⎯⎯	⎯⎯
Videotapes	⎯⎯	⎯⎯
Newspapers	⎯⎯	⎯⎯
Magazines	⎯⎯	⎯⎯
Disk recordings	⎯⎯	⎯⎯
Tape recordings	⎯⎯	⎯⎯
Maps	⎯⎯	⎯⎯
Pamphlets	⎯⎯	⎯⎯
Study prints	⎯⎯	⎯⎯
Historical pictures	⎯⎯	⎯⎯
Documents	⎯⎯	⎯⎯
Artifacts	⎯⎯	⎯⎯
Art collections	⎯⎯	⎯⎯
Manuscripts	⎯⎯	⎯⎯
Posters	⎯⎯	⎯⎯

Using an encyclopedia

An encyclopedia is one of the best all-around basic research tools you have at your disposal. Use an encyclopedia to answer the following questions. This will help to familiarize you with both the organization of the encyclopedia you use, and with the kind of information which can be found in an encyclopedia.

1. Who was Piet Mondrian, when did he live, and why is he famous?
2. What is the meaning of the word "philosophy" and from what language is the word derived?
3. Who was the founder of the method of treating mental illness known as psychoanalysis?
4. What is the traditional religion of India?
5. What does a nation's gross national product (GNP) represent?
6. What is the term of office of United States senators?
7. What is the fundamental theorem of calculus?
8. About how many miles (kilometers) is the earth from the sun?
9. Where are the ailerons located on an airplane?
10. Who were the Brontë sisters and why are they famous?
11. What was the Saskatchewan Rebellion, when did it take place, and why is it important in Canadian history?
12. In what year did Louis Joliet and Father Jacques Marquette travel through the Wisconsin region?
13. What is the capital, official language, official name, and form of government of the state of Bahrain?
14. What is biofeedback?
15. Who was George Boole, when did he live, and why is he famous?
16. What is the only breed of dog that cannot bark, and where was this type of dog originally bred?
17. What two novels did Daniel Defoe write and why is he important?
18. What are the three degrees of comparison that are used in English grammar?
19. What is the oldest university art museum in the United States?
20. What is the name of the longest river in the world, where is it, and how long is it?

Research checklist

Many students approach the job of using a library to do research with a great deal of fear and confusion. This is because students often fail to clarify in their own mind exactly
what information they are trying to find and how they
should go about finding this information. Using a library to
do research is not difficult to do if you are able to go about it
in a systematic, orderly way. Use of the following checklist
could help you to approach library research with greater
confidence.

OK

1. Decide firmly on the subject of your research
   project. _____

2. Use available reference works to identify the
   content limits and divisions of the topic you
   have chosen. _____

3. Use the card catalog to pinpoint books that
   deal with the topic you have chosen. _____

4. Use the *Readers' Guide* to pinpoint articles
   and periodicals that might deal with the topic
   you have chosen. _____

5. Check for any other materials the library
   might have. _____

6. Ask the librarian for help and advice throughout the course of your research project. _____

A guide to study skills

Are your grades as good as they could be? Would you like to get better grades in your classes? Most students do not get the kind of grades they are capable of getting. This is because few students approach study in a systematic, organized way.

This unit discusses basic techniques you can use to make your studying more effective. It presents a plan for efficient studying. And it describes special techniques that can be used for studying specific subject areas, such as mathematics or foreign languages.

8

The contributors of this unit are Dr. Nicholas P. Georgiady, Professor in the Department of Educational Leadership, Miami University, Oxford, Ohio; and Dr. Louis G. Romano, Professor in the Department of Administration and Higher Education, Michigan State University, East Lansing, Michigan.

1. Why study?

"Why study?" This is a question that is asked by some students. Many students feel that studying is a waste of time. The reason for part of this attitude is that many students do not understand what studying is. When they hear the word "study," they imagine themselves locked in a quiet room, nose buried in a textbook.

Studying is not necessarily limited to textbooks. You can study nature by walking in the woods to observe plant and animal life. You can learn how to repair a small motor by watching an expert mechanic. You can learn how to develop photographic negatives by studying the process from a book, or viewing a film or filmstrip, or studying the techniques of a friend who knows how to develop negatives. You can study by reading, observing, listening, or doing.

In school you are involved in many learning activities. You will use some of this learning right away. And some of this learning you will need in the future. But both kinds of learnings demand you master certain information and certain kinds of skills.

For example, you must study mathematics so that you have number skills for immediate use such as doing your math homework or passing tests. Yet such mathematical skills as counting money and balancing a check book are required of people throughout their lives.

Whatever the information or skills, memorizing them does not make for lasting learning. You must understand the information or skill. The best way to reach understanding is by studying...studying which may involve listening to the teacher, or doing something on a worksheet, or reading, or discussing, or just thinking.

212

There are many other reasons why you should make the effort to study. Knowledge is changing rapidly. There are more things to be learned every day. And the things to be learned are growing more complex. Culture and technology are advancing so quickly that many people are being "left behind."

You will find that studying does not end in school. To keep up in a modern society, you must study throughout your life.

For example, what a mechanic in the 1920's learned about the early model T Ford is of little use today. The mechanic's skill in repairing a model T Ford would not help to repair a modern eight cylinder, high-powered engine. Not only is the engine itself a more complicated mechanism, but so are the tools needed to repair a modern engine. A mechanic today must be able to study a car manual, and be able to translate the procedures and ideas on the printed page into action in the garage.

And what about the cars of the future? Will there be atomic powered cars? Will cars be powered by electricity? Whatever the case, you must develop study skills to keep up with changes in culture and technology.

So, it is important that you learn how to learn, or learn how to study. For you will find you need continuous study to meet the challenges of the future. Schools cannot do the whole job of educating. Schools do not have enough time. You will have to continue learning long after you have left school.

Other reasons to study

Every person has goals that he or she would like to reach. These goals may be immediate or long range, academic or social, intellectual or physical goals.

Your immediate goal may be to graduate from high school. Your long-range goal may be sucess in a career.

Academically, you may want to read blueprints so you can plan to build a house. You may attend night school where you are taught how to read blueprints. Or you may study blueprint reading with an architect friend. Socially, you may want to improve your skill in the card game of bridge. So you study one of the many books written on this subject.

In physical skills, you may want to improve at golf or some other sport. This goal can be reached by studying the sport with the help of a professional. Whatever your goal, studying is the important ingredient if you wish to be successful.

You and your goals

The wrong reasons for study

Some students avoid serious studying at all costs. Such students believe the only value in studying is that it enables them to "pass", to get a grade that is acceptable and helps to keep parents satisfied. Little or no thought is given to the poor study habits that are being developed. And this is a serious mistake. The development of poor study habits now can affect your life for many years to come.

One of the worst study habits is cramming. Cramming is the kind of studying done the night before an examination in a desperate attempt to "learn" everything at once. Cramming is short-sighted. Learnings are not likely to be remembered for long. And actual understanding is usually not achieved.

You need a program for study

In contrast to cramming, some students practice a program of regular study and review. When you practice a coordinated program of study, you are more likely to understand the material you are trying to learn. When you gain understanding of some skill or piece of information, in a sense you "own" that knowledge. It can never be taken away from you. Long after school and examinations are a distant memory, the knowledge you gained will still be yours.

A well-designed program of study is a must if you wish to learn. But you must make a personal commitment to such a program if it is to work. These are *not* simple tasks. It is much easier to turn on the television set or listen to rock music than to stick to a study plan or to practice many study skills. How to listen, how to read efficiently, how to take notes, how to plan a study schedule, how to remember facts, and how to take a test are just a few of the study skills you will have to master. To acquire these skills will take effort.

So you can see that attending school and going to class is not enough. In order to get the most out of your educational opportunities, time must also be devoted to studying. You must know how to get the most out of the study time that is available to you. The sections that follow will provide some practical advice on how to accomplish this goal.

2. How should you plan your studying?

Studying is lonely. You are the only one who can develop good study habits for yourself. This is especially true when you are trying to prepare or map a personalized study schedule.

Your school day is organized for you. But the time after school and on weekends is free time. Subtracting time for sleeping, you probably have about 60 hours per week that is free time.

How do you make use of your free time? Do you spend a lot of time watching television, listening to music, or just "fooling around?" Do you spend too much time on a particular extracurricular activity such as sports? Then do you complain that you do not have enough time to do your homework?

You can solve your problem if you are ready and willing to *budget* your free hours. If you carefully plan how you will spend your after-school time, you will find that you have *more* time for study and pleasure rather than less.

Many students do not believe this. A typical answer to this suggestion is, "Even if I plan, there still isn't enough time to complete what I have to do." This statement is nothing more than a crutch. It takes courage and action to analyze how you use *and abuse* your free time. You must have the courage to admit to yourself when you are wasting time. And you must be determined to *stick to* whatever personal schedule you make.

Finally, remember that haphazard study habits are inefficient, and inefficiency wastes valuable time. Without a plan of action or study schedule many assignments will be left incomplete or skipped over altogether. Research continues to show that successful students usually work according to some kind of formal plan.

Your personalized study schedule

The first step toward organizing your time is to find out exactly what you are doing with your time. Keep a list for one week of everything you do. This list should include class attendance, studying, going to a movie, or talking on the phone—everything you do for a week. Without this information, you will be unable to judge if you are using your free time wisely.

What follows is a sample of a list of typical daily activities that might be prepared by a student. After such a list has been done for each day of a week, the student would compile and record weekly totals for the categories shown at the bottom of the list.

USE OF TIME CHART
MONDAY, OCTOBER 9

Hours	Activities
6:30 - 7:30	Dress and breakfast
7:30 - 8:00	Transportation to school
8:00 - 9:00	English class
9:00 - 10:00	Read magazine in study hall
10:00 - 11:00	Math class
11:00 - 12:00	Gym class
12:00 - 1:00	Lunch
1:00 - 2:00	Social studies
2:00 - 3:00	Went to library—met with friends
3:00 - 4:00	Science
4:00 - 4:30	Hung around at drug store
4:30 - 6:00	Played tag football
6:00 - 7:00	Dinner
7:00 - 8:00	Listened to rock records and talked on phone
8:00 - 9:00	Watched TV and talked on phone
9:00 - 10:00	Watched TV in bed

_____ Time in class
_____ Time studying outside of class
_____ Time in social activities
_____ Time not accounted for

This is the kind of list you should now begin gathering. After you have totaled your time, you will probably be surprised at the amount of time you have wasted or are unable to account for.

You should not be discouraged by this. Yours is not an uncommon problem. But the desire and will to solve this problem is. *You* must decide that you wish to solve this problem. *You* must be convinced that you *can* and *will* make better use of your time. And, finally, *you* must have the determination to stick to whatever time schedule you prepare for yourself.

After examining your totals for the week, you should recognize that time is precious. Its use should be planned to gain the greatest advantage. Time can be used to aid and benefit worthwhile activities. Or time can be frittered away with nothing gained.

Procrastination and disorder are two factors which work against the effective use of time. Procrastination, or "putting off until tomorrow, what you are too lazy to do today," is the great roadblock to an effective study schedule. Your education will suffer unless you are able to acquire the habit of completing tasks on time. Good work habits are one of the keys to success.

Good work habits will help you not only in school, but also after your school career is finished. People who are successes in any field will always show good work habits. If you aim at success in school and in life, you will need to be self-directed and assume personal responsibility for the use of your time. And a planned study schedule is the best way to make sure you are using your time most efficiently.

Planning a study schedule

Approach your school work with a definite plan of action rather than asking yourself, "What next?" Begin planning your study schedule by reviewing the *Use of Time Chart* prepared in the last section. The information shown on this chart will tell you what your present schedule is. Ask yourself the following questions while reviewing the chart.

Do I plan in advance how I will spend my daily study time?

Do I schedule study periods so that they precede and/or follow a subject being studied?

Do I study consistently during free hours of the day to avoid last minute "cramming"?

Do I provide for additional time in my daily, weekly, and semester schedules for term papers and other special projects?

Do I provide time for review of lessons daily and weekly?

Do I schedule my social activities so that they do not interfere with study time?

Do I schedule daily periods for recreation?

It is very likely that your answer to most of these questions will be an emphatic, "No!" And this should convince you that you must develop a working study schedule that will meet your study needs. You cannot copy another person's schedule because each schedule must be a personal one. While preparing *your* schedule, keep these ideas in mind.

Plan for required periods of time. Required courses, time for meals, and other required activities such as music lessons, regular doctor appointments, and so forth should be blocked in first so that you have a good idea of what time is available for other activities.

Plan for emergencies. Be ready to make adjustments in your schedule for emergencies. Include an occasional free period in your schedule. This free period could be used to makeup scheduled study periods lost because of some emergency.

Plan ample time for study. For each subject, plan about three to five hours of study a week. Some subjects will need little or no study time. But others may require more time. You must be the judge of how much time certain subjects need. After a period of intensive study, do not plan to move into another intensive study period. Include a rest period. Without scheduled rest periods learning suffers! Try to study within the time limits you have set for yourself. The *kind* of studying you do is more important than the amount of studying you do. And above all, *get started!*

Plan a study session after a particular class. Sometimes this is not possible. Whenever your schedule does not allow it, then plan to schedule a study session as soon before or after the class period as possible. Planning the study of a subject immediately after the class period enables you to work on the assignment while it is fresh in your mind.

Plan for your learning personality. Each student has his or her own learning personality. Are you an "early bird" and seem to learn best in the morning, or are you a "night owl" and seem to learn best in the after dinner hours? If you are an "early bird," then plan to include as much of your intensive study or review during morning hours.

Plan to study the same subject at the same time each day. Consistency is important. If you know that at 10 A.M.

each day from Monday to Friday you will be studying science, then you will find that you are prepared mentally to study science at that time. You need mental preparation to concentrate.

Plan for review sessions. Set aside at least one hour each week for review of each subject. Also, plan for additional review time prior to a quiz or an examination.

Plan for some free time in your schedule. Every scheduled hour of the day need not be set aside for a particular subject. Some free study time in your schedule will permit you to take care of emergencies, to schedule more time for activities of your liking, or to have additional time for extra study of a particular subject.

Plan for leisure, recreation, and chores. "All work and no play makes Jack a dull boy" as the old saying goes. Physical activity is just as important as mental activity. Therefore, it is important that in your schedule you set aside some time for physical activity. This time need not be for an active sport. Taking a brisk walk can be a satisfying break between study periods.

Plan for specific tasks. After you have blocked in your specific subjects and other activities, be sure to provide space to write descriptions of specific tasks. These descriptions should include such things as pages to read, number of problems to complete, and so forth. Your entries should be something like the following:

Math: Read pp. 17-18
Do prob. 1-6 and 17-21.
Review p. 15.

Making your study schedule

Keeping these guidelines in mind you are now ready to make your own personalized study schedule. Incidentally, it is important that you be realistic when preparing your schedule. A common mistake made by students preparing their first study schedule is to try to do the impossible. These students set aside every free hour for study, and provide little or no time for rest and relaxation.

Such a schedule quickly becomes a "grind." If you make this mistake, you will probably not stick to your schedule long enough to find the value in it. Keep in mind that the schedule is intended to make your work easier and to give you greater satisfaction and freedom than you now have.

What follows is a sample of what a typical study schedule for a week might look like. Study this sample for some guidelines as to what your study schedule should be like.

Study schedule for one week

Hours	Monday	Tuesday	Wednesday	Thursday	Friday	Saturday	Sunday
6:30 A.M.	dress and breakfast					dress and breakfast	
7:30 A.M.	transportation to school					employed	
8:00 A.M.	English	English	English	English	English		
9:00 A.M.	*study English*	*study math*	*study math*	*study English*	*study math*		
10:00 A.M.	math	math	math	math	math		
11:00 A.M.	phy. ed.	*study social science*	phy. ed.	*study math*	phy. ed.		
Noon	lunch	lunch	lunch	lunch	lunch	lunch	church, personal activity, special study and review
1:00 P.M.	social studies	social studies	social studies	social studies	social studies	recreation	
2:00 P.M.	*study social science*	*study science*	*study social science*	*study science*	*study social science*		
3:00 P.M.	science	science	science	science	science		
4:00 P.M.	free	free	free	free	free	free or *study*	
5:00 P.M.	*study science*	*study	*study	*study social science*	*study science*		
6:00 P.M.	dinner	dinner	dinner	dinner	dinner	dinner	
7:00 P.M.	*study math*	*study math*	*study math*	*study	social activity or *study*	*study math*	
8:00 P.M.	*study English*	*study English*	*study science*	study		social activity	
9:00 P.M.	free time: recreation, reading, special study, sleep, and so forth.						

*Study period, but not designated for a particular study.
Used for review or a subject needing more time.

In your time schedule be sure that you follow the guideline which points out the need for describing the *specific tasks* to be completed in each subject.

Besides a daily time schedule, you may want to prepare a long range schedule or calendar of important days. What follows is an example of such a long range schedule.

Calendar of important days

Week	1st	2nd	3rd	4th	5th	6th	7th	8th	9th	10th	11th	12th
Dates	9/1 to 9/3	9/4 to 9/10	9/11 to 9/17	9/18 to 9/24	9/25 to 10/1	10/2 to 10/8	10/9 to 10/15	10/16 to 10/22	10/23 to 10/29	10/30 to 11/5	11/6 to 11/12	11/13 to 11/19
English				test 9/20				test 10/19				test 11/14
French								test 10/17				
Biology					notes due 9/28	unit test 10/7			notes due 10/28		unit test 11/8	
Math										mid-term 11/4		
Art							proj. due 10/14					proj. due 11/15
Drum Lesson		9/10		9/24		10/8		10/22		11/5		11/19
Social				school dance 9/24								school play 11/13
Doctor									exam 10/29			
Committees		car club 9/9	French club 9/14				car club 10/11	French club 10/19			French club 11/9	

The sample schedule shown in the preceding section is for a student who also holds a part-time job. This job takes up some of the time that would usually be used for study.

The working student

More and more junior high and high school students are working at part-time jobs. And for some of these students, working causes study problems and falling grades.

Yet research has shown that students who hold part-time jobs *and* use a study schedule manage to make better use of their time than those who have no job and/or no study schedule. Many working students seem to have the attitude that their time is valuable. These students quickly get used to a set routine. They have less difficulty sticking to a study schedule. Having less time for study forces many working students to budget their time more carefully.

Adjust your schedule

Once you have completed your first study schedule, your job does not end there. You must constantly check your schedule for adjustments. This is best done by trial and error.

After you have tried to work according to your schedule, you will be able to tell if this schedule fits your needs or not. You will be able to tell if you need more time for study in a particular subject, or less time in another.

Do not be afraid to revise your schedule. It will probably take you some time to develop a schedule that fits all your needs—academic, social, and others. Just remember that the effort required to finalize your schedule will be worth it.

Finally, keep in mind that it is not necessary to devote your every waking hour to study to make a good study schedule. Remember, it is the *quality* of hours you spend on study that is important and not the *quantity*.

3. Where should you study?

After you have found any weak spots in your study schedule, and have made the necessary adjustments, make extra copies of your schedule. Post copies on the wall over your study desk and on the inside cover of your notebook. Be determined and consistent in following your study plan. The best plan will do no good if it is ignored.

Surroundings can make a difference

Developing and following an efficient plan is an important part of your overall study program. But it is not the only part. The best study schedule can be made less effective if your physical surroundings are not good.

There are many distractors around you. These must be eliminated if you are to focus your attention on studying. *Studying demands active participation.* Therefore, it is important that you remove everything which competes with studying.

Many students claim that they can work effectively while sprawled out on a couch, listening to the stereo or television, or munching on potato chips and other "goodies." Studies have shown that all of these things detract from careful concentration. You can in fact study with such background distractions. But your study will be both less efficient and less effective.

The requirements for study surroundings will be different for each student. But there are some general guidelines that would apply to everyone. Following these guidelines will help you to create the kind of physical surroundings that will give you a good atmosphere for study.

Study in the same place or room. You should set aside a particular place as your study area. And you should *always* use that place for serious study sessions. The place could be a corner of your bedroom, a den, or, if space permits, a separate room which is intended only for work, study, and concentration. This must not be the place to have a television set, or your stereo outfit, or to set up your hobby. It must not become a recreational area.

You should feel that while you are in this area you will not be distracted until you have completed your studies as scheduled. You must build a "mind-set" for study in this particular room. No visitors, no phone calls, and no other distractions until you have finished your study task.

In addition, be sure that the place you choose is away from normal traffic patterns. For example, it would be a mistake to locate your study area in a place other members of your family would have to cross to get to the bathroom. It would also be a good idea to choose a room with a door that could be closed if necessary.

Have a permanent work surface. Does the work surface allow for good posture? Does it have adequate top surface? How about sufficient storage space? Is it placed to reduce distractions? These are some of the questions you must ask yourself about the work surface you use for study.

Your work surface should be at a height that will permit you a comfortable upright posture with your feet touching the floor. The chair should not be a recliner or lounger. Studying is not done in a horizontal position. Can you reach all of your materials on your desk from your chair? The chair should also provide your lower back and shoulders with support. Improper support will lead to tension and fatigue. And tension and fatigue will distract you.

Your work surface should be large enough to allow you to spread out your notebook, books, and other needed materials. All of your materials should be within easy reach. You will not be able to concentrate if you must constantly leave your work area to get study materials.

Clean your work area before you begin to study. Remove all knickknacks, objects that might steal your attention, and papers and books not related to your study needs. The fewer items you have available to tempt you, the better the opportunity for concentration.

Your work surface should be placed against a wall. There is much less chance for distraction if you face a wall while studying. It is also helpful if there is a window nearby for sunlight and fresh air.

Provide for room comfort. There are certain environmental factors that must be taken into consideration. Good air circulation is desirable. Improper circulation of air will cause lack of oxygen. Lack of sufficient oxygen will reduce both your mental and physical alertness. And you must be mentally and physically alert for maximum learning efficiency.

Room temperature also affects learning. The proper temperature for your study area should not exceed about 70°F (about 21°C). This temperature is ideal for peak mental and physical alertness. A relative humidity of about 50% is also desirable.

Provide needed study tools. The furnishings in your work area should include all the materials and equipment you need for unbroken study. These study materials should be available in your desk drawers, on nearby shelves, or on a bookcase.

A dictionary is a must. You cannot turn in class assignments with misspelled words. A thesaurus is also a good reference book to have available. Other supplies needed include paper, pen and pencils, erasers, stapler, scissors, Scotch tape, paper clips, rubber bands, gummed ring reinforcements, and so forth. If you type, a typewriter is an invaluable tool.

If these materials are not within your reach when you want them, you will break your concentration by leaving your learning atmosphere to search for these materials. You may also be side-tracked and not get back to work until much later, or not at all.

Provide for proper lighting. Always provide plenty of light. Insufficient light and glare from desk tops and papers can produce eye fatigue. Eye fatigue reduces learning efficiency. Good lighting decreases the tension developed during reading. But be careful not to have excessively bright lights. Lights that are too bright can reduce reading speed.

Some final comments

Use of these guidelines should help you to work faster, feel alert, and make better study decisions. And it should also be pointed out that it is difficult to concentrate when you are hungry, sleepy, or run-down. Therefore, to maintain good concentration, you should eat three regular, well-balanced meals a day, and get proper amounts of sleep. When these health habits become a regular routine, you will find that your thinking power will be at full power for efficient study and learning.

4. How should you study?

There are different ways to study

What does the word *study* mean to you? What do you do when you study? Study is a word you use and a thing you do every day. Yet you probably have never thought about what study means and is.

Most students do not know how to study. Many students think studying means sitting down with a book and plowing through it until a lesson is completed. Is reading a chapter or a lesson study? Research shows that it is not. This research proves that the average student learns less than half of the information he or she needs through simple reading of a lesson.

What, then, is an efficient method for studying? This section will show you that there are many different ways of studying. And the section will show you that there are different ways to study different subjects.

The textbook—an aid to studying

Textbooks are the instructional tool you use the most. They include definite aids to point out to you what is important and what you should learn.

Textbooks are usually organized so that the main ideas are placed at the beginning of each chapter or section. Textbook authors often outline the major headings at the beginning of each section. Major points are usually centered and minor points are sometimes indicated. Sometimes these headings are numbered.

Topic and summary sentences are often used in textbooks. Topic sentences at the beginning of a paragraph give the central idea of the paragraph. Summary sentences at the end of the paragraph wrap-up the important idea and refer you back to the topic sentence. Textbooks usually also include some or all of the following aids to learning:

1. *Pictures, charts, diagrams, and maps.* These are included to give clearer meaning to materials in the chapter. The authors use them to visually reinforce important ideas.

2. *Important ideas or words printed in italics or boldface type.* An important statement or word may be printed in *italics.* Usually definitions are printed in *italics* or in **boldface** type. The authors do not use italics or boldface often. When they do, they are telling you that some word or statement is especially important.

3. *Important subpoints in outline form.* Authors will often list important points in outline form.

4. *Use of explanatory footnotes.* Sometimes authors will use footnotes to give greater meaning to materials included in a chapter or section. Footnotes should be read carefully.

Several research studies have been done to help students learn how to study more efficiently. One of these studies resulted in a method for study that has been used successfully by many students. This method is called the SQ3R method. The letters and number stand for the steps that a student follows while using higher-level study skill methods. The term means the following:

One method for learning

1. *Survey.* If your assignment is to read a chapter, first survey it by reading the headings. Authors write textbooks from a well-organized outline. The main points of their outline are usually used as headings in the book. Headings are important clues to the contents of a chapter. In addition, if a summary is available, read this as part of your survey of a chapter. A survey of the headings and summary will give you most of the important ideas in a chapter.

2. *Question.* After reading the headings of the chapter, turn these headings into questions. Questions will help you learn because they will make you think about what it is that you are studying. Now you have a purpose for your learning. This technique may be difficult for you if you have not done it in the past. But with practice you will find that it will grow easier to ask yourself questions. Some authors of textbooks will begin each chapter with a list of questions to be answered in the body of the chapter. Use these questions. Others will include questions at the end of the chapter. In either case, remember that the use of questions will help you to study.

3. *Read.* Now read to answer your questions. Read *aggressively* to answer your questions. Challenge yourself to make sure that you understand what you are reading. Read everything including charts, graphs, activities, appendixes, and picture captions. Remember that everything in a textbook has some purpose. Be thorough in your reading.

4. *Recite.* After you read a section, stop and repeat aloud the major ideas under that particular section. Do this without looking at the book. Answer the questions that you raised about the section, answer these questions in your own words, and give an example. If you succeed, then go on to the next section. But if you fail, then go over the section again. As you recite, you may want to write on a sheet of paper in outline form the ideas you have learned. When you are ready for the next section, turn the heading into *questions*, *read* to answer the questions, then look away from the book and *recite* the answer to the questions. Continue this procedure until you have completed the entire chapter or lesson.

5. *Review.* The final step of the SQ3R method is to *review*. Survey what you have read. Skim over the headings of the chapter, ask yourself what they mean, and what information they contain. Recite the important ideas under each heading. Reread if necessary to be sure that you have answered the questions *without* looking at the textbook. Remember to also review relevant class notes at this time. Reviewing is not something that you should do only at the end of a chapter or before taking an examination. It should take place immediately after you have completed the first 4 steps in the SQ3R method. And it is something you must do consistently throughout the school year.

Using the SQ3R method, you should be able to read faster, pick out important points in your reading, and fix these points in your memory. Also, examination questions will seem familiar because headings turned into questions are usually the points teachers emphasize.

At first, the use of the SQ3R method may be difficult. It requires practice. But the results are worth it.

The teacher—an aid to studying

Your teachers are important aids to learning. Listen carefully and take good notes during class. Teachers will usually present several important ideas during a class period. These important ideas often amplify what is found in textbooks.

Sometimes additional important ideas are presented. Whatever the case, classroom presentations are a valuable aid to learning about the type of information that may appear on examinations. Other teacher aids to look for are the following:

1. The use of lead-in statements such as "This is important," "Remember this," "I'd like to emphasize."
2. The use of the chalkboard, charts, and other visual aids. Preparation of such aids takes time and thought. Teachers use such things to give greater emphasis to important ideas.

When presenting a lecture, a teacher must make good use of the limited time available. Therefore, when planning a lecture, a teacher will usually choose to present important materials that are not easily available to the student, and to give further explanation of important points that are to be found in the textbook. This makes your ability to listen to and learn from classroom lectures very important. What follows are some guidelines that will help you work efficiently in the classroom lecture situation.

1. *Listen aggressively.* Concentrate on your teacher's lecture. What are the major points? As you listen, decide quickly what is important. Record this in your notebook. Be so alert that you are aware of nothing else but your teacher's words.
2. *Sit in the front or center of the classroom.* Sitting in the back of the room or near a door or window will hurt your concentration. Too many distractions may occur. The result will be that you will not hear what your teacher is saying. Sitting in the front or center of the room will enable you to not only hear better, but also be able to clearly see materials placed on the blackboard.
3. *Avoid emotional reactions that might block learning.* Good listeners are aware of this problem. Poor listeners will tune the teacher off the moment they hear an idea with which they do not agree. The aggressive listener concentrates on what is being said and writes his or her notes.
4. *Listen for cues that indicate important ideas.* Writing down every word your teacher says is time-consuming and clutters up your notes with insignificant details. Listen carefully for cues that indicate important ideas. Did the teacher use a voice inflection to make a point

stand out? Did the teacher use a topic sentence, and a summary statement? Did the teacher indicate a number of important subpoints by cue statements such as "the three reasons," "a list of five," or repeat a particular statement, or state, "Listen carefully to this point"? All of these cues will help you in recording important ideas in your notes.

5. *Be ready to ask questions.* Sometimes your teacher will plan for a discussion period. This is the time to ask questions that will help you to clear up anything you missed in the lecture.

6. *Use lined note paper in a loose-leaf binder as your notebook.* The loose-leaf binder allows for flexibility. Notes on outside readings may be placed near the lecture notes. If there is the need for additional pages, these can be inserted.

7. *Study your assignment before the lecture.* At the conclusion of a lecture, your teacher will probably announce the topic for the next lecture. Study the related textbook materials *before* the lecture. This will enable you to have a mental picture of the ideas to be presented by your teacher. The lecture will become more meaningful, and you will also have another aid in obtaining the best notes.

8. *Develop your own shorthand.* Some teachers speak rapidly, or do not pause to give you an opportunity to write careful notes. Therefore, it is essential that you develop your own system of shorthand. For example, skip unnecessary words and do not worry about grammar. Drop suffixes like -*tion* and -*ing*. Abbreviate words whenever possible.

9. *Learn to take notes in outline form.* You cannot take down every word your teacher says. Therefore, you must learn how to prepare an outline. As you listen, your notes should include only the *important* ideas. Good notes are an outline and not a word for word record of a lecture.

10. *Write down examples given in the lecture.* Your teacher will probably use examples to clarify particular points. Include the examples in your notes. They will help you to a greater understanding of the main idea.

11. *Review your lecture notes.* Most notes need editing to put them into the most useful form. Well-organized notes will improve your retention of these materials. Notes should be reviewed and reorganized the *same day* they are taken.

Each subject you take in school has *different kinds* of things you have to learn. Because of this, you must approach the study of each subject in a slightly different way. What follows are some suggestions for the most efficient way to study various subjects.

Foreign languages. The study of a foreign language can be difficult. This is especially true if you are not interested. Examine your reasons for taking a foreign language. Although there may not be an immediate goal other than fulfilling a requirement, knowledge of the language may be useful in the future.

A thorough understanding of English grammar is important to success in the study of a foreign language. There are certain grammatical terms that you must know. Usually the teacher will identify these terms. If you are not familiar with them, then look them up in an English grammar book or dictionary.

Reading through a lesson without stopping to translate each new word will help you to learn the general meaning of the selection. Reread the selection to fix the general meaning in your mind. Also, review the previous lesson to increase your ability to remember new vocabulary words and new verb forms.

Self-recitation practice of new vocabulary words and conjugation of verbs is invaluable. Use 3" by 5" cards with foreign words on one side and English equivalents on the other for drill. As you master a word, delete it from your "active" set of cards and add it to a "review" set. This procedure will leave you with a manageable set of "active" cards. Remember to study your "review" set periodically.

Phonograph records and tapes will help you to learn the language. Reading a foreign newspaper and conversational practice with other students will also strengthen your knowledge and ability to use a foreign language.

Mathematics and science. Mathematics and science, like foreign languages, must be studied daily. They are cumulative subjects. What you learn today will be needed if you are to understand tomorrow's lesson.

For example, if you have not learned the simple arithmetic processes taught in the early grades, then you will have great difficulty in advanced mathematics. Ask your instructor to give you self-review tests for arithmetic fundamentals and science fundamentals. Find your weaknesses and concentrate on drill work.

Read ahead before classtime. Then you will be able to tell what in the classwork is repeated from the textbook, and what is in addition to the textbook. This procedure will enable you to decide what notes to take during classtime.

Solving a mathematics problem can be difficult. First, you should carefully *read* the problem *twice* to determine what things are given, what principles and relationships are stated or implied, and what it is to be found or proven. Write down the essentials before you set the problem up. Concentrate on analyzing the problem rather than hurrying into the computation. Sometimes you can draw a diagram which will give you a better picture of the facts, principles, and relationships. Now apply your computational skills. Estimating your answer before you do your computation can be helpful. But be sure to check your answer.

To study for an examination, keep up with your daily work and review your mathematics and science notes periodically. Ask your instructor for assistance if you have difficulty with particular problems. Record important formulas and principles on notecards. Use these cards for recitation and drill.

After an examination, rework the problems in which you made mistakes. This is a valuable learning experience.

English grammar and composition. There are many self-help texts available in local bookstores. Check yourself on grammar, capitalization, punctuation, and sentence structure by taking the tests in a self-help text. After you have scored the tests and know your errors, do the following:

1. Study the rules.
2. Correct your errors.
3. Practice using the correct form daily.
4. When in doubt use an English grammar handbook.

Spelling is a problem for many students. Most common misspellings are words called "spelling demons." Learning these words is a sure way to improve your spelling ability. Again, you should obtain a self-help text for spelling. Such a text will include a list of commonly misspelled words.

Fill-out some of the spelling tests. Correct your tests. If you have errors, do the following:

1. Visualize each misspelled word in every detail.
2. Spell each word aloud.
3. Write each word out.
4. Check for difficult spots in each word.

Finally, words are sometimes misspelled because they are mispronounced. Always check words you are not sure of for the correct pronunciation.

In English composition there are guidelines that will help you to improve your writing. They are:

1. Define your central theme clearly.
2. Develop an outline and follow it.
3. Keep in mind the principles of good composition (unity, coherence, emphasis, and adequate development).
4. Be concise.
5. Proofread your finished paper.
6. Do not be afraid to make revisions.

Most importantly, be yourself when you write. Do not try to imitate someone else's style of writing. If you are unsure of punctuation, grammar, or spelling, refer to an English composition book and a dictionary. These should be available to you at all times.

Social studies. Reading a social studies book requires certain study skills. First, try to visualize what is on each printed page. There are often many pictures, maps, charts, and graphs. These will help you to "see" what the author is writing about.

Second, the social studies use a whole new set of terminology. Learn these new words. Such words are often printed in italics or boldface type. A glossary is usually included at the end of each chapter. It should be studied carefully.

Third, be sure to do the activities and the exercises at the end of each chapter. These permit you to test yourself and see if you can apply the social studies' concepts that were taught in each chapter.

5. How can you pass tests?

There is no way out

Tests...tests...tests. As someone said, "Tests will be as inescapable to you as death and taxes." But there is no need for you to be frightened of taking a test. Ask yourself the following questions before a test: Did I prepare a study schedule and follow it? Did I provide for the best physical atmosphere for study? Did I use the SQ3R approach to study? Did I listen intently to the lectures? Did I take good notes? Did I organize and review my lecture and reading notes? If you are able to answer "Yes!" to these questions, then you should have little to worry about.

However, no matter how well you do, you might wish to do even better. If so, this section is for you. The following suggestions will help you to do a better job when taking examinations. These suggestions will make you "test-wise."

Getting ready

As in the story of the race between the tortoise and the hare, preparation for good test performance demands regular study rather than an ambitious sprint at the end of the race. To delay studying until right before an examination is foolhardy.

According to many people, cramming is beneficial. But most experts state that cramming is the poorest way to study. And some believe that cramming is actually bad for a number of reasons.

Cramming can cause tension and anxiety to block learning. Also, the facts you cram the night before a test will be forgotten as soon as the examination is over.

Furthermore, crammed facts are learned out of context. They will have little or no relationship to an understanding of important concepts. You will not be getting full value out of the subject. Last-minute preparation will not give you the confidence that you will need to take a test. Cramming will mean that your planned schedule for a particular night will be disrupted.

You will do better in examinations if you keep up with your work and review your reading and lecture notes *regularly*. And the best way to remove anxiety about examinations is to know your subject *thoroughly*. Not only is preparation important, but so is remaining cool at all times. These guidelines should help you to calmly prepare for an examination. Study them carefully.

1. *Try to learn your teacher's test-making habits.* Some teachers give objective tests while others prefer essay tests. And some teachers will give both objective and essay questions on the same examination. Usually your teacher will tell you which type of examination you will be given. Memorization of facts, dates, and names is required for objective examinations, while for essay examinations you will need to study general concepts and theories.

2. *Review what you do not know.* Time is important to you. What you know well need not be included in your review. Study only those things you should know better, or you do not know at all.

3. *Organize your notes from various sources.* Your notes from lectures, reading, and discussions should be organized so that information about each topic is in the same section of your notebook. Remember, *recitation* of the information to yourself from memory is an important study skill. Practice reciting to yourself until you have mastered the information.

4. *Construct sample questions.* You will have had experience with this procedure as you change the major headings in your textbook to questions. Now take the information that you have mastered and construct questions that you think your teacher might ask. You will be surprised at the number of questions that you have asked yourself that will be found on the actual examination.

5. *Study with two or three other students.* This procedure can be very helpful or it can be a complete waste of your time. Plan to work with students who you know have carefully planned their study and are ready to take the examination. This study session should take place about a week before the examination so that if there are any questions that need further study on your part, you will have the necessary time available.

Above all, avoid turning this into a social situation.

6. *Develop a good attitude about taking examinations.* Think positively about examinations. They are given to help you judge your progress in a particular subject. Having a positive frame of mind will help you to work at top efficiency when taking an examination. And this will usually mean a good grade.

7. *Be prepared physically.* It is important for you to be in good physical condition when you take a test. Your mind will not function at its best if your body is not in good physical shape. You should have enough sleep the night before the test. And you should start the day of the test with a good breakfast.

8. *Be confident.* If you have studied and are well-prepared for a test, you will have confidence in your ability to do well. Lack of self-confidence can cause you to be nervous, and will hurt your efforts to do well.

9. *Have the necessary test materials.* Be sure to bring all the materials you will need to take the test. These would include such things as paper, pencils, eraser, and any other materials your teacher instructs you to bring. Have two or three pencils so as to avoid wasting time if a pencil point breaks.

10. *Arrive a few minutes early.* If you arrive a few minutes early, you will be able to get seated comfortably, and you will not waste testing time getting settled. This is important, especially if you will be taking a timed test.

11. *Above all, relax.* If you *know* you have prepared well for an examination, then do not worry. If for some reason you cannot avoid worrying, then take several deep breaths. This will help you to relax.

Face to face with the examination

The time has come for your teacher to pass out the examination. Now is the time when panic can set in. Again, remind yourself that you are prepared. Take the attitude, "I can beat the test!" There is nothing like having a winner's attitude. As you study the examination, keep these points in mind:

1. *Follow directions exactly as given.* Read the directions carefully, not once but *twice.* Be sure you understand all the directions *before* you begin. If you do not understand something, raise your hand and ask about it. Students often fail tests because they do not follow directions. Do not let that happen to you.

2. *Skim through the test.* Before you actually begin taking

236

the test, skim through it to see how long it is and how many parts it has. This overview will give you some idea of the character, scope, and difficulty of the test.

3. *Budget your time.* Make a 30-second survey of the examination to determine how much time will be needed for each essay question or for each section of the objective test. Once you have determined the amount of time, pace yourself accordingly. For example, if an essay question counts for 20 points out of 100, then 1/5 of the examination time should be given to writing the answer to this question. You should remember, however, to cut this time down so that there will be time at the end of the hour to go back and re-read your answer in order to make corrections and additions. Above all, whether it is an objective or essay test, *answer the easy questions first.* Then, return to those questions which you are not sure of. If it is a lengthy test, and time is extremely important, it is best to make a guess on any question you are not sure of and continue on to another question. Put some notation by test items that could use further consideration, or items which you must skip for the time being. However, avoid skipping too many times. It takes time to read the test items over again. Answer all questions when there is no special penalty for wrong answers. Taking a chance can result in getting a higher score.

4. *Check your answers.* If time permits, check *all* of your answers. Do not be afraid to change an answer if you think it is incorrect. Studies have shown that you generally increase your score when you make *thoughtful* changes.

Different kinds of tests require you to take different kinds of approaches. Each kind of test will present you with special problems. And each kind of test has certain key features that can help you to do better, if you recognize these key features. What follows is a description of the more common kinds of tests you will take, and a discussion of what some of the key features of each kind of test are.

Each kind of test is different

The objective test. Objective tests require either short answers or a choice of the best answer from answers that are provided. Usually these tests examine your knowledge of factual information. This type of test is popular because it can cover a large body of information in a small area of space. The test may also be graded quickly and easily. Objective tests may include any or all of the following kinds of questions: multiple choice; true and false; completion; classification; matching; and rearrangement. Some general guidelines to follow which may be helpful to you when taking objective tests are:

1. *Read each question carefully.* Make sure you read the entire question carefully. Pay special attention to the specific details. Sometimes in your haste to complete a test, you may overlook an important detail in a question.

2. *Re-word any statement you do not understand for clearer understanding.* If you come across a statement that you do not understand, try changing the wording. It may help you to arrive at the right answer.

3. *If there is no penalty for wrong answers, guess.* Check the directions to determine if you will be penalized for wrong answers or if only correct answers will be counted. If there is no penalty for wrong answers, guess. Otherwise, answer only the questions you are sure of.

4. *Answer easy questions first.* Bypass difficult questions and come back to them later. Watch your time so that you do not spend too much time on any particular question. Plan enough time to make an "educated guess" for questions that you are not sure of, *and* enough time to check your answers.

5. *Your original answer may be the best answer.* Do not change the original answer unless you are absolutely sure that it is incorrect. Your first choice is more likely to be correct. It is a good rule not to make changes in your answers *on impulse*, although carefully considered changes usually will help you to improve your score. Be cautious when changing anything.

6. *Check for mechanical errors.* Always check your answers to be sure you did not make any mechanical errors. Did you record the correct number or letter for your answer? For example, for a given question you might decide that "a" is the correct response, but accidentally you record "d" as the answer. Also make sure that each answer corresponds to the right question.

7. *Check the order of answers in rearrangement questions.* Check the directions for each test item to know exactly what the item wants you to do. This is especially crucial in test items which ask you to arrange facts or dates in order of importance or in chronological order.

8. *Mark computerized or machine scored tests properly.* More and more computerized or machine scored tests

are being used. These kinds of tests require special precautions. You should be sure that you are using the right kind of pencil. The wrong kind of pencil will not permit the machine to score your test. Usually your teacher will provide the special pencils. With machine-scored tests it is important that you make a dark, heavy mark. Erasures should be *clean.* Failure to mark or erase your test items properly will result in errors in scoring. You should also avoid making unnecessary marks on your test paper when taking a machine-scored test.

9. *Watch for traps.* "Trick" questions are sometimes used to keep you on your toes. Although you may consider them "traps," they are necessary to challenge you. In reality, most are simple questions, and if you are alert you will answer them correctly.

Some of the more common kinds of objective tests contain certain clues that will help you to work with them more successfully. What follows are some hints that will increase your chances of passing certain kinds of objective tests.

1. *Completion tests.* Sentence completion items are test items which require you to fill in an answer of either one word or a short phrase.

   Example: The name of the largest planet is _____.

   Hints: Read each question carefully for any cues that may be contained in the question. For example, sometimes the author of the test will provide blanks for each question equal to the number of words needed to complete the test item.

   Check the word that is found immediately before the blank(s). If the word is "a," the first word you fill in the blank(s) should begin with a consonant. If the word is "an," the first word you fill in the blank(s) should begin with a vowel.

2. *True/false tests.* These tests contain items that require you to decide if the given statements are true or false. Each question must be true in every sense in order to be correct, or it is false.

   Example: T F 1. The dinosaur is a prehistoric animal.

   T F 2. Man lived during the period of the dinosaurs.

Hints: Watch out for words like "always," "never," "no," "every," "all," and "entirely" in true and false items. A statement may appear to be true, but if these words are used and there is an exception to the statement, then the statement is false.

Examine each item for misleading information. Sometimes you might believe a statement to be true because most of the information in the statement is true. But if there are any erroneous facts contained in the statement, then the statement is false.

Try not to read too much into a question. In most cases the instructor is not trying to "trick" you. Apply the statement to what you have learned in lectures or from the textbook.

3. *Matching tests.* These tests usually consist of two columns or series of items. You must "match" one item in column one with another item in column two.

Example:

Column 1	Column 2
___ 1. Edison	A. Composer
___ 2. Chopin	B. Inventor
___ 3. Churchill	C. Statesman

Hints: Answer the questions you are sure of first. Then study the remaining choices for answers to the difficult questions. Be sure to mark out choices as you use them.

The essay test. Essay tests differ from objective tests in that essay tests require you to write in depth about a few questions instead of covering many areas of knowledge with short answers. When answering essay questions you must provide a lot of information in an *organized* manner. As with objective tests, there are guidelines to follow which can help you do well on essay tests.

1. *Read each question, and then follow with a second reading.* First, read *all* of the questions. Then read them a second time to see if any of the questions are related. Answer first the questions that you are best prepared for.

2. *Check the verb portion of each question; that states what you must do.* Understand what is meant by and what is called for in such critical words such as "analyze," "explain," "evaluate," "compare," "contrast," "examine," "list," or "give." Be sure you follow exactly what you are supposed to do. If the teacher asks for a list, then do not

give lengthy coverage of the topic...*only a list.*

3. *Organize your answers well.* Writing down what comes into your head first, and then going on from there can only develop into a poorly written essay. Make a sketchy outline of key words identifying the ideas you wish to cover. Keep in mind that an organized essay answer tends to get the higher grade.

4. *Number the main points in your essay.* Your teacher has to correct many papers. Numbering the main points in your answer will enable your teacher to easily see the organization of your answer. Again, your chances for a good grade are increased.

5. *Elaborate on a point when it is necessary.* Be explicit in your essay. Sometimes it is important to give an illustration or expand on a point to make your answer clearer to the reader. This type of elaboration is not "padding." Irrelevant padding will result in a lower grade.

6. *Answer all questions.* Never leave a question blank. If you run short on time, make sure that you at least write the outline of the main ideas you intended to cover. The outline will show your teacher that you know the answer, but time did not permit you to elaborate. A sketchy answer might receive at least some credit.

7. *Write legibly.* There is nothing more disturbing to a teacher who has many papers to read than poor penmanship. Some instructors will try to read the answers while others will give up in disgust and mark down the illegible paper. Research has shown that papers which are legibly written usually receive at least a passing grade.

8. *Proofread your answers.* Check your answers for good grammar, proper punctuation, and correct spelling. This is necessary for easy reading and understanding of what you are trying to say. Poorly constructed sentences and paragraphs can change the whole meaning of your answer.

Activities

The unit-end activities have been designed to help you to practice and gain the ability to use the various study skills described in this unit. Please do not write in this book, but place your answers on a separate sheet of paper. Where appropriate, answers to the activities can be found in the **Answer Key** that begins on page 290.

Understanding the unit

Review your understanding of important points in this unit by answering the following questions.

1. Why is cramming considered to be a bad study habit?
2. What does research continue to show about how successful students usually work and study?
3. What is the first step toward organizing your time for effective study?
4. Can you name two factors that work against the effective use of study time?
5. Why is it unnecessary to devote every waking hour to study in order to have a good study schedule?
6. Why is it important to eliminate any possible distractors from the area in which you intend to study?
7. What are five important factors you should consider when choosing a place where you should study?
8. Which instructional tool do the majority of students use the most?
9. What are some aids to learning that are usually included in most textbooks?
10. What does SQ3R stand for?
11. How should use of the SQ3R method help you to study more effectively and efficiently?

12. Where should you sit in a classroom in order to get the most out of a lecture situation?
13. What is the most important factor in the study of foreign languages?
14. What is the best way to remove anxiety over the taking of an examination?
15. What are the two different kinds of tests that most teachers use?

Listening skills checklist

The classroom lecture is one of the most important learning situations in which you will participate. It is during the classroom lecture that you will discover what your teacher believes to be the key learnings you must know. Yet many students fail to take classroom lectures seriously. Complete the following checklist, evaluating yourself as honestly as you can. Each incorrect response may indicate a listening skills deficiency that could affect your success in class.

	Yes	No
1. Do I listen aggressively, concentrate on the teacher's words, and stay on the alert for major points?	____	____
2. Do I sit in the back of the room or near a door or window where distractions may occur?	____	____
3. Am I able to avoid emotional reactions to the teacher's statements, reactions that could block learning?	____	____
4. Do I listen for word cues from the teacher that indicate important ideas?	____	____
5. Am I always ready to ask questions when some point of information needs to be clarified?	____	____
6. Do I use lined note paper in a loose-leaf binder as my notebook?	____	____
7. Do I study my assignment before the lecture?	____	____
8. Have I developed my own shorthand to improve note-taking speed?	____	____
9. Do I try to take down every word my teacher says?	____	____
10. Am I careful to write down any examples my teacher may use to clarify points?	____	____
11. Do I carefully review my lecture notes?	____	____

A guide to school activities

What kinds of activities do you enjoy? Do you belong to any school clubs or organizations? Extracurricular activities are an important part of the total educational program for every student. The right amount of participation in an activity or club will help to make you a more well-rounded person.

This unit describes the requirements for participation in various extracurricular activities. It provides information you can use to make a wise choice among various activities. And it gives you some suggestions that will help you to participate in an activity more successfully.

The contributor of this unit is Dominic J. Piane, Instructor, University of Chicago Laboratory Schools, Chicago, Illinois.

1. What can you learn outside your classroom?

Extracurricular activities and education

Your hours at school are filled by classes. Studying often takes up many of the hours you spend away from class. For many students, part-time jobs fill additional hours. And, of course, you want time for social activities.

This means you may have trouble finding time for extracurricular activities. So why should you consider devoting some of your precious time to school activities outside the classroom? And why does your school sponsor and support such activities?

The answers to these questions are simple. Extracurricular activities offer opportunities to practice skills that have been taught in the classroom. Extracurricular activities also offer you a chance to develop new skills. And extracurricular activities can be just plain fun.

Schools support extracurricular programs in order to contribute to their students' education. This makes the extracurricular program a necessary part of a school's educational package. And this makes your participation in extracurricular activities worthwhile.

So extracurricular activities can be an important, useful, and enjoyable part of your education. But what kinds of things can you learn through your participation in extracurricular activities? What kinds of skills can you acquire?

Learning by doing

You can benefit physically, intellectually, and socially from participation in extracurricular activities. For example, you can improve muscular coordination and physical dexterity by playing a sport. You can gain self-discipline by taking part in debate. You can increase self-confidence by acting in a class play. You can experience a spirit of cooperation as part of the school band. And you can learn how to work as part of a group through membership in a club.

Different kinds of activities offer different kinds of benefits. Therefore, the kind of activity you decide to join will be important. And since most extracurricular programs stress "doing," the degree to which you actively participate will be crucial.

The opportunity to learn by doing is perhaps the single most important benefit you can get through participation. Much of the "learning" that you derive from your formal educational experience is abstract. That is, you are dealing with concepts and ideas that often seem unrelated to the "real world." Often, you have little chance to test the usefulness of what you learn in school. And because you cannot test and apply these concepts and ideas, you really do not understand them.

But in extracurricular situations this is not always the case. Extracurricular activities usually *do* give you the opportunity to test, to apply, to discover if various concepts and ideas work in practice.

For example, you may not understand the process by which government officials in the United States are elected simply by reading a political science textbook. However, actually organizing and then carrying through a campaign for election to a club office will give you insights that cannot possibly be gained through a textbook or a classroom lecture.

Your practical application of concepts and ideas will help you achieve a fuller understanding of them. And putting these concepts and ideas into practice will help you retain such understanding.

Extracurricular activities help you learn things that cannot be learned within the regular curriculum. Quite often, the content of such activities will provide you with an opportunity to supplement, or extend in-depth, content that is only touched upon in the classroom.

Different kinds of learnings

At this stage of your educational experience, you are being exposed to a lot of basic information in a very short period of time. This information is presented to you with very little regard for your personal likes, dislikes, and aptitudes.

This is probably as it should be. Your school's job is to give you a foundation of basic knowledge upon which you will be able to build. This foundation of knowledge is so broad that there is not the time available to provide you with many choices as to what you will study and should learn.

This is where extracurricular activities can meet an important need. Here are some guidelines for participation in extracurricular activities.

1. Pick and choose from among those activities that will supplement classroom learning. Try to gain from an extracurricular activity a deeper understanding of the subjects you encounter in the classroom.
2. Get involved in activities for which you have some particular aptitude or interest that can be more fully developed.
3. Use your participation in extracurricular activities to broaden the range of your personal experiences.

For example, many schools cannot provide broad classroom experiences in the arts. Experiences in drama, music, photography, and other arts usually cannot be obtained in the normal classroom situation.

This means that a student who wants to fully develop an interest or aptitude for the arts and things artistic must go outside the normal classroom situation. The answer to such a student's problem is involvement in some extracurricular activity.

An appreciation of drama can best be gotten through participation in a school play. A photography club will probably teach you more about this art than you can learn in any textbook. And a school band or orchestra is one of the best ways to develop a love for and understanding of music.

So you can see that there are many benefits you can get from an extracurricular activity. Remember that your classroom learnings are the most important part of your total educational experience. The classroom experience is basically the reason you are in school. But a careful choice of extracurricular activities will help to make your classroom learnings more meaningful. Participation in such activities will help make you a more well-rounded person, increase the number of your interests, and sharpen your skills.

Some things you can learn

As was stated earlier, participation in extracurricular activities offer the opportunity to practice skills learned in the classroom and a place to develop new skills. Well-organized and well-run extracurricular activities offer you a base from which you can "reach out," if you want to.

For example, these activities permit you to deal in different ways from the classroom situation with fellow students and with faculty members. Extracurricular activities present you, the student, with situations in which you can express your ideas on an equal footing with other students and, more importantly, with teachers. Thus, participation in extracurricular activities can teach you a variety of skills that will be increasingly useful as you grow up.

However, it is also important to keep in mind that extracurricular activities supplement and extend what you learn in a classroom. For example, participation in a foreign language club can help you with your foreign language classes. Field trips to museums, restaurants, or other communities can help you to understand and appreciate the contributions to contemporary American life various ethnic groups have made.

Membership in the school band, orchestra, or chorus often leads to participation in musical groups outside of school. Many famous professional musicians began their career when they joined a school band.

An ecology or science club can permit you to put into practice knowledge and skills you have learned from a textbook in the classroom. Field trips can help to enhance your social skills.

And there are other benefits that are less obvious. There is no better place for you to meet new people and make new friends. As part of an extracurricular activity you can meet people who have the same interests as you do.

Finally, some activities, such as athletic events, debate tournaments, or band contests, involve competition. This competition will give you the opportunity to experience the discipline needed to prepare for the achievement of a specific, well-defined goal. It can also teach you important lessons about sportsmanship.

Be an asset if you join

You can get a lot out of an extracurricular activity. But you must be ready to contribute your time and effort. Approaching an activity with the proper attitude can mean the difference between success and failure.

Be prepared to do what is required of you. Be at the right place, at the right time, with the right attitude, and ready to work. Be flexible, ready to adjust to changing situations when you have to. Be prepared to accept responsibility and use your initiative if the situation requires. If you decide to participate in an extracurricular activity, keep these things in mind and try to practice them. If you do, then there is no reason why you will not both enjoy yourself and have a valuable learning experience.

2. How should you choose a club or activity?

You will probably choose to join a club or activity that interests you. This will be true even if you have had no experience with the subject of the club or activity.

However, some organizations have special requirements.
For example, to belong to a school orchestra, you must be
able to perform with some skill on a musical instrument.
Depending upon the policy of your school and the type of
program being offered by its music department, junior and
senior high school may be too late for you to join such an
activity.

Some sports programs work in much the same way. Much
of the necessary athletic training may be done at lower
grade levels. By the time you are in senior high, it may be too
late to join.

One solution to this problem is private instruction. But a
word of caution. Private music or sports lessons cost a lot of
money. And such lessons usually take up a lot of time. You
must think carefully and decide if the result is worth the
investment. It would be foolish to spend money and time on
private lessons only to find that the time spent is causing
you to get lower grades. Remember that the time spent practicing is time that must be taken from studying or other
things.

Besides private instruction, another way to get special
training is to take advantage of programs sponsored by local
park districts. Community parks often offer training in various sports or sponsor leagues for various age groups and
levels of skill. Parks may also offer classes in arts and crafts.
Such classes may not be available in your school. Park dis-
trict programs are excellent places to get training you may
lack. Participation in such programs is often encouraged by
school activity directors and teachers alike. In many cases,

school activity directors and your teachers can recommend worthwhile programs. In any case, it would be a good idea to consult with them before you begin your search for a program.

There are also instructional camps specializing in sports or the arts. Qualified instructors and interested students are brought together in these camps for several weeks of intensive training. Some of the large national camps bring both instructors and students from all over the world together. The training you can get at such camps can be very valuable. And the experience of studying with well-known instructors and meeting new people who share your interests can be very exciting.

But, as before, you must be careful of the cost in time and money. Because these camps employ some of the best-known instructors, costs are high. Weigh carefully the costs and benefits. Here again, your school activity director and your teachers can be a source of valuable advice.

There are also many private sports leagues you can join to get training and practice. As in park-sponsored leagues, these private leagues are divided by age group and levels of skill. Such leagues exist for baseball, football, ice hockey, soccer, and other major sports.

Not all extracurricular activities require a background of training. Many programs, sports or arts, start training students at the junior high school level. There is no reason to believe that because you are already in junior high school and have no previous training, you will not be able to join one of these activities. On the contrary, the advanced physical and mental development of an older student often more than compensates for a later start. However, do not wait until the later years in senior high school to decide to join the team or activity you like. By then, it may be too late.

How can you find out what activities are offered by your school? The best way is to visit an open house before the actual school year begins. Many schools hold an open house for parents and students sometime before registration. School-sponsored clubs and activities usually have exhibits and representatives at an open house. You will have the chance to meet the faculty advisers who work with the clubs and activities.

Identifying your activity

An open house is a good time to ask questions about what is offered, how to join, and what the requirements of the various extracurricular activities might be.

The school's activity director is usually a good source of information about the extracurricular program. Besides acting as the coordinator of the program, the activity director often plays an active part in recruiting students for participation in the program.

Another place to seek advice is the school's physical education department. Either the chairperson of that department, or the athletic director if the school has such an official, can help you to make a choice. You may even find one of these people contacting you if they think you might be an asset to one of the school's athletic teams.

If you demonstrate a skill in a class that might be put to use in an activity, the teacher may direct you to that activity. For example, the art teacher might feel a student's interest in photography might be put to good use on the school newspaper. Or the physical education teacher might spot a student's potential for some sport in a physical education class or an intramural program.

However, do not wait to be discovered. If you have an interest, find out who to contact and contact that person.

By the way, do not forget your parents as a helpful source of information. They were your age once. Chances are that they were once faced with making a similar decision. In fact, your parents can be the best source of advice when you make your final decision. They know your interests, skills, and aptitudes better than anyone else does.

Finally, talk to students who are already involved in the extracurricular program. You may already have friends in the activity that interests you. They will tell you what you are getting into, usually in a very candid and straightforward way.

A word of caution. Do not join an activity just because your friends are members. The fact that they like the activity or club does not mean that you will. What is right for them, may not be right for you. You may find that you joined an activity because of a friend, but that the activity itself holds little or no interest for you. This is the sure way to an unsatisfying, unsuccessful experience.

Try a service club

Most schools sponsor several extracurricular organizations that provide services to others. These clubs perform services for the school or the community. Doing things for others can be a very rewarding experience. And many students find service organizations to be the best way to participate in extracurricular activities.

Ecology clubs may clean up school grounds and community parks. Social service clubs may volunteer to help the elderly or to work in local hospitals. Whatever the club and whatever the job, the members of such service clubs benefit both themselves and others.

Student government is a service organization that often draws much participation. The thought of being partly responsible for the operation of the school may appeal to you.

The advantage of service clubs is that their activities will expose you to the same kinds of problems that must be solved by adults in actual work situations. Participation in any service club can be a very educationally rewarding experience.

An important commitment

After you have investigated and evaluated the activities offered, you are ready to make a decision. After you join an activity remember that you have made a commitment and you will be expected to live up to it.

This is more important than you might think. Colleges look closely at an applicant's record of extracurricular participation. And so do prospective employers. That is because this record is a reflection of the applicant's total development.

If you have good grades and are also active in the rest of your school's life, colleges and employers believe that you have a better chance of being successful in a college career or job. Through your involvement you have demonstrated that you are able to make a commitment and stick to it. And you have demonstrated how well-developed you are socially since you must be able to work with others in extracurricular activities.

A problem of time

It is natural for everyone to want to share with others the results of his or her work. It would be disappointing to belong to a drama club that never gave a public performance. Belonging to a football team that only practiced would not be much fun.

In fact, many activities would have little student involvement if it were not for the fact that they gave students the chance to perform for the public.

Such performances, and the practices that must come before, take a lot of the student's time and energy. This investment of time and energy is a necessary part of any program that offers satisfaction to those who participate. Anything worth doing justifies the effort that goes into it.

However, there is a problem. Some students spend so much time on an extracurricular activity that schoolwork begins to suffer. You must keep a balance between study and the activity. You cannot permit yourself to become so involved in an outside activity that your grades drop.

The responsibility for keeping this balance rests entirely with you. Faculty advisers and coaches are often not aware of a student's scholastic difficulties until it is too late. If you begin to experience difficulties, seek help immediately. Go to your faculty advisers for assistance. Your counseling department can also help.

A similar problem results when a student joins more activities than he or she can handle. The opportunities available to students in a good extracurricular program are numerous—possibly too numerous. Students sometimes commit to too many activities.

As was mentioned earlier, most activities, while offering great rewards to those who participate, also make great demands. School plays always rehearse after school or in the evenings. Performances always take place on evenings or weekends. Musical organizations usually perform in the evening. And school bands are often away from school during the school day for such things as parades and concerts. Sports involves both home and away games. While these conflicts present no problem for the student who can handle the work, they can compound problems that may already exist for the weaker student. And when the same student is involved in two or three of these kinds of activities, the result is usually scholastic disaster. Pick and choose carefully from among conflicting activities. Avoid the mistake of overextending yourself.

Participation in too many extracurricular activities is as bad or maybe worse than not participating at all. In fact, the one problem that is as serious as nonparticipation is too much participation.

School administrators are constantly confronted with the problem of excessive time demands placed on students by outside activities. This can become a problem with any activity if you allow activities to become too demanding on you. The hours you spend in a rehearsal, on the practice field, or for any other activity have to be limited. It is your duty to allocate your time properly. And it is wise to involve yourself in only one major activity.

You, as a student, must weigh the benefits gained from an activity against the cost in time and energy. Many times students deceive themselves into thinking there is not much involved in the commitment to activities. After all, extracurricular activities are more pleasant than study. However, if you attend practice for some activity and neglect study because you are too tired when you get home, you are only hurting yourself in the long run. Five minutes of glory on the playing field is not worth that cost.

You probably already set aside special time for study. Why not do the same for time spent on an extracurricular activity? If for any reason you begin to feel that your schoolwork is beginning to suffer because of your participation in an extracurricular activity—drop it!

Schedule your activities

There may be pressures to stay in from a lot of people and for a lot of reasons. But you cannot allow pressures to change your decision. Remember, you are the only person who really knows how much you can or cannot handle. And remember to turn to your counselors and faculty advisers the moment you feel you may be getting into trouble. The faculty members cannot do a thing for you if you do not keep them informed. They are there to help you succeed. If you hide the fact that you are having study problems, you will only fall deeper into trouble.

Some kinds of extracurricular activities require much less time and energy than others. That does not mean such activities are unimportant. Such activities may be just what you are looking for. The stamp club, the radio club, the chess club can give you the benefits of participation while taking a minimum of your time. That is why it is important to investigate the school's activity offerings thoroughly. Only then will you be able to make an intelligent decision about which activity to join.

It is foolish for anyone to try to do something that he or she is not capable of doing. Yet many students join activities that make greater demands than these students are able to fill. The efforts needed to be successful in such an activity is often greater than any benefit that may result.

Stay within your capabilities

This is especially true in sports. Many students get involved in sports that are too physically demanding. The result is these students often invest much energy in the sport at the expense of academic work. They are often crushed when a coach advises them to drop out or cuts them from the team.

Often, too, it is outside pressure that puts a student in this position. Comparison to other family members, whether intended or not, can do great harm. An older sister or father who was a successful athlete does not ensure your success. And it does not mean that you too must try to be a successful athlete. The same applies to other activities. Your brother's musical ability will not necessarily make you a great musician.

By all means, seek and heed the advice of the people close to you. But make the final decision yourself. You know best what your interests and abilities are. You are the one who has to do the work in the end.

A means and not an end

Participation in activities is a means to a well-rounded education. It is "something extra" that can help you develop skills and abilities not covered in the classroom.

However, for some students activities become the goal. And this is a serious mistake. You must keep participation in extracurricular activities in its proper perspective.

For example, you may be successful at an activity in your school. Because of your success, you begin to consider the activity as a lifetime career. There is, of course, nothing wrong with this as long as you do not allow your academic work to suffer because of something that only *might* be true.

You may be a great athlete or a fine singer or an accomplished artist in your school. But that does not ensure success in those fields in the outside world.

You may find that the competition for the few positions available is too stiff. Think of the number of people who want the status and money that goes with success in the three career fields that have been mentioned. Now try to imagine the number of people who actually "make it" in those career fields. You will find that there are very few by comparison.

It is much wiser to use activities for enjoyment or relaxation and concentrate instead on your academic work. The work you do in the classroom is more important by far than anything you may do outside. You are building now for tomorrow. Because of this you must keep your academic work and your extracurricular activities in reasonable balance. The student who makes the wrong choice seriously risks his or her future. But the student who makes the correct choice takes the first step toward a happy and fulfilling life.

3. Do you belong to a club?

To start a club or activity of any kind, you must begin with a group of enthusiastic students. The responsibility for starting and organizing a club should rest with the students who will then belong to the club.

Organizing a club

A faculty adviser should be on hand to help. But he or she should stay in the background as much as possible. The adviser should get actively involved only when he or she is needed. Most of the responsibility for the active management of the club should be left to the students.

So the first requirements for organizing a club or activity are enthusiasm and interest. If enough people are interested and continue to be interested, a successful club or activity can be organized and operated.

Organizations need rules. Without rules, members of an organization would not know what to do or how to do it. Rules show what the purpose of an organization is. And rules tell an organization's members what is expected of them.

The need for rules

A club's rules are its constitution. If you join an extracurricular activity that has been operating for some time, there will probably be a set of rules that you will have to accept. If you join a newly organized activity, or are yourself helping to organize an activity, you may find yourself taking part in making a constitution.

This is not as hard to do as it sounds. And there are some things to remember that will make preparing a constitution even easier.

The first thing to do is to decide who will run the club until a constitution can be prepared. The club's faculty adviser could be a big help in this situation. He or she could act as the temporary presiding officer.

Once this has been taken care of, a committee to write the constitution should be formed. Something to keep in mind here is that the smaller the committee, the faster and with less conflict will be the writing of the constitution.

Different kinds of activities and organizations need different kinds of rules. Depending upon what kind of organization you are forming, you may need some special rules. Your faculty adviser can help you decide what special rules your organization needs.

But besides these special rules, there are some things every constitution must have. These general rules set what the structure and operation of your activity will be.

Your constitution should give the name and explain the purpose of your organization. It should describe what the requirements for membership are. The organization's offices should be listed. And a description of each officer's duties should be given. If there are to be any standing committees, the constitution should list and describe them. The time and place where the organization regularly meets should also appear in the constitution.

Finally, the constitution should provide a method for amendment. This is very important. It is difficult to know what the problems of running an organization will be *before* the organization actually begins to operate. You may find that some parts of your constitution are not fitted to your organization. Or you may discover problems that were not thought of during the planning stage. In either case, there should be some set method for changing or modifying the constitution.

Your faculty adviser can be a great help during preparation of the constitution. Remember, he or she has probably been through this before. And most schools require the faculty adviser's approval of any school-sponsored club's constitution. Keep your faculty adviser informed and involved.

Robert's Rules of Order is another good source of information. This book explains the accepted procedures for the efficient running of an organization. Your committee may decide not to follow the suggestions given in *Robert's Rules*. But the book can help by showing you a model of what correct procedures should be. Your school's library probably has a copy. But if not, there should be a copy in your local public library.

After the constitution has been completed and approved by your faculty adviser, it must be approved by the club. This is usually done by vote at a special meeting of the entire club.

A club's officers organize the club's activities. The officers make sure the club follows its constitution. And the officers run the meetings, making sure the club follows its original purpose.

The club's constitution should provide for a slate-making committee. This committee selects a list of candidates for office from the membership. Nominations for office may also be made by club members at a general meeting. Election to office is usually by secret ballot. Descriptions of the duties of some club officers follow.

The president. The chief officer of the club is the president. The president's duties include managing all meetings both of the general membership and of the executive board. The executive board is a committee made up of the elected officers and the club's faculty adviser. The president is also responsible for preparing an agenda for each meeting. The executive board usually helps to prepare the agenda. The president is also a member of all committees.

The vice-president. This officer is the second-ranking officer of the club. In the absence of the president, the vice-president assumes the president's duties. This office is almost as important as president. So it is important to select a competent person to fill it.

The recording-secretary. The person who holds this position takes the minutes, or notes, at all meetings. The recording-secretary keeps the general records for the entire organization, except for the treasurer's notes.

The corresponding-secretary. This officer is responsible for all of the correspondence of the club. The corresponding-secretary is usually responsible for notifying the members when a meeting is to be held. And the corresponding-secretary takes care of any mailings or notices that have to be sent out. The two secretarial offices are sometimes combined.

The treasurer. This person takes care of all of the organization's money. The duties vary considerably from one organization to another. But this is a difficult job to do in any situation. There is a great deal of responsibility involved in the handling of money. For this reason, great care should be taken in the choice of a person to fill this office. The treasurer's duties include making financial reports to both the executive board and the general membership, the collection of dues and other fees, and the payment of any bills.

It is a good idea for a person who has been elected to this office to spend some time learning how to keep a simple ledger. Here is an example of such a ledger.

Date	Description	Receipts	Disbursements	Balance
10/1	Balance brought forward			$25.50
10/3	Dues	$ 9.00		34.50
10/9	Class gift		$15.00	19.50
10/12	Paper supplies		7.59	11.91
10/17	Paper drive	46.50		58.41
10/24	Refreshments		22.63	35.78
10/28	Candy sale	11.80		47.58
TOTALS		$67.30	$45.22	

Keep a five-column ledger showing *date,* a *description of the transaction, receipts, disbursements,* and *balance.* The description column should list the source of a receipt or the reason for a disbursement. The proper dollar amount should be entered in the appropriate "receipts" or "disbursements" column. This dollar amount is then added to (receipts) or deducted from (disbursements) the previous balance so that there is always a record of the current balance. The receipts and disbursements should be totalled at the bottom of the page at the end of each month, and the balance carried forward to start the new month's ledger sheet. The club's faculty adviser should be notified of all financial transactions. And the monthly ledger sheet should be checked and initialed by the faculty adviser.

At each month's meeting, the treasurer should make a financial report. Here is a simple way to organize a monthly treasurer's report.

```
┌─────────────────────────────────────────────────────────────┐
│                                                               │
│             TREASURER'S REPORT: October                       │
│                                                               │
│   1) Balance brought forward from                             │
│         previous month                                $25.50  │
│                                                               │
│   2) Receipts                                                 │
│         Dues                          $ 9.00                  │
│         Paper drive                    46.50                  │
│         Candy sale                     11.80                  │
│         Total                                          67.30  │
│                                                               │
│   3) Balance after receipts                           $92.80  │
│         (total of 1 & 2)                                      │
│                                                               │
│   4) Disbursements                                            │
│         Class gift                    $15.00                  │
│         Paper supplies                  7.59                  │
│         Refreshments                   22.63                  │
│         Total                                          45.22  │
│                                                               │
│   5) Balance at end of month                          $47.58  │
│         (deduct 4 from 3)                                     │
│                                                               │
└─────────────────────────────────────────────────────────────┘
```

At the end of each year, before a new treasurer takes office, there should be a complete audit of the books by an audit committee. The audit committee should issue a yearly financial report. The treasurer's report for each month and the yearly report should become part of the recording-secretary's notes.

Finally, whenever money is collected, the amount should be entered into the ledger *immediately*! After the tally is checked, the money should be turned over to the faculty adviser for safekeeping. The faculty adviser should count the money again and check the ledger to be sure the two totals agree. After that, the faculty adviser should initial the ledger to show that the figures have been checked and the money has been accepted.

The faculty adviser. While the faculty adviser is not an elected officer, his or her job is as important as any officer's. The faculty adviser should always be informed about what is going on. It is a good idea to have the faculty adviser present at all meetings. He or she should be included in all committee meetings and board meetings. And in some schools, the faculty adviser also has veto power over the decisions of the club membership.

Clubs need a purpose

No matter how well-organized your club is, it will not succeed unless it has a well-defined purpose. When your organization works on revisions of its constitution, it would be a good idea to review the purpose of the organization and check to be sure this purpose is still workable. It is one of the main duties of the faculty adviser and officers to make sure a club sticks to its purpose.

Keep the club's purpose as well as the rest of the constitution as simple and straightforward as possible. Remember, these are the rules your club members wrote and agreed to follow. If purpose and constitution are vague or hard to interpret, the result will be a lack of progress. And if an organization stops showing progress, it will lose members and eventually may fall apart. Officers and members alike must be interested in the progress of the organization. If interest declines, the entire organization will decline.

Tips for successful participation

To have the right to say anything about the administration of an activity, you must actively participate in that activity. You must attend meetings. That is the first requirement. You must let people know your opinion and the reasons for that opinion. Keep informed about what your club is doing or planning to do. Work hard on behalf of the club you join. It is not enough to just be a member. To get the most out of an activity, you must have a positive attitude and you must demonstrate enthusiasm. Do not wait for someone to ask you to participate; volunteer on your own. You will do no good for your club or yourself if you just sit on the sidelines and criticize the performance of others.

Good communication will help you participate more fully in an activity. When you get important information that should be passed on to other club members, jot it down and keep track of it. If, for some reason, you get secondhand information on any important matter, go to the source and check it out. Taking a little time can save a lot of confusion later. Do not be the person responsible for starting or passing a rumor. Ask questions when you are given information. Be sure you have correctly received the information.

Almost all of the functions of an activity depend upon good communication. Too often good ideas fail because of poor communication. Communication should be simple and straightforward. If a piece of communication is to be written, show it to the faculty adviser for his or her approval before you pass it out to the membership. Do not let a good idea fail because you did not get information out quickly enough or because you were unable to get your ideas across in writing.

The ability to write a memorandum or report is important to good communication. Here are a few tips on how to write a clear, understandable memorandum or report.

1. Use everyday language that is easy for everyone to understand.
2. Say what you have to say in as few words as possible.
3. Re-read and re-write as needed.
4. Use your best handwriting or, if possible, use a type-writer.
5. After you have finished, re-read again for mistakes.
6. Show the memorandum or report to your faculty adviser for his or her approval.

The better you are able to communicate your ideas, the more fully you will be able to participate in any extracurricular activity.

Holding a business meeting

For many people, the most boring part of an activity is the holding of business meetings. While the purpose of an activity, be it photography, stamps, chess, and so forth is the main reason people have decided to form or join a club, business meetings are a necessary evil. Financial matters are arranged and policy decisions are made at business meetings. The activity itself must usually wait until the business meeting has been completed.

All of the advice given in this section pays off only if the club holds efficient business meetings. Meetings that have no direction waste time. Such meetings will cause members to become bored and to lose interest. What follows are some suggestions that will help you hold fast and efficient meetings.

Call the meeting to order. The minutes of the previous meeting are then read by the recording-secretary. At this time any corrections that have to be made in the minutes are recorded. The corresponding-secretary's report is the next order of business, followed by the treasurer's report.

After these reports have been given, any old business left unfinished from previous meetings is discussed. There should be specific items listed in the agenda under old business. After the old business has been completed, the meeting should consider new business. Here also, there should be specific items listed in the agenda. Any items not on the agenda that the general membership wishes to bring up at the meeting should be discussed under new business. After discussion of new business, the meeting is adjourned.

Each item listed on the agenda should be given a specific time limit. Meetings have a way of getting out of control if speakers are allowed to go on and on with any single item on the agenda.

The president should have prepared notes to help him or her keep the purpose of the meeting clear. He or she should begin the meeting on time, control the amount of time spent on any single item, and end the meeting on time.

The president should avoid dominating any discussion. Instead, he or she should guide and aid discussions. The president must recognize people before they can speak. In that way the president controls the time used by each speaker. The president must stop any speaker who begins to dominate a discussion, and must make sure that everyone has a chance to speak.

The president should try to get opinions from as many different points-of-view on an issue as possible. But he or she should remain impartial. The president has to encourage participation at meetings. The quickest way to discourage participation is for the president to take a stand on an issue before it has been fully discussed.

Making a club work   What do you need to have a successful organization? The organization must have a worthwhile purpose, clearly stated in the constitution. The constitution must be well-written. And you and other members must be willing to follow it. If the constitution needs to be changed, do not hesitate to change it.

In addition to a well-written constitution and a well-defined purpose, you must have sound leadership. The leaders must be able to carry out the duties of their offices to the letter of the constitution. Clear, accurate record keeping is important. This would include committee reports, financial records, and the records kept by the corresponding-secretary and the recording-secretary.

The program that the organization is offering to the students must stimulate membership. The membership must feel a sense of direction and progress toward specific goals. Stimulating events and programs should be offered.

Activity

The unit-end activity has been designed to help you to retain and put into practice some of the suggestions discussed in this unit. Please do not write in this book, but place your answers on a separate sheet of paper. Answers to the activity can be found in the **Answer Key** that begins on page 290.

Participation checklist
Check your level of participation in extracurricular activities by answering the following questions. An incorrect answer may indicate a deficiency that could limit the effectiveness of your participation in extracurricular activities.

1. Do you try to get information about the activities and goals of an organization before you decide if you will join it?
2. Do you make an effort to take part in the leadership of an organization after you join it?
3. Do you make an effort to understand the "other side" of issues that come before your organization?
4. Are you able to communicate your position on issues that come before your organization?
5. Do you volunteer to do various jobs?
6. Are you able to keep the purpose of your membership in mind?
7. Have you learned to delegate authority?
8. Do you depend on your organization's faculty adviser for help with difficult situations?
9. Are you selective about the number of activities in which you try to participate?
10. Do you avoid making unrealistic commitments to organizations?

A guide to
your future

What are you going to do when you get out of school? Have you chosen a career area in which you would like to work? Too many people do not make a conscious decision to enter a specific career. Instead, they drift into a career that leaves them unhappy and unfulfilled.

    This unit presents some guidelines you can use to help you make a well-informed career decision. It discusses the important features of many occupations. And it tells you what sources to go to for additional career information.

The contributor of this unit is Dr. Jerry J. Anderson, Instructor and Student Council Advisor, Oak Park and River Forest High School, Oak Park, Illinois.

1. What are you going to do?

Plan ahead

An intelligent career choice does not come about without planning. Choosing a career is a very difficult and important thing to do. If your choice is suited to your ability and personal needs, the possibility of your having a happy and rewarding life will be much greater. So you can see that it is most important not to leave this choice to chance.

There is no simple answer to the question as to when you should choose a career. But school counselors agree that by the time you are a freshman in high school you should begin to have some idea of your general career interests. Your high school program should, to a large degree, prepare you to follow up on those interests.

But this does not mean that you must make a definite choice of occupation sometime during your high school career. This is not so. But you should at least have some idea of general career interests and should be planning to follow up on those interests.

Choosing a career interest

The task of choosing a career can be simplified by following three basic steps:

1. Determine your abilities, your aptitudes, your interests, your personality characteristics, and your general physical condition.
2. Study occupations to determine their requirements, duties, and other significant characteristics.
3. Based upon the results of 1. and 2., try to match yourself with an occupation.

Be aware that the three steps outlined are an over-simplification of the process of vocational choice. The making of a career choice does not just happen all of a sudden.

Instead, it is the result of a series of decisions made over many years. It is the total impact of these decisions that largely determines final career choice.

Guidance counselors generally identify three periods of decision making:

1. The period of fantasy, before 11 years of age, when you believe you can be anything you wish.
2. The stage of tentative choices, between 11 and 17 years of age, when your choices are made largely on the basis of interests.
3. The realistic period, 17 years of age to young adulthood, when you come face to face with reality, and begin to finalize your choice.

As you begin to take a realistic view of the world, you will see that no field can give you everything you want. You will begin to understand that your final career choice will be a compromise choice. You will probably pick a career in which you will be able to make as much as possible of your interests and abilities while satisfying as many of your values and goals as possible.

While there is no definite list of "do's" and "don'ts" in making a choice of occupations, here are five steps you should do *before* you make a final decision.

A choice of occupations

1. Study any occupational choice from every angle. Learn all that you can by reading everything you can find on the occupation that interests you and do this *before* you start any formal training for your chosen occupation.
2. Make a checklist of your social, psychological, and financial needs. Then decide if a particular occupation measures up to your personal needs in all areas. How close does it come? You may have several choices. Which choice comes closest to meeting your needs?
3. Choose from occupations which you will enjoy and which you are psychologically suited to handle. These are important criteria in the decision-making process. It is very unlikely that you will succeed in an occupation that does not meet these criteria. Take advantage of psychological aptitude tests that are available. In the hands of a qualified counselor, such tests can be invaluable in helping you to make an occupational choice.
4. Find out if there are special physical, mental, or emotional qualifications necessary for success in the occupation of your choice.

5. Discuss your career plans with several people already established in the occupations you are considering. You will get a clearer picture of both the favorable and unfavorable sides of the job. Find out about the actual work you would have to do. Be sure to ask about the day-to-day experiences that in the long run make an occupation agreeable or disagreeable.

You must decide   The things that should influence you most in your choice of careers are high school courses in which you did well, reading about careers, friends and teachers in the field that interests you, and, hopefully, some actual work experiences. A special note of caution is in order at this point. Do not allow your parents, teachers, or counselors to decide on an occupation for you. This is not to say that you should ignore the advice of your parents, teachers, and counselors. Such advice is often very helpful in assisting you to make a career choice. But the point is that *you* and *you alone* will have to live with the results of that choice. The final decision must be yours.

2. What are some career choices?

There are over 20 different ways of classifying jobs. Classifications depend on the purpose for grouping the jobs. Jobs may be grouped according to interests. And jobs may be grouped according to estimated levels of intelligence that may be required to do them.

Classifying jobs

What follows in this section is an overview of some of the many kinds of occupations people work at today. Remember, before you make any choice of occupations it is very important for you to know what jobs there are, what these jobs require, and what they offer to the worker. Occupational choices should be matched against what you hope to get from, and what you have to give to, an occupation.

It is important to have a sound understanding of occupations. This fact has been highlighted by many studies. In these studies, several thousand manual workers across the nation have been interviewed. When asked about work experience, how they got jobs, and why they changed jobs or stayed on a job, only one out of five of the workers surveyed indicated that the first job he or she took was in the occupation he or she had planned to enter while in school. The others took the first job they found. And many took whatever job was found for them by parents or friends.

Lack of planning hurts

Perhaps more importantly, the studies found that this lack of career planning continued through many people's working years and that job horizons were extremely limited. These workers had no information on alternative occupations and job opportunities for which they might qualify. And to make matters worse, these workers were not even aware that career planning and guidance services were available to them.

| Many kinds of jobs | During this decade, somewhere between 30 and 34 million young people will enter the labor force. According to the U.S. Department of Labor publication *Occupational Outlook Handbook*, most workers today are in service occupations. Service occupations include careers in areas such as education, health care, trade, repair and maintenance, government, transportation, banking, and insurance. Less than half of today's work force is in industries that produce goods. These include jobs in agriculture, construction, mining, and manufacturing. The projection is that there will continue to be more jobs in the 1980's in service-producing industries than in goods-producing industries. |

Other projections include the fact that as industries continue to grow, they will become more complex and more mechanized. The result will be that jobs will become increasingly specialized. Career possibilities will grow in some, shrink in others.

White-collar workers (professional, managerial, clerical, and sales) now outnumber blue-collar workers (craftsmen, operators, and laborers). And they will continue to do so.

Professional occupations will probably be the fastest growing. Service occupations will be close behind. Fastest growing service occupations will include workers who assist medical professionals in hospitals, food services, home care for the sick and elderly, and police officers. Clerical workers, including computer operators, machine operators, record keepers, and secretaries make up the next fastest-growing group.

What follows are descriptions of various career areas and some specific occupations within those career areas. These descriptions should give you a good idea of the scope and requirements of many of the occupations typically available today.

| White-collar workers | White-collar jobs generally require a fairly high level of intelligence, and study or training past high school. Length of time of extra study and training varies for different white-collar occupations. Categories of white-collar occupations include the following: |

Professional and technical workers. Typical professional occupations include veterinarian, college adminstrator or teacher, county agent, accountant, engineer, physician, teacher, social worker, chemist, architect, lawyer, author, religious cleric, editor, musician, actor, and actress. These jobs require a high degree of mental activity in complex fields, superior intelligence, abstract mental ability, extensive training, and commitment to high standards. Senior college and postgraduate training are usually required. High scholastic ability is essential for professional training, and personality factors are important in most professions.

Typical technical occupations include draftsperson, laboratory technician, surveyor, aviator, television technician, athlete, dancer, and optometrist. These jobs also require extensive training and experience, with emphasis on technical and mechanical details. Technical occupations usually require less training in theory than professional jobs. High school graduation plus post-secondary technical training is usually required.

Managers, government officials, and small business-people. Typical managerial occupations include retail or wholesale manager; hotel, motel, and restaurant manager; ship's officer and engineer; contractor and business executive; advertising agent; factory manager; credit manager; purchasing agent and buyer; postmaster; government inspector; store manager; and public officials. Duties usually involve responsibility for policymaking, planning, supervising, coordinating, and guiding the work activity of others. So these jobs typically require sound judgment and the ability to handle people.

Clerical and related workers. These jobs include bookkeeper, cashier, office clerk, stenographer, typist, shipping clerk, mail carrier, telephone operator, transcriber, receptionist, secretary, broker, messenger, and office machine operator. Good communication skills are necessary since these jobs involve preparing, transcribing, transferring, and systematizing written communications and records. The need for communications machine operators is increasing rapidly.

Sales workers. Important occupations in sales include salesperson, canvasser, demonstrator, real estate agent, salesclerk, and insurance representative. These jobs include performing sales transactions or closely related work. Although above average intelligence is required, personality is very important. A thorough knowledge of the product and of the field is becoming increasingly necessary in selling. Technical education as well as training in sales techniques and distribution is increasingly demanded.

| Manual workers | Manual jobs usually require greater physical rather than intellectual skills. Training concentrates on the development of certain kinds of manual dexterity and mechanical ability. Categories of occupations for manual workers include the following: |

Craftspeople and related jobs. Occupations in this area include baker, weaver, milliner, seamstress, cabinetmaker, upholsterer, printer, carpenter, toolmaker, machinist, electrician, auto mechanic, tailor, stonecutter, furrier, engraver, and painter. These jobs are essentially craft and manual occupations. Most require thorough and comprehensive knowledge of certain special techniques. A high degree of manual dexterity and mechanical ability are essential as well as considerable independent judgment and a strong sense of responsibility. Comparatively long training periods are often necessary. Post-secondary technical training, apprenticeship beyond high school, or trade training are increasingly being required.

Operatives. Typical operative occupations include machine operator, truck driver, gas station attendant, power sewing machine operator, welder (an occupation that will probably have the highest demand in the next few years, according to the latest *Occupational Outlook Handbook)*, apprentice, truck driver, miner, laundry worker, telephone or electrical lineperson. These jobs require manipulative ability limited to a fairly well-defined routine. Independent judgment is of secondary importance, and training periods are comparatively short.

Laborers, except for farm and mineworkers. Typical laboring occupations include laborer, packer, yard worker, fieldworker, construction laborer, fisherman, longshoreman, teamster, roadbuilder, gardener, lumberjack, repair worker. Physical exertion is the principal requirement. Little or no training is required. Good physical condition is of the first importance.

Service workers

Service jobs require many different kinds of skills. The amount and kinds of skills required depend upon the individual job. But nearly all service jobs involve close contact with the public. Therefore the right kind of personality is almost as important as proper training. Categories of service occupations include the following:

274

Private household workers. Occupations of typical household workers include housekeeper, maid, cook, and governess. These jobs involve service in private homes. Personality factors are most important since all such jobs require the employee be able to get along well with the employer.

Other service workers. Service occupations, other than household, include security guard, firefighter, police officer, waiter, cook, barber, beautician, porter, elevator operator, and hospital attendant. These jobs involve the protection and guarding of property and individuals as well as requiring personal contacts and associations. Personality factors and a service point of view are important. Trends show an increase in personal service occupations as well as indications of demands for increased training requirements. High school graduation is often desirable.

Farm workers

Agricultural jobs vary greatly in levels of training. Some agricultural jobs require specialized training and a college education. Other agricultural jobs require physical dexterity and stamina. Categories of agricultural occupations include the following:

Farmers and farm owners. Typical farmers' occupations include ownership of dairy, cotton, fruit, grain, livestock, or poultry farms. Suitable land and equipment are required as well as practical and theoretical knowledge of agriculture. High school education, including specialized agricultural education, is desirable. Some specialized forms of agriculture require college training.

Agricultural laborers. Typical farm laborers' jobs include general laborer, picker, stocktender, and greenhouse worker. These jobs require limited training. Training is usually secured on the job. Physical qualifications are important, and much of the activity is seasonal.

For more information

There are several sources of information on career guidance in general as well as for specific occupations. You may have overlooked the more obvious sources such as the public library, your school's library, your teachers and guidance counselors, employment offices at businesses, and counselors from state employment services. Be sure to take advantage of all of these during your career search. Here are a few specific sources of information you may wish to contact for career information and guidance.

U.S. Dept. of Labor
Bureau of Labor Statistics
Washington, D.C. 20212

U.S. Dept. of Labor
Women's Bureau
Employment Standards Administration
Washington, D.C. 20210

National Vocational Guidance Association
1607 New Hampshire Avenue, NW
Washington, D.C. 20009

American Vocational Association
1510 H Street, NW
Washington, D.C. 20005

A valuable source of job information that is often ignored is your state department of education. You can usually obtain lists of accredited schools offering training in the specific occupation that interests you. When writing to any source, be sure to be specific about the kind of information you want and what career areas you are interested in.

3. What happens after high school?

Whether or not you should plan to go to college is a problem to which there is no simple solution. An investment of a large sum of money and four years of your life is not to be taken lightly.

And remember that the main business of college is study. College involves much more studying than you have done in the past. Not everyone is able to carry the load.

If you have the ability and the motivation needed to finish a four-year program, college can give you a rich educational and cultural background. However, the college dropout rate is high. Even if you qualify for admission, the odds of your graduating are about 50-50. The most common reasons for failure are lack of interest or motivation, financial difficulties, and lack of good work and study habits.

Here are a few suggestions that will help you decide whether or not to go to college.

1. Be sure you are not going to college because of social prestige.
2. Have enough money to pay for at least the first semester or quarter.
3. Be sure you are able and willing to withstand long hours of individual study and preparation because, to a very high degree, you will be on your own in college.
4. Make sure you get counseling help from school counselors, teachers, other qualified members of the community, and parents before you make a decision.

Think about college

High school testing programs are important to all students, whether they are college-bound or not. However, some of the tests will be especially important to you if you have decided that college is for you.

Testing can help

Tests are used to help you learn how to help yourself. Tests can show you what your current ability level is. And they can also predict your ability to learn certain skills in the future. Most schools use tests to place students in various course levels and to help students make a career choice.

A typical high school testing program usually includes the SCAT (School and College Ability Test). This test is usually given in your freshman year. The SCAT attempts to measure abilities that are related to success in academic learning. Verbal ability is measured by vocabulary and sentence completion items. Mathematical ability is measured by items involving computation and arithmetic reasoning. The language portion of the test, the *Stanford Achievement Test*, includes language usage, punctuation, capitalization, dictionary skills, and sentence sense.

College testing generally begins during the junior year in high school. The PSAT/NMSQT (Preliminary Scholastic Aptitude Test/National Merit Scholarship Qualifying Test) is given in the fall. The PSAT/NMSQT is an introduction to the college testing program. It measures skills in the verbal and mathematical areas. Although these tests are not used for college admission, they can give you a prediction of how you might do on college admissions tests. The National Merit Corporation also uses the scores from these tests to determine National Merit Scholarship winners.

This series is followed by the SAT (Scholastic Aptitude Test) and ACT (American College Test) in the spring.

The SAT also measures your verbal and mathematical skills. The tests are scored from a low of 200 to a high of 800. Scores in the 500 range on each test are considered average and are often acceptable for college admission. However, colleges also take into account class rank, involvement in extracurricular activities, and recommendations.

The ACT also measures your abilities in skills areas that are required to do college work. There are four tests: English, mathematics, social science reading, and natural science reading. Each test is scored on the basis of a low of 1 to a high of 36. Your final score is the average of a composite score of all four tests. Scores in the range of 20.3 are considered acceptable at most colleges, along with class rank and other related factors.

Keep in mind that if you intend to go to college, you cannot avoid taking the SAT and ACT tests. Virtually all colleges and universities consider acceptable scores on both the SAT and the ACT to be part of their admission requirements.

You may also choose to take an additional series of tests

called Achievement Tests. The Achievement Tests are directly related to the school curriculum. Each is an hour-long test in a specific subject matter area such as English composition, American and European History, mathematics, biology, chemistry, physics, French, German, Hebrew, Latin, Russian, and Spanish. The tests are often required by colleges for placement purposes. However, they are not designed to be used as devices for college admission.

While most students take the SAT, ACT, and Achievement Tests in their junior year, you may wait until your senior year to take them. If you took these tests in your junior year, you may also choose to take them again in your senior year.

Many high schools also offer an Advanced Placement Program. Students enrolled in advanced placement courses in English, math, science, language, history, and art may gain college credit by passing an advanced placement test.

Choosing a college

Should you decide that college is for you, you will have over 3,000 colleges from which to choose. You should first discuss your career ideas with your high school counselor. Very likely your counselor's advice will be that you write to several colleges and request their catalog. The college catalog is an invaluable source of information. Be sure to pay particular attention to such items as admission requirements, courses in your field of interest, and costs. The catalog will also supply information about scholarships, student loans, work-study programs, and housing.

Additional sources of information, and ones that should not be overlooked, are alumni of colleges that you are interested in. Colleges will give you the names of recent graduates who live in your area. You should interview some of these graduates for information and opinions about the college from which they graduated.

If you need a scholarship

There are a variety of both general and special scholarships available to deserving students. These scholarships range from the National Merit Scholarships to those granted by various state and local sources. It would be impossible to make a list of available scholarships since they vary considerably from state to state and within various localities. Here again, your best and most reliable guide is your high school counselor. The counselor is generally up-to-date on what kinds of financial aid are available for both the college bound and non-college bound student.

A college checklist

As you can tell from the preceding material, the decision for college is a complex one. There are many things you have to be aware of and many things you have to do. Among the most important things you must remember to do are the following:

1. Deciding that college work is for you.
2. Discussing your decision with your parents and counselor.
3. Taking the SAT and ACT tests.
4. Discussing the results of the SAT and ACT tests with your parents and counselor.
5. Studying the catalogs of schools in which you are interested.
6. Selecting which schools you will apply to.
7. Applying to the schools which offer the program you wish to pursue.
8. Evaluating your financial needs and gathering information on how these might be filled.
9. Deciding, with advice from your parents and counselor, which specific college or university that has accepted you, you will choose to attend.

These procedures are time-consuming. You would be wise to make your initial decision on college as early in your junior year in high school as possible. And you should *not* wait until the last minute to begin the application/selection process.

Think about vocational education

Remember that college is only one of many very good options open to you as you leave high school. It is not the answer to all of your career possibilities. Most counselors agree that the main factor in securing a good job, and being reasonably satisfied with it, is the ability to do that job and to do it well. One reason why many students believe that a four-year college degree is necessary is simply that they are not aware of the many alternatives.

A college degree does not necessarily mean that you are going to be competent, happy, and successful. In fact, it is not even a sure guarantee of financial success. You may be amazed to learn that a skilled workman can and often does earn as much if not more than many people holding college degrees.

Education other than that offered in the four-year college program has been often referred to as "vocational" education. There is no doubt that it has suffered from an "image problem." The very word "vocational" seems to imply second-rate, something less than desirable. The national attitude has been that vocational education is for somebody else, someone who is unable to earn a college degree.

The negative view of vocational education is diminishing as many students become increasingly disappointed with college education. The growing scarcity of jobs for college graduates, especially in the liberal arts, is encouraging many high schoolers to redirect their career plans toward vocational training. It is sad but true that in many cases young people are graduating from college unprepared to enter any occupation.

If your main reason for attending school is to gain an occupational skill, you should seriously consider vocational education. Most junior colleges and virtually all public community colleges offer vocational courses.

There are over 7,000 privately owned trade and technical schools that specialize in occupational training. These schools offer you training for jobs such as computer programmer, data processor, cook and chef, medical and dental assistant, radio and television broadcaster and engineer, airline pilot, electronic technician, police officer, and health service worker.

Labor unions offer job training programs in the form of apprenticeships. An apprenticeship involves on-the-job practice plus related classroom instruction. Many private employers, especially large corporations, often provide job training which includes a variety of employee training programs. These programs usually include instruction in additional skills for job advancement or job transfer, supervisory training, and management development.

Home study courses are another way you can learn a vocational skill. Such courses often offer subjects that you may not find in a local school. The skill being taught often requires specialized equipment, for example a radio or television kit.

And do not overlook the daytime and evening courses offered at most vocational schools and adult education centers. Under cooperative work-study programs offered by many schools, you may receive school credit for on-the-job training and related in-school instruction.

Choosing a vocational school

Here are a few suggestions that might help you to choose a vocational school. First, and most importantly, discuss your vocational plans with your high school counselor. Your counselor is usually in the best position to help you obtain and evaluate information about vocational school programs. Ask companies that offer the kinds of jobs you are interested in to give you the names of schools that offer good training. Write to these schools for a catalog. Vocational school catalogs should describe offerings, requirements, length of training periods, and tuition costs.

Once you have settled on a school, find out if it is accredited and by whom. Be sure to carefully read any enrollment or registration blanks before you complete and sign them. If possible, visit the school and see for yourself what it has to offer. Do not hesitate to ask the school for the names of former students and employers who have hired them in your area. Contact these people, and ask their opinion of the school.

Most private trade schools are reliable institutions, but some are not. Beware of such practices as salesmen who try to rush you into signing a contract or paying tuition in advance. And steer clear of schools that "guarantee" jobs upon completion of the course. Reliable information about vocational, trade, and technical schools can be obtained from the following sources:

National Association of Trade
 and Technical Schools
2021 L Street, NW
Washington, D.C. 20009

National Home Study Council
1601 18th St., NW
Washington, D.C. 20009

Council of Better Business Bureaus, Inc.
1150 17th St., NW
Washington, D.C. 20036

Bureau of Apprenticeship and Training
Manpower Administration
U.S. Department of Labor
Washington, D.C. 20210

Vocational testing opportunities

The general high school testing program has been discussed earlier. But should you consider a vocational career, there are vocational tests which are a good way to learn more about your vocational aptitudes. Most of the tests you take are designed to find out how much you have learned in school. But there are no right or wrong answers on vocational aptitude tests. Instead, these tests are designed to measure how you "feel" about the things asked.

Two of the most commonly used vocational aptitude tests are the Strong Vocational Interest Blank (SVIB), and the General Aptitude Test Battery (GATB). While there is no test which will answer positively that you will or will not succeed in a particular occupation, these two tests are reliable enough to pay attention to. They can tell you what your underlying needs and values are and what kind of person you are or would like to become. These tests help you to take stock of your experience and to develop a deeper understanding of your assets and limitations in relation to the world of work. Again, consult your guidance counselor about the possibility of taking such tests. Most high schools administer the SVIB and GATB only on request.

You may need money

Whether you are college bound or thinking about vocational education, money can be a problem. There are a variety of financial aid programs designed to help needy students achieve their educational goals. To determine how much aid you actually need, some schools are participating in the College Scholarship Service (CSS) Need Analysis Program. It is a nonprofit organization which helps the schools to determine a student's need for financial aid. The forms and instructions are usually available from the financial aid office of the school which you hope to attend.

Most schools are using the so-called "package" concept to help needy students. It usually means that the student receives a combination of grant, job, and loan. Since scholarship funds are usually limited, this program permits a school to help more students than it would be able to by the granting of outright scholarships.

The major sources of student aid come from the educational institutions themselves, organizations interested in training people for a particular field, organizations interested in providing educational opportunities for particular groups, state governments, and the federal government through a wide range of programs, each designed for a particular need.

Money to further your education, academic or vocational, is available. However, it is up to you to pinpoint the sources of this money. Use your initiative, dig for the information, and do not be afraid to ask questions. As with so many other pieces of your career picture, this is largely up to you.

4. How do you get a job?

Learn from others

All of the questions you might have about getting and holding a job cannot be answered in this section. That subject would take a book in itself. But consideration can be given to the questions that most young people seem to have on their mind. Remember, what may be good advice for another job-hunter may not fit your individual needs. You will have to make your own decisions. But you can learn from the knowledge, mistakes, successes, and failures of those who have already been through the process of looking for a job.

Finding an opening

There are many different ways of getting a job. Depending on the type of job you want, some ways may be more important than others. If you live in or near a large city, check to see if an employment directory is available. This is a guidebook that lists the services and agencies that are ready to help you find a job. Local offices of your state's employment service should have such a guidebook.

One of the best ways of getting leads on jobs is through your friends and relatives. As a matter of fact, most beginning jobs are obtained in this way, and there are several reasons for this. If you have a friend or relative who has a good employment record with a company, he or she is likely to be asked to recommend the names of possible employees.

This is often referred to as using "pull." Should you use this technique? Most counselors agree that there is nothing wrong with using this approach—providing you have the ability, interests, and other characteristics that will make you a worthwhile employee. However, unless you can really deliver the goods on a job, it is unfair to take advantage of friends and relatives.

Your state employment office provides many services for you. If you have a definite vocational goal in mind plus the necessary training, the office will attempt to place you in a suitable job. It will also assist you in learning about your abilities and interests through testing and counseling.

Another source of job leads is through employment agencies that are operated on a private basis for profit. These agencies usually have the employer pay a fee for securing the kind of worker that is wanted. However, the job applicant sometimes pays the fee for securing the position, and the fee is usually a percentage of the beginning salary. It is always a good idea to investigate the reputation of any private employment agency before registering with it. Take particular care to read the contract that you will customarily have to sign. Most private agencies are reputable, but your local Better Business Bureau can help you to make sure.

Nearly all schools assume some responsibility for placing graduates in jobs. In most schools, the placement service is well organized and operates effectively. In others, it may be less efficient. In any case, the school as a placement agency has many advantages for you. Employers realize that the school, better than any other agency, has a thorough knowledge of its pupils and their potential for certain kinds of jobs.

The daily newspaper can put you in touch with prospective employers. Watch the "help wanted" advertisements and leads on new industries and businesses that are locating in your community. Be wary of ads that are general in nature and vague as to the kind of position available, but seem to promise expense accounts, high salaries, and other unusual advantages. After you have replied to some ads, you will be able to distinguish the desirable from the less desirable.

Federal, state, and local government agencies are the biggest employers in America. Almost every kind of possible job can be found in one or another government service. Most of these positions operate under civil service policies and regulations. This means they are filled by means of competitive examinations. If you are interested in working for the government, you will find notices announcing federal government jobs posted in your local post office or federal building. Similar announcements of state and local government jobs can be found in state and municipal buildings.

Some individuals may have a special problem finding a job because of a physical or emotional difficulty. Every state maintains a bureau of vocational rehabilitation in partnership with the federal government. Any handicapped person, 16 years of age or older, who can reasonably be expected to profit from rehabilitation services, may apply for help.

Some helpful hints   Suppose you are looking for the first job. What are some important first steps? Here are a few that could prove helpful.

1. Select a type of work that is in line with your abilities, aptitudes, interests, and training.
2. Prepare a one-page Personal Data sheet to take along when you go for your interview. Include personal and health information, education, special training, records of work experience, positions of leadership held, and names and addresses of three references.
3. Have clearly in mind what you have to offer the employer in the job for which you expect to apply.
4. If you are arranging for an interview by letter, be certain that the letter is well prepared and properly written. The letter should be typed and not more than one page in length. Use short, concise sentences. Enclose with your letter a self-addressed, stamped envelope for reply. If the request for an interview is made by telephone, make sure your call is businesslike and courteous. Speak distinctly and with confidence.
5. Be certain that you are appropriately dressed and groomed for your interview, and *be on time.* Be yourself and self-confident.
6. Should you be given an application blank to complete prior to the interview, read it carefully, and complete it in ink clearly and legibly. Provide information on all items which apply to you.
7. During an interview, speak freely, distinctly, positively, and to the point. Be interested, enthusiastic, and, above all, sincere. Be a good listener, but do not hesitate to ask questions which you believe are pertinent. Volunteer important information if it is being overlooked.
8. Avoid giving the impression that you are interested only in the pay. Be sure, however, that you understand clearly what wages you are to receive.
9. It is a good idea to write the prospective employer a brief thank-you letter after the interview. It gives you the opportunity to reiterate your interest in the job.
10. Do not be discouraged if you do not get the first job for which you apply. Most people do not. Try again until you get the kind of job you want.

The interview is the single most important step in the entire process of getting a job. There is little chance of your even being considered for a job without an interview. Business executives have been asked to list things they look for during interviews that seem to indicate an applicant would prove successful on the job. Here are some of those things, listed in order according to the number of times they were mentioned by professional interviewers.

Surviving an interview

1. Active participation in extracurricular activities, especially in college. Election to offices in student groups.
2. Hobbies and recreational interests which have cultural value.
3. Active interest in community affairs.
4. Wide reading interests, with an awareness of current events.
5. Clarity of thought, intelligent response to questions, convincing manner of speaking.
6. Pleasing voice, ability to talk freely and fluently with good diction and grammar.
7. Confidence, self-assurance, and ease during an interview.
8. Friendliness, with a sense of humor.
9. Neatness, cleanliness, and a well-groomed appearance.
10. Intelligence in planning for a career with a clear knowledge of company and product.
11. Good scholastic record, and a willingness to start at the bottom and work up. More interest in long-term opportunity than in starting salary.

Once you get a job, here are a few tips on how to keep it.

Holding that job

1. Be ahead of time and listen to all instructions carefully.
2. Be friendly to all fellow employees. Watch their method of doing things and ask them for suggestions and help when needed.
3. Be systematic in what you do. Have a plan of operation. When you make a mistake, do not try to cover up. Report it to the boss and learn how to avoid making that same mistake again.
4. Learn the company's rules and regulations. You can avoid many pitfalls if you know company policies.
5. Get enough rest each night so that you will be alert on the job and be able to do your work cheerfully.
6. Learn names of department heads and fellow employees as soon as you can. Keep busy, be prompt, and be patient.

Activities

The unit-end activities have been designed to help you to retain and put into practice some of the suggestions discussed in this unit. Please do not write in this book, but place your responses on a separate sheet of paper.

Your personal résumé

When you are looking for a job, often the first impression a prospective employer has of you is from your résumé. A résumé is a summary of your personal, educational, and employment history.

Most prospective employers will request that you submit a résumé *before* a decision is made as to whether or not you should be granted an interview. And for any job opening, a prospective employer might have dozens of résumés from which to choose three or four interviewees. So the impression created by your résumé is a vitally important one. The résumé should be short, precise, well-written, and neat. A typewritten résumé usually creates a more favorable impression than a handwritten one.

Practice writing a personal résumé. While there are many recommended formats, all suggest that the following information be included:

1. Name, address, and telephone number
2. Date of birth
3. Educational background, including the name and address of schools attended, if graduated or not, and degrees attained (if applicable)

4. Employment history, beginning with the most recent position held, including
   a. Name, address, and telephone number of each employer
   b. Dates of employment
   c. Position or positions held
   d. Description of the duties and responsibilities of each job.

Remember, be brief and be positive. Your résumé must convince a prospective employer that it is worth his or her while to interview you. It is the first step toward getting the job you want.

Interview practice

Job interviews are a frightening experience for many people. And this is unfortunate since nervousness during an interview has cost many people the job offer they wanted.

One good way of avoiding costly mistakes during an interview is to practice. Review the material in section 4 of this unit. Then ask a classmate or friend to join you in the role play of a job interview. Alternate role playing the situation of the interviewer and the interviewee.

Try to identify areas in which you had not properly prepared for your "job interview," and concentrate upon making good any deficiencies. The more you practice and the more you work at developing an "interview technique," the more at ease you will be in real-life job interview situations.

Answer Key

Each unit of this book concludes with an activity section. The activity or activities have all been carefully designed to help you reinforce your understanding of the ideas, skills, and techniques presented in each unit. Some of these activities simply suggest various procedures that might be followed to improve skills in certain problem areas. But others ask that specific answers be given to specific questions. Answers to the activities follow.

Unit 1: page 21

Study habits checklist
The following answers indicate that the student has a well-developed program for efficient study over the long range.

1. Yes	7. Yes	13. Yes
2. Yes	8. Yes	14. Yes
3. Yes	9. Yes	15. Yes
4. Yes	10. No	16. Yes
5. No	11. Yes	17. Yes
6. Yes	12. No	

Unit 2: pages 42-43

Readiness checklist
No specific answers are required for this activity. However, it is suggested that such a checklist be kept on a daily basis until the habit of "checking" for tools and supplies is developed.

Improving participation
No specific answers are required for this activity. However, if the student's response to half or more of the questions is "sometimes" or "never," this could indicate classroom behavior deficiencies that would be general enough to be noted by the teacher.

Unit 3: pages 76-79

Understanding the unit
1. Because you cannot speak as rapidly as you can think, subvocalization slows down your WPM rate.

2. You might survey a book if you wanted to get an idea of its shape and contents before you actually began reading it. And you might survey a book if you were reading it simply for practice or pleasure.

3. $\dfrac{\text{number of words read}}{\text{time in seconds}} \times 60 = \text{WPM reading rate}$

4. The best way to set a purpose for your reading is to decide in advance what your end product, what you have to get out of the material you are going to read, needs to be.

5. Underlining the main ideas will force you to decide what is important as you go along. Underlining will also be useful later if the material is to be reviewed.

6. If you come to a word you do not know in a reading assignment, circle the word, use context clues to try to guess the meaning of the word, and read on. After you have completed the reading assignment, look up the meaning of any unfamiliar word, and write the meaning down for future reference.

7. You should slow your WPM reading rate when you are reading hard, very technical, poetic, or unfamiliar material.

8. You should use the skills of skimming and scanning when your purposes for reading are searching for information from among a mass of material or reviewing books or notes for tests.

Find the main idea

The main idea in each paragraph is contained in sentences (1), (4), (13), and (15).

Using context clues

1. A *domino* is a half-mask.
2. *Dieseling* describes a condition in which an internal combustion engine continues running after the ignition has been turned-off.
3. *Defamatory* remarks are remarks that hurt a person's reputation.
4. A *precipice* is the edge of a cliff.

Reading for details

1. There are many kinds of marking or coding that could be used when studying this passage. The following would be one example:
   a. circle the technical terms;
   b. underline or star the sentences containing main ideas;
   c. comments on the main ideas written in the margins;

d. a general comment on factual accuracy.
2. A *clepsydra* is a kind of water clock.
3. An atomic clock is tuned according to the vibrations of atoms and molecules.
4. An atomic clock can be accurate to within a few seconds in 100,000 years.
5. Atoms can also be used to mark the passage of time through a process called *carbon dating* that measures the decay of carbon 14 atoms.
6. This second system is not very accurate, usually measuring time to within hundreds of years.

Unit 4: pages 111-115

Test your outlining skill

The following is the most logical and consistent outline of the data as given. Note that the subheads could be given in any order.

I. Evidence of pollution
  A. Contaminated fish
  B. Increased cost of water purification
  C. Undesirable levels of algae
II. The causes of pollution
  A. Industrial wastes
  B. Pesticides used for farming
  C. Inadequately treated sewage
  D. Thermal pollution from nuclear energy plants
III. Solutions to the problem
  A. Laws limiting industrial emissions
  B. Pesticide controls
  C. Sewage treatment regulations
  D. Maximum water temperature regulation

Using verbs properly

1. a. blew; b. blown
2. a. burst; b. burst
3. a. broke; b. broken
4. a. brought; b. brought
5. a. came; b. come
6. a. dived, dove; b. dived
7. a. dragged; b. dragged
8. a. drank; b. drunk
9. a drowned; b. drowned
10. a. flew; b. flown
11. a. gave; b. given
12. a. was; b. been
13. a. led; b. led
14. a. rode; b. ridden
15. a. ran; b. run
16. a. shrunk, shrank; b. shrunk, shrunken
17. a. stole; b. stolen
18. a. swung; b. swung
19. a. threw; b. thrown
20. a. wrote; b. written

Using commas properly

1. I have made my scratch outline, done my reading, and taken notes.
2. The President of the United States, who has greater responsibility for this country's welfare than any other person, is also Commander-in-Chief of the U.S. Armed Forces.
3. It is time to go in the house, Tom.
4. On July 4, 1976, Americans celebrated 200 years of independence.
5. I would like to watch TV, but I have to write my report.
6. "Don't go without me, Mary," Jane called.
7. At the salad bar were cottage cheese, marinated herring, tossed salad, and olives.
8. I went right to sleep last night, and so the thunder did not disturb me.
9. Whenever I have a long, complicated term paper due, I try to work on it for at least a little while every day.
10. "John," she called, "I have something to show you."

Test your knowledge of good usage

1. did
2. doesn't
3. except
4. lain
5. advice
6. am not, anyhow
7. It's
8. I
9. teach
10. have

A checklist of usage

No specific answers are required for this activity.

Unit 5: pages 137-139

Getting ready

No specific answers are required for this activity. However, consistent use of such a checklist should help the student avoid some of the more common problems encountered in the preparation for delivery of a speech.

Give a speech

No specific answers are required for this activity.

Unit 6: pages 176-179

Using the dictionary

1. lb; 16 ounces; about 453.6 grams.

2. Jones's
3. that is; that is to say; namely
4. The symbol is derived from the Latin, *exempli gratia.*
5. A word formed from the first letter or syllables of other words; *Zone Improvement Plan.*
6. A radioactive, metallic chemical element; it was first produced at the University of California.
7. alumni
8. π; ♂, ⊕, or⊖;¶
9. kom′ pərə bəl; in ek′ splə kə bəl; siz′ əm
10. noun, verb, adjective
11. *uninterested,* showing or having no interest: *disinterested,* free from selfish motives: *respectively,* as regards each one in his turn or in the order mentioned: *respectfully,* showing respect: *flaunt,* to show off: *flout,* to treat with contempt or scorn.

Making words

Although additional words could be made from the choices given, the following are some examples of possible answers.

1. lain, an, nil	9. chest, sty, set
2. liar, air, ail	10. heat, eat, at
3. ear, bar, bare	11. our, ruse, use
4. rat, tear, tar	12. ear, real, par
5. urn, runt, rut	13. list, sit, ten
6. deal, led, lad	14. fort, tune, for
7. men, man, an	15. vow, low, wove
8. tea, ear, are	16. fat, her, the

Adding letters to endings of words

1. rodeo	7. ballet	13. kink
2. plump	8. browse	14. misery
3. pinch	9. combat	15. oath
4. locket	10. cube	16. pastel
5. sandal	11. fang	17. pastor
6. booth	12. forge	18. pier

Finding hidden words

1. ore	6. sable	11. alms
2. lap	7. utter	12. vent
3. vender	8. lop	13. lance
4. aria	9. holly	14. raze
5. literate	10. lute	

Adding the correct prefix

1. inexpensive	6. illegal	11. inexact
2. unemployed	7. illegible	12. indivisible
3. immovable	8. irreligious	13. antislavery
4. improper	9. irrational	14. antitoxin
5. impractical	10. atypical	

Complete these sentences

1. submarine	3. Subnormal	5. superfine
2. Subterranean	4. Subsonic	6. Supernatural

Adding the correct suffix

1. selfishness	4. bravery	6. contentment
2. recklessness	5. savagery	7. preparedness
3. dampness		

Unit 7: pages 204-209

Listing in order

AIRPLANE	ERNEST	MONGOL EMPIRE
AJAX	HEMINGWAY	SCULPTURE
ANATOMY	HEMISPHERE	SEA
LUDWIG	HERALD	SEAL
BEMELMANS	RICHARD McBRIDE	SECRETION
BLOOMINGTON	CARSON	SEDATIVE
BOTULISM	McCULLERS	URUGUAY
DENMARK	MADISON SQUARE	VIRGINIA
DIME	GARDEN	WRESTLING
DIVISION	MAINE	FERDINAND
DOG	ANDREW MELLON	VON
HAWAII	MELON	ZEPPELIN

Locating sources

Information related to each listed topic would be found under the following general numbers.

1. 300-399	11. 500-599	21. 300-399
2. 100-199	12. 900-999	22. 300-399
3. 800-899	13. 700-799	23. 600-699
4. 400-499	14. 500-599	24. 700-799
5. 600-699	15. 700-799	25. 300-399
6. 000-099	16. 300-399	26. 600-699
7. 100-199	17. 800-899	27. 500-599
8. 900-999	18. 300-399	28. 900-999
9. 200-299	19. 500-599	29. 600-699
10. 700-799	20. 900-999	30. 800-899

Using the Readers' Guide

An article about aviation safety. The article appears on page 10 of the January 26, 1981, issue of *U.S. News & World Report.* The article is illustrated.

An article concerning changes in amateur photography. The article appears on pages 220 to 222 (and is continued on additional pages) of the October 27, 1980, issue of *Business Week.* The article is illustrated.

An article concerning employment prospects for college graduates. The article appears on pages 65 and 66 of the January 26, 1981, issue of *U.S. News & World Report.* The article is illustrated.

An article by R.L. Perry about home use of computers. The illustrated article appears on pages 62 and 63 (plus additional pages) of the January, 1981, *Mechanix Illustrated.*

An article by D. Folster about the use of alcohol fuels in Canada. The article appears on page 50 of the March 24, 1980, issue of *Maclean's.* The article is illustrated.

An article by P.L. Buckley about travel by railroad. The illustrated article appears on page 904 (plus additional pages) of the August 20, 1976, issue of *National Review.*

An illustrated article about tornadoes. It appears on pages 12 and 13 of the December, 1979, issue of *USA Today.*

An article about the work of L. Rogers, a U.S. Forest Service biologist who studies bears. The article appears on pages 4 to 9 of the December, 1980, issue of *National Geographic World.* The article is illustrated and includes portraits of Rogers.

Help from newspapers

No specific answers are required for this activity.

Library checklist

No specific answers are required for this activity.

Using an encyclopedia

1. Piet Mondrian was an artist who lived between 1872 and 1944. His rigid, geometric style is a continuing influence on modern architecture and commercial design.
2. The word *philosophy* means "love of wisdom" and is derived from two classical Greek words, *philo* and *sophia.*
3. Sigmund Freud.
4. Hinduism.
5. A nation's Gross National Product (GNP) represents the value of all goods and services produced by that nation during a given period.

6. Six years.
7. $\int_a^b f(x)\,dx.$
8. About 93 million miles (150 million kilometers).
9. On the wings.
10. The Brontë sisters were named Anne, Emily, and Charlotte. All three were well-known 19th century writers.
11. The Saskatchewan Rebellion was an uprising of persons of mixed French and Indian descent in Canada in 1885. The rebellion convinced the Canadian government of the importance of the Northwest Territories.
12. 1673.
13. Manama; Arabic; The State of Bahrain; Emirate.
14. It is a method of learning to control body processes that ordinarily cannot be regulated voluntarily.
15. George Boole was an Irish mathematician who lived from 1815 to 1864. He was the originator of the mathematical system today called Boolean Algebra.
16. The basenji, a hound originally bred in Africa.
17. *Robinson Crusoe, Moll Flanders;* Defoe is known as the father of the English novel.
18. Positive, comparative, and superlative.
19. The Yale University Art Gallery.
20. The Nile River in Africa; it is 4,160 miles (6,695 kilometers) long.

Research checklist
No specific answers are required for this activity.

Unit 8: pages 242-243

Understanding the unit
1. Because learnings are not likely to be remembered for long and actual understanding is usually not achieved.
2. Research continues to show that successful students usually work and study according to a formal plan.
3. To find out exactly what you are doing with your time.
4. Procrastination and disorder.
5. Because it is the quality of the time spent and not the quantity that is important.
6. Because studying demands active participation, it is important to remove everything that interferes.
7. a. Study in the same place or room.
   b. Have a permanent work surface.
   c. Provide for room comfort.
   d. Provide for needed study tools.
   e. Provide for proper lighting.

8. The textbook.
9. Pictures, charts, and diagrams; important ideas or words printed in italics or boldface; important subpoints in outline form; use of explanatory footnotes.
10. Study, Question, Read, Recite, Review.
11. Using the SQ3R method, you should be able to read faster, pick out important points in your reading, and fix these points firmly in your memory.
12. Sitting in the front or center of a classroom will enable you not only to hear lectures better, but also to clearly see any visual aids the teacher might choose to use.
13. A thorough understanding of English grammar.
14. The best way to remove anxiety about examinations is to know your subject thoroughly.
15. Objective tests and essay tests.

Listening skills checklist

Each incorrect response indicates a listening skills deficiency on which the student should work to improve. Correct responses are as follows.

1. Yes	5. Yes	9. No
2. No	6. Yes	10. Yes
3. Yes	7. Yes	11. Yes
4. Yes	8. Yes	

Unit 9: page 265

Participation checklist

Each incorrect response indicates a problem area in which the student should work for improvement. Correct responses are as follows.

1. Yes	5. Yes	8. Yes
2. Yes	6. Yes	9. Yes
3. Yes	7. Yes	10. Yes
4. Yes		

Unit 10: pages 288-289

Your personal résumé

No specific answers are required for this activity.

Interview practice

No specific answers are required for this activity.

Index

Outline, 90-92, 95, 194
   exercise, 111
   final, 107-108
   for a speech, 125-127
   for a term paper, 102
   in textbooks, 227
   in note-taking, 230
   scratch, 102, 106-107